Building Gender Equity in the Academy

Building Gender Equity in the Academy

Institutional Strategies for Change

Sandra Laursen and Ann E. Austin

Johns Hopkins University Press

Baltimore

© 2020 Johns Hopkins University Press
All rights reserved. Published 2020
Printed in the United States of America on acid-free paper

9 8 7 6 5 4 3 2 1

Johns Hopkins University Press
2715 North Charles Street
Baltimore, Maryland 21218-4363
www.press.jhu.edu

Library of Congress Cataloging-in-Publication Data
Names: Laursen, Sandra, author. | Austin, Ann E., author.
Title: Building gender equity in the academy : institutional strategies
    for change / Sandra Laursen and Ann E. Austin.
Description: Baltimore : Johns Hopkins University Press, 2020. |
    Includes bibliographical references and index.
Identifiers: LCCN 2020006003 | ISBN 9781421439389 (hardcover) |
    ISBN 9781421439396 (ebook)
Subjects: LCSH: Women in higher education—United States. | Educational
    equalization—United States. | Women science students—United States.
Classification: LCC LC1568 .L38 2020 | DDC 378.1/9822—dc23
LC record available at https://lccn.loc.gov/2020006003

A catalog record for this book is available from the British Library.

Special discounts are available for bulk purchases of this book. For more
information, please contact Special Sales at specialsales@press.jhu.edu.

Johns Hopkins University Press uses environmentally friendly book
materials, including recycled text paper that is composed of at least
30 percent post-consumer waste, whenever possible.

Contents

Acknowledgments

Informed by the spirit of collegial exchange and support that is a hallmark of the ADVANCE community, this volume has benefited from the contributions of many people and organizations. The work was conducted with generous support from the National Science Foundation under awards HRD-0930097 and HRD-1830185. We emphasize that any opinions, findings, conclusions, or recommendations are those of the researchers and do not necessarily represent the official views, opinions, or policy of the National Science Foundation.

We have learned from the hard work and insightful reflections of many leaders in the ADVANCE community. Colleagues from the institutions we studied took the time for long interviews and conversations, arranged for campus visits, and candidly shared their successes and challenges. They have reviewed our materials and provided comments that helped to improve the content and structure of this book. Our advisory board has been very engaged at key points in our work, offering critically useful guidance, and we thank those colleagues and numerous others who offered their advice. Other colleagues have offered useful comments and validation of the findings. We also acknowledge and express appreciation for the leadership and insights provided by the program officers responsible for ADVANCE at the National Science Foundation. These colleagues include Jessie DeAro, Laura Kramer, Kelly Mack, Beth Mitchneck, Mary Anne Holmes, Dana Britton, Sharon Bird, and Alice Hogan. We are very grateful for the many instances of collegiality, interest, and support we have enjoyed as part of the ADVANCE community.

We also thank colleagues who have worked with us at Michigan State University and the University of Colorado Boulder. Melissa Soto and Dali Martinez served as research assistants at MSU, and Karla Bellingar assisted with adminstrative tasks and transcription. At the University of Colorado Boulder, Anne-Barrie Hunter contributed in early stages, and Melissa Arreola Peña and Devan Daly assisted with administrative and research tasks. Ryan Vachon was the videographer for the StratEGIC Toolkit. Elizabeth Creamer and Kris De Welde provided insightful feedback as evaluators and colleagues. We also thank those whose expertise and professionalism contributed to the production of this book.

We are especially appreciative of the broader ADVANCE community. Over nearly two decades, this group, including administrative and faculty leaders at institutions that have received ADVANCE grants, NSF program officers, and scholars of gender issues and organizational change, has been a source of collective wisdom and encouragement. The work discussed here celebrates and records the vision, dedication, and persistence of this spirited and collegial community. At the same time, this volume takes a forward-looking perspective, sharing insights and strategies for change for institutions and individuals beyond the immediate ADVANCE community. We offer this book for use in both new and ongoing institutional efforts to foster change in support of the recruitment, retention, advancement, and success of women scholars in science, engineering, and mathematics.

Building Gender Equity in the Academy

Introduction

THE RECENT #METOO movement has exposed to public view the persistent, everyday sexism of academic workplaces, among others. By squelching innovation, driving away talent, and distorting interpersonal interactions, exclusionary cultures are harmful not just to women in the academy but to people of all gender identities. Successful challenges to this culture must fix the workplace and not try to fix the women. In this book we offer concrete strategies, based in research, for improving institutional environments for academic women, and we examine how these strategies can be adapted to fit different workplaces for the benefit of all. We focus on the STEM (science, technology, engineering, and mathematics) disciplines, where women are especially underrepresented compared both to their numbers in the general population and to their achievements at earlier stages of STEM education and career paths.

The strategies we describe arose from our multiyear research study of federally supported ADVANCE Institutional Transformation (IT) projects. As the first systemic efforts to change the working environment for academic women scientists and engineers, the ADVANCE projects provide an unprecedented opportunity to analyze the approaches that institutions have used to craft more equitable workplaces, and to understand how such strategies contribute to that goal—not just to hypothesize about what works. In this book we distill our research findings and share tested ideas and examples that can be useful to change leaders and researchers working on equity in academe and in other STEM organizations, from government labs to Silicon Valley tech firms. While our data come from studies of these change efforts in academic STEM departments, we argue that many of the strategies are likely to be useful in other disciplines too. Indeed, as colleges and universities institutionalize their ADVANCE work in order to sustain successful programs and to regularize equity-attentive processes, they commonly make programs available to all faculty members regardless of their discipline, and they implement strategies, such as those for inclusive hiring and equitable leave arrangements, university-wide across departments and colleges. Thus, while gender equity in STEM fields is at the core of the research we carried out, we offer lessons that we believe are very portable to other disciplines, and we suggest adaptable models for improving equity for other groups of faculty whose needs are less well studied but whose lack of visibility and voice is also evident and harmful in the academy.

As evaluators and researchers who study change projects in academic environments, we are often approached by people who know what they need to accomplish but not how to do it. Drawing on the case studies in our data set, we lift general models out of the examples, classifying the interventions used by institutions and describing how each can be strategically adapted (or not) to different campus settings. None of these strategies are one-size-fits-all, but some are more flexible and some less so. A key lesson from our research is that institutional context influences the specific ways that gender inequity may appear and thus influences both the local nature of the problem to be solved and the appropriate choice of solutions. In examining the relevance and potential utility of each intervention in relation to these institutional contexts and needs, our analysis makes the change interventions *strategic*. Our explicit discussion of the possible adaptations and limitations of each strategy will aid people trying to select and adapt approaches for their own organization.

When we began the research presented in this book, we imagined our main audience as people doing equity work in academic institutions. Many seek to improve the inclusion and visibility of women scientists and other groups also underrepresented in the sciences or in academia at large: scientists of color; researchers born outside the United States; lesbian, gay, and bisexual scientists; gender-nonconforming researchers; and disabled scientists. In academic institutions, the people doing equity work include faculty change leaders, academic administrators, and those in cross-disciplinary roles in diversity, faculty development, or teaching and learning centers—and, importantly, women academics themselves, who are tired of being told to "lean in" and are looking for ways to make their own efforts benefit themselves and others.

However, as we have continued the work, we have recognized that our research will also be useful to leaders in institutions of higher education who work on change projects that have different goals but are also transformational in nature, such as improving undergraduate STEM teaching and mentoring. Such leaders may work in institutional roles or in cross-institutional spaces, such as professional organizations or funding agencies. Scholars who study change processes in higher education will also find useful insights in our work.

The book is organized in three parts. Part I examines the long-standing problem of women's underrepresentation and invisibility in STEM higher education. While the number of women earning advanced degrees in science and engineering has risen over time, women remain sorely underrepresented on academic STEM faculties, especially in higher-prestige positions and institutions. The barriers to women's full participation are many: biased evaluation processes for faculty positions and promotions, lack of support for faculty with families and other significant personal responsibilities, and self-perpetuating, homophilous networks that preferentially direct social capital to others of the same gender, race, or social group. Thus, it is essential to address the barriers directly, rather than indirectly by trying to help women navigate them. Part I outlines the need for a systemic approach to gender equity and describes the research study on which the book is based.

In Part II, we identify 12 strategies for change. They are conceptually grouped as institutional responses to four different aspects of gender inequity: biased evaluation processes, unwelcoming work climates, employment structures that do not accommodate personal lives, and inequitable opportunities for advancement. These strategies are drawn from work done by previous ADVANCE Institutional Transformation awardees, and all are real approaches that institutions have used to change the numbers, success, and experiences of women scientists and engineers. We end part II with examples of exciting new ideas being tried by more recent awardees.

In part III, we discuss how to bring these strategies together into systemic change initiatives that are appropriate for specific institutional contexts. Strategically combining several approaches leverages their individual strengths to craft stronger synergies and to make the change efforts comprehensive rather than piecemeal. We describe three cases in which institutions did this, and we compare them in order to identify some broader lessons. We then offer some research-based advice to help readers think through how to design their own comprehensive, strategic, and contextually responsive change plan and carry it out. We end by identifying some areas where we still have more to learn about the implementation, impact, and success of both individual interventions and comprehensive institutional change efforts that deploy several interventions in strategic combinations.

We offer this book in a spirit of collaboration grounded in the sense of connection built from working together on a hard problem, a connection that we have experienced as part of the ADVANCE community. We are truly encouraged that so many people are working together and learning from each other in collective efforts to create the kinds of inclusive and supportive academic workplaces that will enable people to enjoy satisfying, meaningful, and productive careers and that will provide higher education institutions with the full array of talent needed to fulfill their missions.

PART I The Problem, the Solution, and the Study

Chapter One

What's the Problem?

DESPITE DECADES OF effort by federal science funders to increase the numbers of women holding advanced degrees and faculty jobs in science and engineering, women are persistently underrepresented in academic STEM disciplines, especially in positions of seniority, leadership, and prestige. Barriers to women are woven into the fabric of academic workplaces: biased selection and promotion systems, inadequate structures to support people with family and other personal responsibilities, and old-boy networks that exclude even successful women from receiving formal recognition or advancing into top leadership roles. These barriers are enlarged and entangled when multiple marginalized identities intersect for women who belong to nondominant groups due to their race, ethnicity, social class, sexual orientation, citizenship, indigenous status, or physical abilities.

In this chapter, we describe the persistent and patterned underrepresentation of women scholars in academic STEM disciplines. We summarize literature that elucidates the causes of these patterns and explain why it is important that women are visible and successful as faculty members and leaders in academic STEM disciplines.

Underrepresented, Out of Sight

In the United States, women are underrepresented in most fields of science, technology, engineering, and mathematics whether compared to the population as a whole or to the population earning college degrees. This has been true for many years and remains severe, especially in engineering, mathematics, and the physical and Earth sciences.

Economists refer to this phenomenon as "occupational segregation," and they describe two types of occupational gender segregation—horizontal and vertical— both of which are common in STEM fields (Frehill, Abreu, & Zippel, 2015; De Welde & Stepnick, 2015a). Horizontal segregation refers to differences in the distribution of women among different fields or subfields, whether comparing STEM and non-STEM disciplines or within STEM. Examples of horizontal segregation include the low proportions of women receiving US doctorates

- in mathematics and computer science (25%) as compared to humanities and arts (51%) (2017 data from NSF NCSES, 2018);
- in engineering (25%) as compared to life sciences (55%) (NSF NCSES, 2018); and
- within mathematics in the subfield of probability (17%) as compared to statistics (50%) (2010 data from Frehill, Abreu, & Zippel, 2015).

Horizontal segregation continues into the faculty ranks of academic institutions. For example, women represent 17% of doctorate holders employed in four-year US institutions of higher education in engineering, which is less than half the percentage (39%) of doctorate holders in such positions in the life sciences (2017 data from NSF NCSES, 2019).

Comparing the data on STEM doctorates earned by women to the data on faculty, as in the engineering and life sciences examples just mentioned, illustrates vertical segregation: women are clustered in lower-status positions within a particular profession. For example, in the life sciences, the percentage of women earning doctorates has exceeded 50% since 2005, but women make up only 42% of assistant professors, 35% of associate professors, and 26% of full professors (2017 data from NSF NCSES, 2019). At the same time, women are overrepresented in positions such as instructor or lecturer, where they are not eligible for tenure and generally lack job security and prestige. In chemistry, the disparity in representation is even more stark (Peplow, 2019). Vertical segregation also manifests in the types of institutions where women occupy STEM faculty positions. For example, in mathematics, women are more likely to hold full-time faculty positions in bachelor's- and master's-degree-granting institutions (36% and 34%, respectively) than in more prestigious PhD-granting institutions (23%) (2016 data from AMS, 2019). Both types of vertical segregation also lead to lower salaries for women (Bertrand, 2018; Umbach, 2007).

One influence on this pattern is "demographic inertia," a term used to signify the slow pace of change in faculty demographics because individuals often hold faculty positions for a long time and the net turnover of positions is low. That is, full professors today are predominantly men because many were hired as assistant professors 30–40 years ago, when the applicant pool was mostly men. This inertia means that faculty demographics retain the imprint of historical discrimination and bias for many years. But quantitative modeling studies show that demographic inertia alone does not explain the current gender imbalance in faculty populations (Marschke et al., 2007; Shaw & Stanton, 2012; Thomas, Poole, & Herbers, 2015). Failures to equitably recruit, retain, and promote women are also important, and thus each aspect of the employment process—recruitment, retention, and promotion—must be addressed to reach parity.

The same patterns of horizontal and vertical segregation apply to faculty of color, both men and women. For example, Asian Americans are overrepresented in science as a whole (19%) compared to their representation in the US population (5%), but relative to their presence in science they are underrepresented in leadership roles, from chancellor, president, or provost (7%) to dean, chair, or department head (10%), levels where white people are overrepresented (NSF NCSES, 2019). In other cases, the numbers reveal few faculty of color in the STEM professoriate at all. For example, across 90 top PhD-granting chemistry departments, there were only 12 African American assistant professors in 2016–3 of them women—and only 25 African American full professors, including just 1 woman (OXIDE, 2019). In all, African Americans made up only 2.3% of the chemistry faculty in these institutions in 2016, and they were concentrated in just 33 departments, meaning that a majority of chemistry departments reported no African American faculty at all.

The figures in 2016 were just as dire for Hispanic/Latinx faculty (3.1% of all chemistry faculty) and Native American people (just seven chemistry faculty nationwide). Yet that year, African Americans made up 14% of the US population, Hispanic/Latinx people 18%, and Native American/Alaska Native people 1.7% (US Census Bureau, 2016). And chemistry is by no means unique in this respect: in general, people of color are so underrepresented that they are entirely absent from many STEM departments, reflecting occupational segregation by race and ethnicity as well as by gender.

Just as underrepresentation in STEM higher education is not restricted to women, neither is it solely a North American issue. In some countries, women's participation is constrained by their lack of access to higher education at all. Yet around the world, women's share of all higher education enrollment has risen notably since 1970 to near or above 50% (except in sub-Saharan Africa, where it is lower), while women's share of STEM enrollments has not kept pace (Ramirez & Kwak, 2015). Moreover, data across countries and STEM fields show a common trend that women's representation further declines at higher levels of education (e.g., doctoral degrees) and at higher prestige levels of appointment (e.g., full professors; Borello et al., 2015; Frehill, Abreu, & Zippel, 2015; Kessel, 2015; Peplow, 2019). These patterns suggest that internationally, as in the United States, women's presence in STEM is not governed by their qualifications for access to STEM higher education and careers, but by exclusionary structures of STEM fields that privilege men. The data we have gathered about institutional strategies to address issues of equity in representation are based on approaches taken by US institutions, yet these strategies resonate with approaches developed in international contexts and may offer ideas to readers who face the same challenges in other national settings (Dean & Koster, 2013).

Barriers for Women on STEM Faculties

A vast literature addresses the situation of women in STEM, documenting women's numbers and trends, accounting for women's presence or absence in science and the institutions where it is carried out, and capturing the factors that offer challenges and bolster success for women scientists. We do not attempt a comprehensive literature review; rather, we summarize some key points from existing research that are pertinent to the ways that institutions can respond and the interventions that they have designed and implemented.

Bias in Evaluation

"Implicit biases" refer to attitudes and beliefs that affect people's judgment and behaviors in unconscious ways, without our awareness or intention—in contrast with "explicit biases," which we can identify and reflect on, even if we choose to conceal them (Staats et al., 2015). Implicit biases are automatically and unconsciously applied dispositions toward other people based on their gender, race, ethnicity, age, or appearance; they may be positive or negative. They result from exposure to direct and indirect messages, starting early in childhood, from family, friends, schools, neighborhoods, the media, and other interactions. In general, mental schemas or stereotypes are efficient cognitive structures, helping humans to quickly sort and make sense of information coming in from a complex world

(Valian, 1999). Indeed, the fact that bias hastens our mental judgments is the basis of one of the most commonly used tools for research on implicit bias, the Implicit Attitudes Test (Greenwald & Krieger, 2006). But these implicit mental schemas become problematic when they are applied inappropriately, such as when they shape our response to an individual because of her group membership, influence our decisions unfairly, or undermine our stated egalitarian values.

Evidence for implicit bias emerged from research in psychology in the late twentieth century and is now well supported with empirical research (Greenwald & Krieger, 2006; Staats et al., 2015). This research shows that implicit biases are pervasive and robust—everyone has them, even those who are committed to equality and impartiality—and they do affect behavior. Most of our implicit biases tend to favor our own group, but people can hold biases against their own group. However, since they are mental habits, biases are also malleable: with effort and time, implicit associations can be unlearned and replaced with new ones. A variety of strategies to reduce or remove implicit biases have been studied.

Implicit bias around gender affects how women are evaluated at every stage of their careers. This is important because of the accumulation of disadvantage: the impact is magnified over time as small biases are repeated at each of multiple decision points. A famous computer simulation shows that a mere 1% bias favoring men at the first stage of evaluation generates a pool where men are represented 2:1 over women after eight stages of evaluation, such as from entry level to the top level of management in a firm. That is, "a little bias hurt women a lot" (Martell, Lane, & Emrich, 1996, p. 158). At the same time, men benefit from positive biases, receiving a greater benefit of the doubt and a presumption of competence. Academic science and engineering may be particularly susceptible to implicit bias because common cultural schemas of women as nurturing and community-oriented are in conflict with cultural schemas of scientists and engineers as analytical, self-propelled, and action-oriented (Valian, 1999). Moody (2010) described the mental shortcuts and cognitive errors routinely and unwittingly made by decision-makers, offered vignettes showing how these enter decision-making conversations, and identified organizational dysfunctions that exacerbate the impact of these cognitive biases.

Bias affects women's entry into academic posts. For example, several studies found gender differences in recommendation letters for academic positions, including postdocs. Letters for men as academic applicants were longer and more effusive than were letters for women, and the language used to describe applicants reinforced gender schemas that tend to portray women as teachers, students, and collaborators, and men as researchers, professionals, and leaders (Dutt et al., 2016; Madera, Hebl, & Martin, 2009; Trix & Psenka, 2003).

In evaluating job applicants, science faculty rated applications with typical men's names as more competent and hirable than identical applications with typical women's names, and they offered higher salaries and more mentoring (Moss-Racusin et al., 2012; Steinpreis, Anders, & Ritzke, 1999). They were twice as likely to hire a man for a simple mathematical task, even when given information about candidates' performance on a similar task (Reuben, Sapienza, & Zingales, 2014). In all these studies, men and women were equally likely to prefer the male employee. Women are less likely to win prestigious fellowships, even if they have stronger qualifications (Sheltzer, 2018; Wennerås & Wold, 1997), and they are less likely to join the labs run by award-winning male faculty (Sheltzer & Smith, 2014). Other studies show that women candidates for roles stereotyped as male are penalized for being competent or for being beautiful (Johnson, Sitzmann, & Nguyen, 2014; Oh, Buck, & Todorov, 2019; Phelan, Moss-Racusin, & Rudman, 2008).

Bias also shapes women's advancement. To succeed in science, faculty need to get grants, present at conferences, and publish papers. Studies show that women may apply for or win fewer or smaller grants (Bedi, Van Dam, & Munafo, 2012; Hechtman et al., 2018; Kaatz et al., 2016; Witteman et al., 2019) and are provided with lower institutional start-up funds (Sege, Nykiel-Bub, & Selk, 2015). Moreover, some evidence shows that women of color fare even worse than white women in getting grants (Ginther, Kahn, & Schaffer, 2016). Observations of grant review panels at the Swedish Research Council revealed how this happens, identifying problematic patterns (which the council took steps to mitigate) in how gender was discussed, how panel members interacted, and how candidates were evaluated and ranked (Ahlqvist et al., 2013). Seemingly small behaviors and comments can add up, and grant decision-making is often carried out under exactly the conditions under which bias flourishes: time pressure, ambiguous selection criteria, and evaluation of individuals rather than ideas (Carnes et al., 2005).

At conferences, women's presentations occur in venues that are less visible and less prestigious, and this experience is exacerbated for women of color (Isbell, Young, & Harcourt, 2012; Ford et al., 2019; Schroeder et al., 2013). Identical conference proposals are rated lower when they are labeled as submitted by a woman (Knobloch-Westerwick, Glynn, & Huge, 2013). But when women are on the inviting committee, the presence of women in sessions and on panels increases notably (Casadevall & Handelsman, 2014; Sardelis & Drew, 2016).

Women are underrepresented as authors in prestigious journals, and their papers are less frequently cited (Filardo et al., 2016; Holman, Stuart-Fox, & Hauser, 2018; Larivière et al., 2013; West et al., 2013). In economics, where sole authorship is prized, women, but not men, are penalized for coauthoring (Sarsons, 2017). Women's papers are better written but remain in review longer and face tougher editorial standards (Hengel, 2017). Women also are less likely to be invited to review—an important learning opportunity for young scientists and a step toward a potential journal editorship later (Lerback & Hanson, 2017). Further, women are less likely to get the awards that would help them advance to full professorship or into leadership positions (Lincoln et al., 2012). As teachers, women receive lower ratings from students, as shown by experiments where identical lectures are delivered by actors or where identical courses are taught online and the instructor's name is the only clue to gender (Bug, 2010; Fan et al., 2019; MacNell, Driscoll, & Hunt, 2015).

These studies have carefully controlled for other factors, such as seniority or quality of the scholarship being evaluated, in seeking to explain the persistent underrepresentation of women in career-enhancing settings. What these studies and many more point to collectively and consistently is the role of gender bias in the evaluation of scientists, mathematicians, and engineers throughout their careers: as women are en route to faculty positions and as they pursue advancement within their field and institution. While we focus here on gender bias, research also documents pervasive racial bias, as well as biases against disabled people; lesbian, gay, trans, and bisexual people; people from other countries; and those from other groups that are marginalized in US society. Thus, implicit biases are central in hindering progress toward equity in STEM faculties, and several of the strategies we present in part II deal directly with recognizing and countering their pernicious effects. Doing so effectively will benefit a wide range of faculty groups in addition to women—faculty who will in turn enrich institutions with their diverse intellectual and personal perspectives and who will broaden the range of role models and mentors available to students.

Masculinized Workplace Culture and Climate

Implicit bias throttles women's entry into academic science, engineering, and mathematics and hampers their progress within institutions, thus leading to the long-standing and persistent numerical dominance of men on STEM faculties (Marschke et al., 2007). This male-dominated faculty composition in turn has consequences for the STEM workplace environments that women inhabit: cultures become masculinized, and women may be ignored, excluded, harassed, or pressured to "cover" by denying aspects of their identity (Yoshino, 2007). Hall and Sandler (1982) introduced the idea of a "chilly climate," which acknowledges that these everyday experiences of inequitable treatment are in fact a pervasive and systematized pattern in academe. The metaphor of climate communicates something that is "all-encompassing" and "saturates spaces" (Britton, 2017, p. 8).

Depending on the discipline, women may experience this chilly climate in their undergraduate education in a STEM field; they will almost certainly meet with chilly or hostile climates in graduate school, postdoctoral positions, and faculty careers—in their department, at a disciplinary conference, or in a field camp (e.g., Avallone et al., 2013; Aycock et al., 2019; Clancy et al., 2014; Crane et al., 2006; De Welde & Laursen, 2011; Espinosa, 2011; Hall & Sandler, 1982; Seymour, 1995; Seymour & Hewitt, 1997). Studies also document that these unwelcoming climates are exacerbated for women of color and for lesbian, gay, bisexual, queer, and transgender people (Atherton et al., 2016; Bilimoria & Stewart, 2009; Clancy et al., 2017; Hughes, 2018). These masculinized climates may manifest as harassment or microaggressions by students and colleagues, dismissive or inhospitable department and classroom environments, a sexualized work environment, intimidation, bullying, incivility, isolation, or inequitable allocations of work and service responsibilities.

Workplace climate is directly connected to faculty job satisfaction, intention to leave or remain at an institution, and productivity. Yet local workplace environments differ among departments within the same institution; while institution-level policies, practices, and symbols do matter, there is no single institutional climate experienced by everyone. Thus, experiences of workplace climate at the departmental level are particularly important, especially for women, in shaping job satisfaction, affecting productivity, and influencing choices to leave or remain at an institution (Archie, Kogan, & Laursen, 2015; Bilimoria et al., 2006; Britton et al., 2012; Callister, 2006; McCoy, Newell, & Gardner, 2013; Rankin & Reason, 2008; O'Meara, Lounder, & Campbell, 2014; Settles et al., 2006; Sheridan et al., 2017). The department is what connects faculty to the institution; it is the place where faculty experience intellectual connections, mentoring, and leadership—or their absence. Departmental climate and leadership shape faculty members' agency and their ability to take strategic action or adopt intentional perspectives to achieve their desired goals (Campbell & O'Meara, 2014). Leaders affect faculty directly through distributing resources, setting tone, and communicating expectations. Thus, efforts to improve workplace climate and leadership may be especially influential for retaining women and supporting their productivity (Archie, Kogan, & Laursen, 2015; Britton et al., 2012; Laursen & Rocque, 2009). The strategies we describe in part II include several approaches developed by ADVANCE institutions to address these challenges of leadership and climate.

Work-Life Conflict and Career Inflexibility

On a day-to-day basis, academic careers in STEM have significant flexibility: faculty must teach their classes, connect with students and colleagues, and participate in departmental activities, but they have a good deal of latitude in when and where they carry out the intellectual work of course preparation and scholarship. But there is much less flexibility in career progression: advancement in STEM faculty jobs is based on an idealized timetable of progression from a college degree through graduate school, to possibly a postdoc, to a tenure-track job (Ward & Wolf-Wendel, 2004, 2012). Advancement to the next step is based on a single up-or-out decision after a fixed probationary time, so to earn the job security of tenure, a fast start toward productivity and professional recognition is required. This may require long hours in the laboratory or at the computer, and significant professional travel for conferences and fieldwork.

As women have entered the professoriate in greater numbers, it has become clear that this idealized timetable is based on a model of men's careers from an earlier era, when it was assumed that a faculty member had no compelling responsibilities or interests outside work, and certainly no household duties or children to care for. Men were construed as "ideal workers" who were available at any time and were committed to work before any other priority (Williams, 2000). But women's lives and careers often do not unfold in this way (Austin, 2006a, 2006b; Bracken, Allen, & Dean, 2006). Due to both biological reasons and social expectations, women in heterosexual couples tend to carry more responsibilities for children and the household—what Hochschild (1989) called the "second shift," which begins when working parents arrive home—and these responsibilities often lead women to take longer to complete their education, to interrupt their education or career for a time, or to choose fields or jobs that do not demand an "ideal worker" mentality. These differences in women's career paths have lasting consequences for their salaries, promotion opportunities, and status.

Data on faculty career progression show starkly the impact of the work-family conflict (Mason & Goulden, 2002, 2004). At 12–14 years after earning a PhD, men who had "early babies," those born within five years of the parent's doctoral degree, are 20%–24% more likely to have earned tenure in a STEM field than are women scientists who had early babies. Family formation is delayed in academia and in other professions that require advanced degrees, such as medicine and law, but both the delay in having children and the gender gap in the career consequences of that decision are exacerbated for academics compared with lawyers and doctors, who have demanding careers but do not face up-or-out promotion decisions (Mason, Wolfinger, & Goulden, 2013). As a result, tenured women faculty are significantly less likely than men to have children in the household, more likely to have fewer children than they'd have liked, and more likely to be single. At home, women faculty do more housework and more childcare and thus less of the research that tends to count most toward advancing their careers (Misra, Lundquist, & Templer, 2012; Schiebinger & Gilmartin, 2010). For postdocs and graduate students, looking to faculty as examples of how to have an academic career leads to real concerns about whether they can have both an academic career and a family, and many make personal and professional choices based on these considerations (Mason & Goulden, 2002; Mason, Goulden, & Frasch, 2009; De Welde & Laursen, 2011; Loshbaugh, Laursen, & Thiry, 2011; Rice, Sorcinelli, & Austin, 2000). Moreover, these decisions are not strictly individual: academic women are more likely than academic men to be partnered with another academic and are more likely to consider their partner's career prospects when job hunting (Schiebinger, Davies Henderson, & Gilmartin, 2008).

Finally, family is not the only consideration that leads young scholars to question the time demands of academic careers; they also seek to have fulfilling personal lives that offer the time and leisure for exercise, hobbies, and social and community life. Many perceive that this will not be compatible with a faculty career (Rice, Sorcinelli, & Austin, 2000). Across career stages, the reality and perception of how work and life conflict are firmly connected to scientists' job satisfaction and feelings about the work environment more generally. Thus, problems with spillover between work and personal life, or family-unfriendly attitudes among colleagues, may tip the balance for women as they are deciding to leave their position or carry on (Archie, Kogan, & Laursen, 2015). So, concerns about work/life conflict are heightened for women, and they are salient for people of all genders. Moreover, work/life conflict influences the composition of tomorrow's faculty as well as today's, since talented early-career scholars may opt out of future academic careers based on the personal life choices and arrangements they observe among the faculty in their department and their department's responses to those paths (Austin, Sorcinelli, & McDaniels, 2007; Gappa, Austin, & Trice, 2007; Golde & Dore, 2001; Rice, Sorcinelli, & Austin, 2000).

In addition to choices with long-term impact such as family formation, life events such as caring for an elderly family member or a sick child generate short-term demands for time and attention outside the workplace and can increase stress, which reduces productivity. This speaks to the need for another type of flexibility: short-term mechanisms that enable faculty to respond to life events and resume a productive career afterward (Gappa, Austin, & Trice, 2007). Even when these mechanisms are available, however, stigma is often attached to using them. Faculty members may fear that revealing their status as a parent will be interpreted as a sign that they are less committed—less "ideal" as workers (Colbeck & Drago, 2005; Drago et al., 2005). Again, these views have consequences for the institution's ability to attract and retain a diverse and excellent faculty since working in an environment with high stigma around work/life flexibility has consequences for the job satisfaction and likely persistence of STEM faculty of all genders (Cech & Blair-Loy, 2014). Some of the strategies we discuss in part II address these issues.

Inadequate Resources for Individual Success

We have now outlined some of the barriers for women that emerge from biased systems, cultural schemas, and workplace structures built for male career models; these are problems with the institutional spaces where science, mathematics, and engineering faculty work, rather than issues stemming from patterns in women's talents, interests, or capacities. Given these challenges, it is no surprise that women who have entered STEM faculty careers are well qualified for their roles, since these impressive and accomplished scholars have already overcome the "glass obstacle course" of often-hidden barriers (De Welde & Laursen, 2011). Yet the energy, time, and attention they have invested (knowingly or not) to overcome these challenges may detract from their development in other ways. For example, when women are excluded from social and collegial networks, they may not accrue informal knowledge about institutional politics or tricks of the trade that may be crucial to getting ahead in their department or research institute (De Welde & Laursen, 2011). When women become efficient in order to juggle work and family life, they may have less discretionary time to develop a high-risk, high-reward project. They may miss out on hallway conversations that generate opportunities or invitations to collaborate, be denied a voice in informal decision-making, or be perceived as uncollegial or contributing less to departmental life (Gunter & Stambach, 2003; Ward & Wolf-Wendel, 2004). When implicit bias takes a toll on women's chances for a grant, award, or invited conference talk, they may feel discouraged and lose confidence in their ideas or in their ability to communicate them.

With this constant barrage of negative experiences and extra barriers, it is no surprise that many women experience a psychological toll. Feelings of self-doubt promote tendencies to discount their own accomplishments, a phenomenon known as "impostor syndrome": the feeling that their accomplishments are due to luck or hard work rather than talent and that they don't deserve the position or accolades they have earned. While the issues women face are based in biased systems and masculinized cultures, it is easy for women to internalize these obstacles as faults of their own: not good enough, not smart enough, not determined enough. Women in STEM are also subject to "stereotype threat," the heightened awareness that they represent their group in a domain where that group is negatively stereotyped. Stereotype threat leads to lower performance due to higher cognitive loads, increased stress, and reduced motivation (Burgess et al., 2012; Fassiotto et al., 2016). Moreover, when self-doubt manifests as hesitancy, self-deprecation, or apologetic language, these behaviors further play into stereotypes of women as less competent and less successful. Impostor syndrome and stereotype threat may be especially pronounced for faculty who are also marginalized in other ways, including faculty of color, genderqueer and sexual minority faculty, and those from working-class backgrounds.

Attacking the root causes of the systemic issues that lead to impostor syndrome and loss of confidence is important, but it does not produce immediate change in the institutional work environments for STEM women; institutional transformation is slow and uneven. In the meantime, while this hard work is under way, it is appropriate and necessary to provide women with the material and psychological resources to succeed: professional development, mentoring, moral support, and opportunities to learn new skills; develop their talents, resilience, and sense of belonging; and build fruitful external connections and internal confidence.

The Double Bind

Women of color face a double bind: challenges arise from both racism and sexism, but those obstacles are not simply or separately linked to race and gender (Ong et al., 2011). More generally, gender, race, social class, indigeneity, citizenship, country of origin, disability, sexual orientation, and other identity categories combine or intersect to produce different experiences and outcomes for people who are differently positioned within this intersectional matrix (Armstrong & Jovanovic, 2017; Cho, Crenshaw, & McCall, 2013; Corneille et al., 2019). The concept of intersectionality arose and developed within Black feminist scholarship (Crenshaw, 1991), and research shows that many of the barriers we have outlined are more serious for women of color. For example, STEM women of color experience higher levels of harassment than white women or than men of any race (Clancy et al., 2017). These issues may also manifest in various ways for different groups: Black women academics report more isolation than do white women, while Latinas describe high levels of disrespect and accent discrimination (Williams & Dempsey, 2014). Women's experiences also differ by other identity categories, including sexual orientation and gender identity. Lesbian, bisexual, and queer women in science, as well as trans and nonbinary scientists, have reported higher levels of harassment than their straight peers, including forms of harassment specific to their sexual orientation and gender identity (Radde, 2018; Richey et al., 2019).

Often asked to represent both women (of all races) and people of color (of all genders) on committees and task forces, women of color do more institutional service than other groups do. Sought out by students of color, they do much informal mentoring, yet they face resistance and disrespect from white students in the classroom (Corneille et al., 2019; Stanley, 2006a, 2006b). Faculty of color may seek to give back to their communities through scholarship that emphasizes community engagement, community impact, and societal service—models of scholarship that may not be valued in institutional evaluation for advancement or in evaluation for research funding (Corneille et al., 2019; Hoppe et al., 2019; Settles, Buchanan, & Dotson, 2019). The drastic underrepresentation of women of color in STEM is one negative consequence of this intersectionality, while positive consequences include the strong identities and cultural resources from which STEM women of color derive resilience (e.g., González, 2007; Ong, Smith, & Ko, 2018).

One study powerfully illustrated the impact of the intersection of race and gender. Biology and physics professors were asked to rate the curriculum vitae (CV) of a hypothetical candidate applying for a postdoctoral position (Eaton et al., 2020). Each CV was identical, except the candidate's race and gender were experimentally manipulated. In physics, men were rated as more competent and hirable, but women were seen as more likable. Further, race and gender combined negatively, such that Black women, Latinas, and Latinos were rated lowest in hirability compared to all others. In biology, a field with more women, racial but not gender biases were evident in the ratings. Studies like this point out that we cannot assume that strategies or findings from research about women writ large—or about white women, or straight women, or cis women—apply equally to all women or indeed to all fields. In research and practice, we must listen and attend to the varied experiences of women in the academy.

The Importance of Representation

The research demonstrates a number of reasons for women's underrepresentation and invisibility in STEM fields. But so what? Why is women's presence important on STEM faculties? Equal opportunity is fair, and institutions of higher learning should be leaders, not followers, in shaping a just society and offering opportunity to all. As places that seek to attract and nurture scientific talent to tackle pressing global challenges in technology, agriculture, environment, and health, academic institutions should be concerned about the evidence—and it is abundant—that the best and brightest often do not succeed in science due to their gender, race, or background. Diversity is a source of excellence: if a department's faculty is not representative of the nation, it has not tapped all corners of potential talent (Malcom, 1996). Equity in opportunity and advancement, inclusion in decision-making and collaboration, and diversity in thought and lived experience are beneficial in practical ways for the core research, education, and civic service missions of institutions of higher learning (Hurtado, 2007).

Diverse workplaces are more productive, innovative, and creative. Studies of technology research and development (Turner, 2009), patent citations (Ashcraft & Breitzman, 2012), and business profitability (Herring, 2009; Hunt, Layton, & Prince, 2015) demonstrate that gender diversity improves an organization's performance and innovation. In academe, scientific publications with ethnically diverse author lists are cited more often than those with more homophilous author groups (Freeman & Huang, 2015). Woman-led author teams explore different kinds of questions, thus expanding knowledge in new directions (Nielsen et al., 2017; Nielsen, Bloch, & Schiebinger, 2018; Schiebinger, 2008). Research shows how these benefits arise: cognitively diverse working groups craft better solutions to complex problems, make better judgments of others' expertise, and make better predictions in the face of uncertainty (Hong & Page, 2004; Nielsen et al., 2017; Page, 2007, 2017). Page (2017) showed that cognitive diversity—differences in how people perceive, analyze, and apply information and experiences—is related to other kinds of diversity, including differences in gender, race, and social class. In diverse groups, people are more diligent and open-minded, and they are better prepared to make their case because they are less ready to assume that everyone has the same information and perspective (Phillips, 2014). This diligent listening and preparation points to why working in diverse groups is also more demanding: effort is required. Thus, identity diversity leads to the cognitive diversity that fosters innovation and problem-solving.

A diverse faculty is also important for learning. Research on college students has shown that experiences with diversity are positively linked to cognitive growth and to stronger attitudes, behaviors, and outcomes of civic engagement (Bowman, 2010, 2011; Gurin et al., 2002). Most powerful are experiences that are not just "learning about" diversity, such as in a class, but that involve direct interpersonal engagement with people different from oneself and with real-world social issues (Bowman, 2010). Even a single counterexample to a stereotype can change students' notion of who can be a scientist (Laursen et al., 2007). Women's presence in universities as educators, scholars, and leaders shapes the socialization of developing scientists in lasting ways as they learn how to work and interact with a variety of colleagues in the labs and classrooms where they are also learning scientific and practical skills. Moreover, faculty with diverse life experiences and knowledge may bring distinct critical perspectives about what is important to teach and how to teach it. Indeed, it is commonly found that women faculty are highly engaged in teaching innovation, outreach, community-engaged scholarship, and community service—which are all faculty activities that expand and deepen institutions' impacts on their students and communities (Antonio, Astin, & Cress, 2000; Ebert-May et al., 2015; Hayward, Kogan, & Laursen, 2016; O'Meara, 2002; O'Meara et al., 2011; Thiry, Laursen, & Hunter, 2008; Thiry, Laursen, & Liston, 2007).

Finally, women on STEM faculties shape the future as mentors, advisors, and role models to students (Blackburn, 2017). "It's hard to be what you can't see," pointed out Marian Wright Edelman (2015). Due to their historical exclusion from STEM professions, women of all races as well as men of color want to see and interact with faculty who look like them and share some of their life experiences (Estrada, Hernandez, & Schultz, 2018; Griffin et al., 2010; Johnson, 2010). Seeing successful women in STEM is important for women graduate students as they consider and visualize their own futures and scan for examples of women who have achieved academic success and have fulfilling personal lives (De Welde & Laursen, 2008, 2011; Rice, Sorcinelli, & Austin, 2000). Undergraduate research students also watch women science faculty closely to see how they manage their professional and personal lives (Laursen et al., 2010). For these positive outcomes to emerge, students must have not just one or two role models, but enough to see a range of possible future selves and to derive personal conclusions without expecting their role models to be flawless (De Welde & Laursen, 2011; Johnson, 2010). A critical mass of women—and of people from other underrepresented groups—on STEM faculties thus influences the future quality, diversity, and numbers of the STEM workforce, which is crucial to economic competitiveness and human well-being (Etzkowitz et al., 1994).

In the work of improving university STEM workplaces to represent, value, and support women faculty, we recognize a welcome irony: the very fact that women are increasingly present and visible in STEM spaces is what enables women and their allies "to contest the terms of inclusion, . . . to challenge the gendered character of the institutions and organizations in which women now have expanded access" (Ramirez & Kwak, 2015, p. 21). In the so-called post–civil rights era, attention must shift from blatant, legalized discrimination to subtle, implicit biases that put women at a disadvantage, and to their cumulative consequences on a large scale. We must address the fact that "those who benefit from greater opportunity and a reinforcing environment find their advantages compounded, while deficits of support and recognition ramify for those who are comparatively disadvantaged" (Wylie, Jakobsen, & Fosado, 2007, p. 2). In this book, we provide concrete and practical strategies—based in research at institutions that have taken on the challenge, made progress, and learned—for how to go about challenging and remediating those gendered STEM spaces.

Chapter Two

Fix the System, Not the Women

RECRUITING WOMEN INTO STEM fields is critically important to ensure that their voices and talents are part of the scientific enterprise and available to address society's daunting challenges. Recruiting efforts at numerous points all along STEM education and work pathways are important, starting with programs designed to increase interest and persistence in science, technology, and mathematics among school-age girls and young women. Initatives to reform undergraduate education in STEM fields also support STEM diversity. For many students from marginalized groups, traditional teaching methods using didactic approaches have not fostered broad success, whereas high-impact practices that include problem-based learning, peer interaction, and active engagement help to close gaps in success, interest, and persistence in STEM across different demographic groups of students and in diverse institutions (National Research Council, 2015). Fellowships that encourage and support women through graduate work in STEM fields open some doors; initiatives that seek to recruit women into STEM faculty positions open others. All of these approaches are needed to increase the involvement of women, as well as men of color, in the STEM world. Yet these efforts, as important as they are, are not sufficient.

At each stage, recruitment must be coupled with retention. Otherwise, the promise embodied in a diverse group of talented scholars actively involved in the work of the academy instead becomes a revolving door of disappointment and frustration for individual scholars and a loss of opportunity and talent for institutions. Hiring women is important, but that alone does not address fully the problem (Marschke et al., 2007). Women faculty members often experience a lack of fit with the implicit and dominant culture of academe. For example, imagine a scientist, just beginning her new job, who is the only woman in her department. Interactions there follow a hierarchical pattern, with senior scholars asserting their voices more strongly than those newer to the academy. Well-established routines in the department mean that meetings are held early or late in the day. Given her family's early morning routines and after-school pickup times, she often finds these meeting hours inconvenient—yet asking for a schedule change may call attention to her personal needs in ways she prefers to avoid. No one else in the department has young children—at least not that she knows—so she worries that anything that suggests less than full commitment to her department and career may send a message that undermines her success. In addition, she would like some advice about an upcoming grant proposal from a senior colleague who has had funding from the same agency, but wonders if asking for help will make her look unprepared or needy.

As this vignette illustrates, while recruitment efforts may bring more women into the academy to work in STEM fields, the challenge of creating an inclusive workplace is not fully addressed when they are hired. Daily experiences at work pose daunting challenges for women. Some depart; others remain but feel frustrated and are less productive than they could be. In response to discomfort with the traditional system and cultural mores in higher education, many women scholars cope in admirable ways; others choose different career paths.

Thus, addressing the factors that support retention, productivity, and satisfaction is as important as ensuring that recruitment processes challenge implicit bias, proactively seek a diverse pool, and send signals of welcome to all candidates. Many institutions have created programs intended to support women colleagues striving to succeed. Examples of such efforts, whether started by institutional leaders or by women faculty themselves, include support groups, information about childcare options, and dual-career programs to support women whose partners are also professionals. Mentoring programs may help women gain tools and skills to successfully navigate and thrive in the traditional culture of higher education.

Each of these strategies usefully offers support and guidance as women negotiate the explicit and hidden traditions, habits, and expectations of higher education institutions. However, if undertaken as stand-alone initiatives, these efforts often appear to be trying to "fix" the women—that is, their goal is to aid women who are recruited and enter the academy to change their approaches in ways that may help them to find success within the organization as it exists. A more transformational approach—and, we argue, a more sustainable and impactful approach—is to consider the whole organization as a system, including policies, practices, rituals, values, and habits. Then the task is to create an environment that works for all: fixing the system rather than fixing the women. This approach incorporates initiatives and programs that offer support to women, such as mentoring, childcare options, and dual-career opportunities, but it goes further in asking how the entire organization can make adjustments that recognize, honor, and support all employees' interests, needs, and values. Taking a systemic approach means looking closely at the underlying assumptions that inform and permeate all aspects of the institution: how work is done, how members of the community interact, how personal and professional commitments are addressed, how decisions are made, how work is allocated, and who has power and influence.

Taking a systemic approach also means recognizing the need for multiple levers of change. Adding one program or adjusting when meetings are held may be helpful but is far from sufficient. A systemic approach means identifying, developing, and utilizing multiple strategies for change. Which levers to choose and how to combine them depend on the specific institutional context and the needs and interests of faculty (and other employees). Such an approach means taking time to analyze the problem—that is, learning what needs to be changed in the institution—and then inviting, hearing, and using the perspectives of the full range of organizational members in order to design a plan that results in significant organizational change. This kind of approach is what we mean by fixing the system, not the women. It honors the talents of women and people of color, as well as other groups of faculty that have not been fully welcomed into the STEM ranks, and it develops ways to support these colleagues with respect and recognition that their contributions are essential to the organization's well-being and ability to fulfill its missions.

The US National Science Foundation (NSF) recognized the need to address the organizational context for women STEM scholars when it established the ADVANCE program to support institutional transformations of this type. In its flagship program, aptly named the Institutional Transformation (IT) award, ADVANCE offered large (US$3 million), five-year grants to institutions that proposed to take on a comprehensive, system-wide project to identify and remove organizational constraints that lead to gendered biases in institutional policies and processes (see appendix A for a full list of ADVANCE IT awards through 2019).

More modest awards have supported a variety of related, smaller-scale activities based in single institutions, networks, or professional organizations (see DeAro, Bird, & Ryan, 2019; Laursen & De Welde, 2019, for a history of ADVANCE and descriptions of its program tracks).

Rosser (2004, 2010, 2017) has described the transition at the NSF from programs that were focused on providing women with resources to support their own professional growth and advancement, to an approach addressing the institutional environments where women work—a crucial shift in mind-set. From the beginning, the solicitation for ADVANCE grant proposals showed commitment to strategic organizational change that seeks to fix the system, not the women. Early on, meetings of ADVANCE project leaders established a generous and collegial culture of sharing their ideas and learning for the benefit of all. Over time, their practical work and scholarly contributions have built an impressive body of knowledge about just how to go about this transformational work in higher education. In addition to many publications on individual projects and studies, several synthetic works and collections focus on ADVANCE (Bilimoria, Joy, & Liang, 2008; Bilimoria & Liang, 2012; Bystydzienski & Bird, 2006; Fox, 2008; Furst-Holloway & Miner, 2019, and references therein; Holmes, O'Connell, & Dutt, 2015; Laursen et al., 2015; Mitchneck, Smith, & Latimer, 2016; Stewart, Malley, & LaVaque-Manty, 2007; Stewart & Valian, 2018). On the NSF's side, shifts in the ADVANCE program solicitations over time have reflected this growing, community-based wisdom, and they communicate an increasing collective awareness of the urgency and complexity of these changes (Laursen & De Welde, 2019). ADVANCE has also become an international model for the transformation of institutional structures and cultures in higher education and beyond (DeAro, Bird, & Ryan, 2019) and thus has been an excellent laboratory for studying and understanding organizational change to strengthen the visibility, success, and leadership of women on STEM faculties.

Studying Systemic Change to Advance Gender Equity

As higher education researchers, members of the ADVANCE community, and evaluators of several ADVANCE projects, we often have been asked for advice and suggestions about strategies to promote organizational change. With such queries in mind, we initiated a multiyear study to investigate the strategies used in the federally funded ADVANCE institutional initiatives, each of which was seeking to develop more equitable environments for women in STEM fields. We wanted to learn what strategies these institutions were using, how their chosen strategies contributed to systemic institutional change efforts, and how the strategies were tailored for specific institutional contexts. We also wanted the research results to be useful to practitioners serving in a variety of institutional roles and to scholars and researchers interested in organizational change.

Our multiyear study, conducted primarily between 2010 and 2014, with additional work from 2015 to 2018, used a mixed-methods approach guided by literature and theory on organizational change and faculty work. We chose for our primary study sample the first 19 institutions that received ADVANCE IT grants (awarded 2001–2004) to tackle gender equity change goals in a systemic fashion (see appendix A, Cohorts 1–2). These institutions had finished (or nearly so) their formal ADVANCE projects by the time we began the study, and thus we believed their leaders could offer reflective insights on what they had accomplished and learned.

Using document analysis, interviews, and case studies, we explored several questions:

- What strategies have been used to create institutional environments that encourage the success of women scholars?
- Which strategies work and which don't? Why?
- What strategies are useful to include in a change plan, and how does institutional context relate to the choice of strategies?

We began by reading the annual and final reports of these 19 institutions and cataloging their activities to understand what they had undertaken, why, and with what results. Drawing on observations from this document review, we interviewed leaders of these projects to learn in more detail about their approaches to change and the lessons they had learned. We then selected 5 universities—diverse in geographic location, aspects of organizational characteristics and culture, and strategies and approaches used—as case studies for intensive on-campus visits. During these multiday visits, we talked with nearly 200 people—ADVANCE leaders, senior university leaders, faculty members, and others—who generously shared their perceptions of their institutional context, change strategies, what worked well, what worked less well, and why. Our research team used careful methods of coding and analysis, guided by social science literature, to reach the conclusions we share in this book. Our advisory board helped us with key decisions throughout the research process, as did other generous colleagues whom we consulted. Our research methods are described thoroughly in appendix B.

The primary focus of our research was on institutions in the first two cohorts of NSF-funded ADVANCE Institutional Transformation awards. Then, to incorporate new ideas generated over time as later IT projects built on the initial work, and to explore various organizational change processes that we came to realize were relevant to successful change, we designed and conducted a working meeting with selected leaders from ADVANCE IT projects funded in award Cohorts 3–6 (awarded 2006–2012; see appendix A). Held for two days in August 2015, the workshop had 14 participants, some representing specific ADVANCE IT awards and others representing scholarly and practical expertise on gender, inclusion, STEM, and the academy. The meeting was organized around questions about the role of context in organizational change, and the organizational change processes that were important. Data collected in this workshop added nuance and examples but confirmed that our overall findings from the institutional sites we had studied earlier continued to be robust and relevant. In a second workshop, held in November 2018, we explored similar issues with a group of 20 attendees, including practitioners and scholars from ADVANCE projects in Cohorts 5–8 (2010–2016; see appendix A) and from other types of institutional change work.

As our research has unfolded, we have shared results and emerging lessons through the StratEGIC Toolkit: Strategies for Effecting Gender Equity and Institutional Change (www.strategictoolkit.org), which we developed in 2014–2016 to highlight our findings (Laursen & Austin, 2014a). This web-based toolkit identifies 13 strategic interventions that are often used to change institutional structure, practices, and cultures, and the toolkit also features 15 institutional portfolios that show how different institutions combined these interventions into comprehensive change initiatives. Video resources include interviews with ADVANCE leaders from a variety of institutions discussing their own projects and institutional contexts, and short documentaries that address cross-cutting issues of institutional change. The toolkit was designed to provide institutional leaders with support to be strategic in choosing interventions and adapting them to their own settings. This book updates and expands the work of the toolkit and gathers our findings and advice in a unified resource for institutional leaders.

The Content and Structure of the Book

The purpose of this book is to share strategies for effecting systemic change for the purpose of creating greater gender equity in US higher education institutions. While the strategies we highlight are specifically drawn from change initiatives to advance gender equity, our research suggests that these strategies are also often adaptable to support other change goals and initiatives. At the same time, we emphasize that strategies to support change should not be considered to be generic or one-size-fits-all. Rather, gender inequity, like many other challenges facing institutions, manifests in different ways depending on the institutional context. The selection and use of any intervention should depend on the specific needs of the institutional context and the specific institutional problem to be addressed. We offer this book as a resource for organizational change teams: we present interventions that others have used, explain their variations, and highlight when and how they may be useful—or not—in particular contexts.

Earlier in part I we discussed the problem of gender inequity and the need for a systemic approach. This defines the problem space for the solutions presented in part II: 12 strategic interventions, identified from the research study we have described, that institutions have used to change the numbers, success, and experiences of women scientists and engineers. In these chapters, we classify the interventions captured in our research into four categories: interrupting biased processes; rebooting workplaces; supporting the whole person; and fostering individual success.

In discussing approaches to *interrupting biased processes*, we recognize that cultural gender schemas create implicit biases that lead people to think of women as lacking the analytical and logical skills associated with doing science. The strategies in chapter 3 offer ways to disrupt the influence of such biases on recruitment, hiring, promotion, and advancement decisions: inclusive recruitment and hiring (Strategy 1); equitable processes of tenure and promotion (Strategy 2); and strengthened accountability structures (Strategy 3).

In discussing methods for *rebooting workplaces* in chapter 4, we emphasize that both formal structures, such as policies, procedures, and roles, and informal norms, which include cultures, symbols, and messages, shape the everyday experiences of women scientists and engineers. Examining and amending these workplace features so that they are supportive rather than demeaning can improve work environments. Applying the following strategies helps to reboot the workplace at scales from the department to the institution: development of institutional leaders (Strategy 4); approaches to improving departmental climate (Strategy 5); and enhanced visibility for women and gender issues (Strategy 6).

The set of strategies in chapter 5 for *supporting the whole person* recognizes that women typically bear more of the load for family responsibilities due to both the biology of childbirth and gendered societal expectations. Institutions can take concrete steps in policies and practices to enable women to thrive as academic scientists and engineers at the same time as they live fulfilling personal lives: support for dual-career couples (Strategy 7); flexible work arrangements (Strategy 8); and practical, family-friendly accommodations (Strategy 9).

Chapter 6 focuses on *fostering individual success*. These strategies recognize that while systemic change is essential, it is also typically slow and uneven across the parts of an institution. Thus, higher education institutions also need to find ways to support women as individuals as they make their way through the current flawed system: faculty professional development programs (Strategy 10); grants to individual faculty members (Strategy 11); and mentoring and networking activities (Strategy 12).

Chapter 7 presents promising strategies that are emerging from the work of more recent ADVANCE IT projects. These offer additional conceptual frameworks and practical actions, beyond the 12 strategies identified in our work, that have been tested on at least one campus. Because they are newer, they have been less widely deployed than those we studied in depth, but they include distinctive rationales and designs that institutional change teams may wish to consider in formulating their change plans.

In part III of the book we focus on building and enacting a change portfolio—that is, how institutions can combine these strategies in synergistic ways that increase their impact. Creating an effective plan for advancing change goals requires more than selecting strategies for their individual values and impacts. Rather, an effective plan involves selecting strategies for the ways in which they suit the particular institutional context and for the impact they can have through their connections and synergies. In chapter 8, we highlight three institutions—Case Western Reserve University, the University of Texas at El Paso, and the University of Wisconsin–Madison—and the change portfolios they created to advance gender equity in their particular contexts.

Each case study examines the major features of one Institutional Transformation project and how the institution's context influenced the project team's identification of core problems for STEM women faculty on their campus, their choice of interventions to pursue, the design and implementation of those interventions, and the success or lack of success of the chosen interventions singly and combined. Together, these case studies make clear that more can be accomplished when multiple levers of change are brought to bear on the problem, and in chapter 8 we review some key lessons learned from the case studies.

In chapter 9, we distill from the research general advice for institutional teams that are planning and implementing comprehensive change plans. To develop a strategic and systemic approach, teams must frame the problem, analyze their own context, and select strategies and interventions with an eye toward how they will combine. As they implement the plan, they must also build a leadership team, develop ways to elicit buy-in and forge alliances, evaluate their work, and plan for sustainability.

Audiences for This Book

We hope this book will be useful to several audiences:

- institutional change leaders engaged in advancing gender equity in their institutions
- change agents working in higher education who can see ways to adapt the ideas in this book to serve their particular change goals
- leaders in national organizations, societies, and networks that support change initiatives at the institutional level and more widely
- scholars who study change in higher education

Members of these audiences will read and use this book in different ways, but we think the research-based strategic interventions, the institutional examples, and our central argument that change requires strategic thinking and planning offer insights of relevance. We believe that leaders who are seeking to advance gender equity in their institutions—both those in administrative roles and those in faculty roles—will find ideas that can aid them in designing and advancing their own distinctive change initiatives. Readers from agencies, such as the National Science Foundation, that support such work should also find that this book speaks directly to their efforts. We present snapshots of change interventions that AD-VANCE institutions have used, but the ideas are likely to have practical relevance to other institutions that are organizing efforts in support of gender equity, with or without an ADVANCE grant.

We suggest several practical ways that leaders might use this book:

- A team charged with developing a proposal for organizational change to advance women faculty might review this volume for ideas. Perusing the strategies may stimulate conversation about the specific problems and issues to address at their institution, data they need to gather, and elements of their context that are relevant to possible change strategies. Reviewing the case studies may help them to see how interventions can be combined to respond to specific institutional contexts and to have different kinds of impact.

- A committee working on a specific intervention—mentoring, for example—might focus on that specific strategy, using the material here as a conversation starter or as a checklist to work through possibilities, variations, and potential benefits and limitations.
- A senior institutional leader might share these materials when making a charge to a faculty task force focused on improving the institutional climate for women.
- An ADVANCE campus leader, experienced in many of these approaches, might review the strategies and case studies for fresh ideas to invigorate or extend the excellent work already under way on campus.

Some of the approaches discussed in this book may aid those leading other change initiatives in higher education beyond efforts to create more inclusive environments: reforming undergraduate STEM education, planning major curricular changes, improving the mentoring of developing scientists, or reorganizing the relationship between cocurricular and academic life on campus. In conversation, leaders have told us they see ways to adapt ideas in this book in service to their own change goals. Leaders with a range of change goals tell us they have experienced resonance with our overall thesis: systemic change in higher education requires analyzing the institution's specific challenges, then identifying and implementing a set of interventions that can work in synergy to respond to those challenges within the specific institutional context.

Higher education leaders may also find ideas and stimulation for their work in national higher education organizations, disciplinary and professional organizations, cross-institutional and discipline-based networks, or funding agencies. These organizations' priorities and projects often highlight change goals related to faculty development, curricular innovation, inclusion and diversity, or connections between institutions and the community.

Finally, we suggest that this book will be useful to researchers who study change in higher education. The lessons that we offer add to a growing body of work about how change occurs in higher education and what strategies are most effective. Our findings should resonate with those studying change, adding further data and institutional examples to emphasize the importance—arguably, the necessity—of taking a systemic approach when seeking to address the complex challenges and opportunities confronting higher education institutions today.

Limitations of the Book

As excited as we are to share what we have learned about strategic interventions and design in support of institutional projects to advance gender equity, we know there are limitations. We have based our claims on our study of a set of institutions that participated in the early years of the NSF's ADVANCE program. We are confident in what we have learned, and we have supplemented our case study research with other sources of information to stay abreast of work by institutions with more recent ADVANCE awards. Our workshops and conversations tell us that the strategies we have highlighted continue to be relevant and frequently used. At the same time, our data set is not all-inclusive; later ADVANCE institutions have developed new ideas and made more effective use of theory in guiding their work. The ADVANCE program has increasingly recognized how women's experiences are shaped by the intersection of their gender with other identities, especially their race and ethnicity (Laursen & De Welde, 2019). More recently funded ADVANCE grantees have increasingly sought to take such intersectionality into account in explicit ways, and this attention is important and groundbreaking. We are grateful to scholars Mary Armstrong and Jasna Jovanovic for their insights on how early ADVANCE institutions attended (or did not) to intersectionality in change initiatives (Armstrong & Jovanovic, 2015, 2017; Jovanovic & Armstrong, 2014).

Both the societal landscape and the scholarly terrain of gender and equity have developed and changed over the years of our research, and they continue to shift. In particular, expanded notions of how gender is understood and enacted inform much current work around equity. Understanding gender as distinct from sex and as a multidimensional spectrum rather than a simple binary classification, where possible in this book we describe interventions that are addressed to people of all genders, but we do not alter descriptions of research studies that considered binary samples of men and women. We also recognize the dearth of research about the experiences and perspectives of transgender, nonbinary, and genderqueer academics (Beemyn, 2019; Harris & Nicolazzo, 2017). As middle-class white women with the benefit of considerable education, we recognize that our understandings are shaped by our own experiences of privilege based on race and social class as well as our experiences of marginalization by gender. And we continue to learn.

We acknowledge the importance of other scholars' research based in institutions with ADVANCE grants, some of which we cite throughout this book. In particular, we direct readers to the cross-program analysis in the volume by Bilimoria and Liang (2012) and to more recent work by Stewart and Valian (2018) on lessons from ADVANCE programs. The latter was published as we conducted our own research, and their work offers insights that parallel many of our findings. We also recognize that much good work to advance inclusivity and gender equity is under way across higher education institutions that we have not studied. Our discussion of strategic interventions is not intended to be comprehensive nor to exclude other effective and creative strategies. Our goal is to share the set of interventions that we have found from our research to be useful options to consider when designing strategic change efforts to nurture more inclusive environments for women. We studied institutional efforts specifically focused on gender equity in STEM; however, we believe that these efforts are relevant beyond STEM, and there is growing evidence that they strengthen the quality and level of equity for all in academic workplaces. At the same time, we recognize as a limitation of our work that our findings are based on a particular set of interviews, workshops, and cases that we have studied. We look forward to learning more as other researchers and institutional leaders add to the shared body of knowledge.

Finally, we recognize limits to the concept of institutional transformation itself. This is slow and incremental work, a ratcheting process rather than a revolution. Archimedes is said to have claimed he could move the earth if he only had a long enough lever and a place to stand—but those are not trivial preconditions. Likewise, for the work of institutional transformation, there are limits to what can be accomplished from inside any institution with the levers of change available to any project team. Just as changing the situation of one woman does not change the institutional system, changing one institution at a time does not change broader societal systems nor remove the sexism, racism, homophobia, and misogyny embedded in them. Our research draws on the actual experiences of people on campuses with ADVANCE IT projects in seeking to understand what has been attempted and accomplished. This pragmatic approach is distinct and complementary to scholarship that explores the theoretical possibilities of transformation or that considers how to envision and build a new and equitable academy from the ground up.

PART II   Strategies for Change

Overview

IN THIS PART, we describe 12 types of strategic interventions that institutions have used to change the numbers, success, and experience of women scientists, mathematicians, and engineers. We classify these interventions into four categories: interrupting biased processes, rebooting workplaces, supporting the whole person, and fostering individual success. Each type of intervention focuses on a particular set of problems and challenges faced by women academics in STEM, and each offers a response to those challenges that can be incorporated into an overall change plan.

Any of these strategies could be included in an institution's portfolio for fostering organizational change to support women scholars in STEM fields. They are not necessarily best practices; rather, they are possible options whose value depends on how they fit into a specific institutional context and the particular local problems that institutional leaders wish to address. Each type of intervention has benefits but also limitations; each can be conceptualized, designed, and implemented in a variety of ways. These interventions become strategic when they are selected and implemented in direct relationship to the goals for organizational change and the particularities of the institutional context and when they are carefully combined and connected in an overall plan for advancing institutional change goals.

The discussion of each strategy is organized in a similar format:

- *Introductory comments* offer a succinct statement of the focus and scope of the strategy.
- *Rationale* reviews how the strategic intervention is relevant to organizational change initiatives focused on gender in STEM fields.
- *Purpose* defines the specific goals of the strategy or intervention.
- *Audience* indicates whom the strategy or intervention targets or intends to affect.
- *Models* include the variations and elements that can differ in the overall strategy or intervention, and they indicate choices about optimal elements of the strategy, which may depend on the specific institutional goals and context.
- *Examples* provide numerous and varied institutional instances of how the strategy has been used and may be distinguished by model type.
- *Evaluation* offers evidence, where available, for how institutions have assessed the value and impact of the strategy; we highlight particular evaluation findings when available.
- *Affordances and limitations* include the benefits that can accrue from using the strategy, as well as possible drawbacks to consider, depending on the specific variations used.
- *Summary* provides our general assessment of the strategy and its potential contributions as part of an institutional change portfolio.
- *Further reading* offers resources for learning more about the strategy.

All cited works appear in the reference list at the end of the book.

This common structure for presenting the strategies is derived from our analysis, and we recognize that different aspects of each are more or less important to readers' evaluation of the strategy and its relevance to their own institution. For some strategies, we have modestly adjusted the format to better accommodate the nature and amount of information available; for example, we have combined sections to avoid redundancy. When citing a specific institution as an example, we indicate in parentheses the cohort in which the institution received its ADVANCE IT award. This is relevant because ADVANCE IT projects evolved in structure and design as the NSF's solicitation evolved (Laursen & De Welde, 2019); awards to institutions in different cohorts varied in both what was allowed and what was innovative at the time, and our research did not sample all cohorts equally. Throughout the book, unattributed direct quotations are from interview data. To preserve respondents' anonymity, we do not identify the speakers. The full list of awardees is listed by award cohort and year in appendix A. Our study samples and the qualitative research methods used to identify the strategies are described in appendix B.

Chapter Three

Interrupt Biased Processes

The influence of widely held mental schemas about gender means that it's hard to think of women as good at the analytical and logical skills we associate with doing science. This type of implicit bias influences evaluation processes throughout the academy, but there are ways to disrupt the application of biases in recruitment, hiring, promotion, and advancement decisions.

THE CONCEPT OF implicit bias is based on a substantial body of work from cognitive science and social psychology, which shows that even well-intended people make unconscious assumptions that influence their judgments. These assumptions may surround names and personal characteristics related to race, gender, ethnicity, religion, and/or physical ability, or may involve stereotypes of certain fields, institutions, and job descriptions. These patterns of association (schemas) are psychologically efficient and may represent some common characteristics of group members, but they are inaccurate when applied to individuals simply because they belong to the group. Valian (1999) pointed out that in the United States, women have made greater and faster progress in joining the profession of medicine than they have in science and engineering. She argued that this difference is in part due to our ability to reconcile mental schemas of physicians as healers with schemas of women as caring and nurturing, while the same schemas of women as nurturers mentally conflict with schemas of engineers as rigorous and analytical. This makes it harder for us to see women as good engineers than to see women as good physicians. Such biases are pervasive and robust: as described in chapter 1, both men and women hold similar biases in terms of gender. Implicit bias toward one's own group may manifest as impostor syndrome or as internalized sexism, racism, or homophobia (Clair & Denis, 2015; DiAngelo, 2012).

A major contribution of the ADVANCE movement has been to develop practical, evidence-based strategies for addressing bias in some of the evaluation processes that occur throughout an academic career: hiring, tenure, promotion, peer review of publications and grant proposals, and consideration for awards and honors. Such evaluations are generally conducted through faculty-governed processes that are particularly susceptible to implicit bias because these processes are informal and collegial, using criteria that are often not standardized and involving decisions often made under pressure of time. Highly educated people—perhaps especially those trained in the sciences—may be likely to see their views as "objective" and informed by evidence rather than recognizing their own biases and acknowledging cultural influences. Moreover, studies show that even when presented with evidence about gender bias, men are more likely than women to dismiss or resist the evidence, while women more readily acknowledge its reality (Bird, 2011; Handley et al., 2015; Moss-Racusin, Molenda, & Cramer, 2015). Because men predominate in positions of power, such responses can enable bias to influence decision-making in academic institutions. Therefore it is essential to take active and continuing steps to recognize bias and find ways to disrupt it in institutional evaluation processes, such as the strategies developed by ADVANCE institutions. It is also important to acknowledge that not all bias is implicit: explicit bias is also real and relevant to faculty experiences. Faculty members must be empowered to respond actively to hateful language and behaviors, and institutional processes must be examined for discrimination, especially against groups that are not fully protected by the law, such as lesbian, gay, and gender-nonconforming faculty.

Strategy 1. Inclusive Recruitment and Hiring

The interventions described here increase diversity in recruiting and hiring new faculty. Some seek to diversify the pool of applicants that a hiring committee considers, while others aim to ensure fairness in evaluating applicants' credentials. A few are proactive in trying to meet the needs of highly ranked diverse candidates and induce them to accept a job offer if one is made.

All of these interventions are distinct from efforts to create a positive institutional environment that will be attractive to candidates—yet some of those broader efforts too may be helpful in recruiting and hiring women. For example, support for dual-career couples (Strategy 7) may attract strong women candidates and encourage them to accept a position if offered. Strategies 10, 11, and 12 describe interventions that support new faculty professionally after they arrive on campus, and Strategies 8 and 9 address policies and practices that enhance work/life balance. Such approaches may enhance candidates' positive impressions of the campus and their interest in the position, but they do not primarily target recruitment and hiring.

Rationale

While women's presence among earners of advanced STEM degrees is rising, women are still substantially underrepresented on STEM faculties and especially in high-status research institutions (NSF NCSES, 2019). Hiring a new faculty member creates an obvious opportunity to increase the representation of women and other people from groups that have been historically marginalized. Faculty colleagues hired today will shape the department and institution many years into the future through their teaching, research, community engagement, and leadership. Excellence in these domains is enriched when the faculty collectively represent a rich mix of interests, perspectives, talents, and backgrounds. This diversity stimulates intellectual discourse, reflects the population, and offers inspiration and mentoring to students of all backgrounds. Moreover, because human talents are widely distributed, a search for excellence cannot be exhaustive unless it welcomes applicants of all types and fairly evaluates their potential to contribute. As Stewart and Valian (2018) noted, diversity is intrinsically coupled to excellence, and this message speaks to faculty values and lies at the heart of the academic ideal to responsibly engage and debate ideas for their intrinsic worth.

A focus on hiring may yield fruit, but because faculty careers are long, it is a slow way to increase the representation of white women and people of color of any gender (Marschke et al., 2007). Hiring cannot be a revolving door: inclusive hiring must be coupled to effective retention measures that foster the success and happiness of new faculty members. This both optimizes the individual's development and protects the university's investment. Indeed, replacing a faculty member is much more expensive than retaining one already hired since it may take up to 10 years to recoup the start-up costs of hiring a new STEM faculty member with external funds brought into the institution (National Research Council, 2007). Schloss and coauthors (2009) made similar calculations of the high cost of turnover among clinical faculty in medical schools.

An important tool in making recruiting and hiring processes more inclusive is the research on implicit or unconscious bias (or, more simply, bias). Search committees benefit from having ways to identify and counter the biases in their own minds and to challenge biased statements when they arise in discussions. Because it is evidence-based and because it shifts the focus of conversation from discriminatory behavior to biases that we all hold but can actively work to neutralize, educating faculty about implicit bias has been a powerful tool for reframing conversations about diversity in the context of recruiting new faculty colleagues.

Purpose

The basic purpose of interventions related to recruitment and hiring is to increase the number of women in a department or institution. In STEM fields where women are strongly underrepresented, an initial goal is often conceived in terms of reaching a "critical mass" (Etzkowitz et al., 1994). This concept holds that a minority group, such as women in science, is easily marginalized when the group is very small, but as the group's size and participation grow, the relationship between minority and majority groups shifts. The minority group becomes self-sustaining and self-organizing, and members may gain power and authority that were "previously beyond their grasp" (p. 51). However, as Etzkowitz and coauthors (1994) note, growth in numbers without fundamental change in the structure of the workplace does not alter working conditions for the minority. Thus, initiatives to hire women in STEM must be coupled with other institutional changes that address structural biases and enable women to succeed on equal terms.

Because of their importance to departments, hiring decisions offer good opportunities to educate faculty about inclusive search and hiring processes and to initiate meaningful conversation about the many dimensions of excellence and how to evaluate it. Engaged leaders can raise the profile of these issues, link excellence and diversity as shared values, and model norms of behavior. Moreover, the excitement of making a new hire who belongs to an underrepresented group may have high symbolic value in units where the numbers of women are low, such as computer science. This symbolism is especially salient for women students, who may be closely watching their faculty as role models and representatives of success in their chosen field and who are looking to faculty and departments to communicate inclusive values (De Welde & Laursen, 2011; Griffin, 2020).

Audience

In ADVANCE institutions, educational efforts were most often targeted to those with authority in hiring: members of departmental hiring committees, chairs or heads, and deans who make and approve hiring decisions. Administrative leaders are key not only in leading and overseeing recruitment and hiring, but in setting a tone for others who are involved. Campus affirmative action/equal opportunity (AA/EO) officers and human resources (HR) professionals were also frequently included in training and monitoring efforts. These educational activities were often augmented with measures to address the structural elements of recruiting and hiring, such as procedures for oversight and approval of a department's recruiting plan or its "short list" of desired candidates (see also Strategy 3). Careful deliberation was encouraged through incentives to encourage departments to apply inclusive hiring practices—and with accountability measures if they did not.

Some activities at the later stages of the hiring process targeted prospective faculty candidates, as ADVANCE projects sought to provide equitable and informative campus visits or to convince a preferred candidate to accept a job offer.

Models

Similar to institutional efforts on tenure and promotion (Strategy 2), efforts toward inclusive hiring made use of both structural and educational models, but educational efforts were generally emphasized. Institutions nearly always deployed multiple activities to affect the hiring process from start to finish.

EDUCATION

Many institutions developed education or training for faculty evaluators who were part of the search process, with dual goals to ensure procedural fairness and to reduce bias in evaluating applicants. The key content of such trainings included search guidelines and operating procedures, best practices for evaluating candidates, and how to conduct interviews and campus visits. Recruitment topics addressed search committee composition, the use of inclusive language in job postings, the value of a broad job description in casting a wide net for applicants, and strategies for the proactive recruiting of women and other minority candidates. Best practices often emphasized the implicit bias literature and recommended ways to catch and curb bias, whether one's own or others', and engaged people in discussing case studies or scenarios (e.g., Bird, 2011). Information about campus visits addressed issues such as avoiding bias-based and overly personal interview questions and providing opportunities for candidates to have their questions answered outside the formal interview process.

Project leaders commonly noted the success of an evidence-based and interactive presentation style in these educational efforts. Variations in the design and format of such efforts included the following:

- Whether the training was encouraged or required.
- Whom the training targeted: search committee chairs, department chairs, or all search committee members. This choice was related to campus size and the number of searches going on.
- How the training was offered. Formats included in-person single or multipart workshops, videos, and online self-paced modules, such as the Faculty Recruitment Best Practices tutorial developed at the University of Rhode Island (Cohort 2, https://web.uri.edu/advance-women/files/Recruit _Handbook-downloadversion.pdf).
- Who led the training. Often, ADVANCE program personnel developed and piloted the training, sometimes with the help of external consultants, and then they engaged other faculty, AA/EO personnel, or HR staff in extending the training more broadly. Visiting scholars with appropriate expertise could also be used to promote the need for inclusive hiring.

At Case Western Reserve University (Cohort 2), search committee training was customized to each department, drawing on information from a one-on-one meeting with the search chair. Case also developed a program of cultural competency training, completion of which was required of all faculty within a year of their hire. This course focused on "faculty life in the lab, classroom, and department and raise[d] awareness about the impact of various kinds of bias on the campus climate, as well as how it impacts the success and retention of women faculty and faculty of color."

Training was often augmented by brochures, manuals, or online guidebooks. For example, the University of Puerto Rico at Humacao (Cohort 1) developed and promoted *A Guide for Affirmative Action in the Recruitment of Faculty Personnel*, which was vetted by the university's legal counsel to ensure that it met the needed standards, and this guide continued to be used for some time.

At Kansas State University (Cohort 2), the ADVANCE program assisted departments in reviewing their websites for equitable language and other positive or negative signals that they might inadvertently give, based on an analytical tool developed by Burack and Franks (2006), the Gender Equity Website Evaluation Rubric (https://www.k-state.edu/kawse/advance/publications/docs/website-rubric .pdf).

The University of Nebraska–Lincoln (Cohort 4) gathered and organized data to present to department chairs about hiring, graduation demographics, and potential hiring pools in their fields at the local and national levels and in peer institutions. One goal was to dispel erroneous beliefs about the availability of women and of men of color as potential candidates in each field and to provide realistic benchmarks. Sharing this information at the "departmental data breakfast" became a tradition.

INCENTIVES

Some institutions deployed incentives to improve departments' attention to diversity throughout a search process.

Extra funding for early recruiting was used to target graduate students and postdocs from underrepresented groups in order to garner their interest in the institution even before they were actively job hunting. For example, an initiative in the engineering school at Kansas State (Cohort 2) called Recruiting to Expand Applicant Pools supported senior faculty to take recruiting trips to sites or meetings likely to have large numbers of potential women candidates. Recruiters identified specific candidates in advance and set up short meetings to engage their interest in Kansas State.

The University of Texas at El Paso (Cohort 2) provided funding to bring an extra interviewee to campus if that candidate would add to faculty diversity. This practice resulted in hiring women in proportions above their representation on the interview short list.

The University of Montana (Cohort 2) developed a two-for-one hiring practice whereby a committee could request to hire two candidates rather than one, if both candidates would enhance the department's diversity.

To improve data collection on diversity in hiring, the University of Michigan (Cohort 1) required departments to collect and submit demographic information about their search process (including interviews, offers, and hires) if they wished to be eligible for special funding opportunities from the provost's office.

The University of Rhode Island (Cohort 2) targeted hiring through its Faculty Fellows program, which provided two- or three-year fellowships for women who then transitioned into tenure-track faculty lines. ADVANCE worked with the provost's office to provide up to $20,000 in start-up funds and to offer matching funds for new proposals that included the fellow as a co-investigator. This approach attracted departments' interest, drew attention to the ADVANCE project, and led to the hiring of 10 women who became very successful. Departments that received a faculty fellow were required to provide a mentoring plan for her and were asked to participate in specific programs, such as the departmental climate workshop (see Strategy 5). Project leaders observed that these very strong hires had positive effects on faculty views of women scientists' capabilities and dispelled myths that there are too few good women to hire.

BUILDING THE APPLICANT POOL

Most efforts to build the applicant pool focused on extending the reach of the job advertisement and ensuring that its language was inclusive. Broader descriptions of the search field, skills, and ways a candidate could demonstrate excellence cast a wider net and signaled a forward-looking view of the field and the potential contributions a new colleague could make (Tuitt, Sagaria, & Turner, 2007). Other approaches were intended to speak directly to diverse candidates, for example, job descriptions that explicitly showed how the faculty role engages with diversity through teaching, mentoring, or community-engaged scholarship (Smith et al., 2004).

Lehigh University (Cohort 5) took a distinctive approach to building its applicant pool. Drawing on literature that suggests women are attracted to interdisciplinary work in STEM, Lehigh sought to make cluster hires in STEM interdisciplinary programs. In this mid-size institution, the cluster hiring approach was seen as a faster way to build a critical mass of women than waiting for positions to open in each department. A set of related support structures was also designed so that the new hires could be successful in conducting interdisciplinary work and receiving tenure and promotion. At Lehigh, interdisciplinary work was seen as a way to broaden faculty networks, facilitate mentoring, and reduce isolation. Yet such positions could have been risky for individual faculty members if evaluation standards were not also adjusted and support mechanisms provided (Munoz et al., 2017; Sá, 2008a, 2008b). Thus, an important element was education of faculty members—not only those involved in searches, but chairs, deans, mentors, and others who are essential in enabling new faculty members to succeed and in fairly evaluating interdisciplinary scholarship for tenure and promotion (see Strategy 5).

ACCOUNTABILITY

Some institutions added or altered steps in their search procedures to ensure that applicants received equal treatment and that search committees had been diligent in their efforts.

At the University of Maryland, Baltimore County (Cohort 2), the provost required all departments to submit a written plan detailing how each new faculty search process would create a diverse and inclusive pool of candidates. Chairs of departments and search committees attended a workshop about conducting an inclusive search.

At Case Western Reserve University (Cohort 2), deans could return the short list of candidates to the department without approval for on-campus interviews if the list did not reflect the diversity of the national pool. In turn, deans and department heads were held accountable for progress on diversity as an element of their annual reviews.

At the University of Montana (Cohort 2), deans reviewed demographic data provided by the human resources office and signed a statement: "I have reviewed the composition of this candidate pool and found it to reflect national availability of diverse faculty by race and gender in this field. In cases where the pool is not fully reflective, an exhaustive effort to obtain a diverse candidate pool has been made."

At the University of California, Irvine (Cohort 1), equity advisors (EAs) based in each college held signature authority at several stages of the search process (see Strategy 3). Initially, the Search Activity Statement provided information about the composition of the search committee, the language for the job posting, and venues and duration for advertisements. The EA could thus ascertain that the search committee was implementing the best practices that had been shared in educational sessions for the committee. Before people were invited for campus visits, the EA reviewed the short list of candidates, along with information about the recruitment pool and national availability in the field. Based on this information, the EA might ask questions of the search committee or consult the dean. The EA's signature on the form was required before the search could proceed. This process asked search committees to proactively identify steps to generate a diverse applicant pool and to retrospectively reflect on how effective these steps had been.

Some institutions found it highly productive to work with their human resources personnel and/or AA/EO officers. ADVANCE projects provided these colleagues with data on national faculty composition, unconscious bias, and strategies to improve searches, seeking to develop allies and ensure that all involved were on the same page. Human resources staff could also transfer this knowledge to processes for hiring staff in nonfaculty roles, which would be a way to have broader influence on compositional diversity at the institution. For example, the University of Montana's (Cohort 2) Partnership for Comprehensive Equity (PACE) project found that many of the recruiting practices it had espoused became part of general university hiring standards. Likewise, at Utah State University (Cohort 2), the involvement of AA/EO and human resources personnel was key in sustaining hiring-related initiatives after the institution's ADVANCE grant ended.

LANDING THE CANDIDATE

A number of interventions addressed the final stage of the search process, when departments host campus visits and work to convince their preferred candidate to accept a job offer.

- *Equity in negotiation and start-up.* Hunter College (Cohort 1) reviewed start-up packages offered to faculty and prepared a template for offer letters. Kansas State (Cohort 2) included start-up packages as a topic in its training for department heads and provided a template with categories for items that might be included in a start-up package. Such approaches seek to minimize differences in start-up resources that may arise from gendered differences in negotiation tactics, improve the transparency of the negotiation process, and ensure that all new faculty have from the outset what they need to succeed.
- *Opportunities for growth.* Some institutions made a point to alert candidates to faculty development opportunities, such as grants or mentoring programs. The University of Colorado Boulder (Cohort 1) incorporated its early-career leadership workshop, which was developed under an ADVANCE award, into new faculty offer letters. The letters highlighted this professional development opportunity and described the stipend paid for successful completion.
- *Dual-career and work/life policies.* Providing information on work/life policies was widely thought to signal institutional commitment to the support of women scholars, as was support for dual-career couples (Strategy 7). Approaches included publicizing such information on institutional websites and proactively highlighting such policies to candidates during campus visits.
- *Confidential inquiries.* Many ADVANCE projects created opportunities during campus visits for candidates to meet with people who were not members of the search committee, so that candidates could ask confidential questions (e.g., about childcare, elder care, dual-career options, domestic partner benefits, and the local community and culture). These campus resource people were equipped with the information to answer likely questions; people taking these roles in various situations included ADVANCE leaders, other senior faculty women, and faculty members of color. At the University of Montana (Cohort 2) this group was formalized as the Council of Recruitment Advisors.

- *Welcome packet.* Some campuses prepared welcome packets that outlined resources for faculty, such as the ADVANCE program, lactation centers, partner-hiring networks, and relocation services. Additional information about the community might include area maps, brochures of local attractions, visitor guides, K–12 school information, and special interest resources such as newspapers or cultural centers for particular ethnic or religious groups.
- *Research support.* At the University of Maryland, Baltimore County (Cohort 2), departments could apply for funds to support a graduate research assistant for the new hire when she arrived on campus. The department in turn committed to working with the new hire to develop a faculty development plan and to find a mentor. This award sought to help new faculty quickly start a successful research career at a teaching-intensive institution.

LOOKING TO THE FUTURE OF THE FACULTY

In the early years of the ADVANCE program, some ADVANCE IT projects sought to strengthen the pools of women and minority scholars who might in the future apply for faculty positions by enhancing the interest and qualifications of people who were currently pursuing undergraduate STEM majors, completing graduate school, or seeking postdoctoral positions and who could become future faculty. One common model for this type of intervention was workshops, brown-bag lunches, or panels on academic (and other) career paths. These sessions typically targeted graduate students and postdocs of all genders. Other gatherings focused on networking, entrepreneurship, and "speed mentoring" with a CV review. Often these efforts were spun off from early-career faculty development activities that were already under way, and reframed for an audience of potential future faculty.

The University of Maryland, Baltimore County (UMBC, Cohort 2), offered a two-day workshop on "what it takes to be successful" for 60 graduate students and postdocs each year, targeting women and others from underrepresented minority groups. The Faculty Horizons program drew 800 applicants in four years. While UMBC did not recruit a workshop participant for its own faculty as a result of this program, leaders noted a positive effect on faculty attitudes and beliefs about the presence and qualifications of minority candidates, and workshop participants were hired at other institutions.

Some institutions developed or strengthened work/life policies for postdocs and graduate students. For example, Virginia Polytechnic Institute (Virginia Tech, Cohort 2) offered financial assistance to departments for supporting graduate students during pregnancy and childbirth. Leaders at Columbia University (Cohort 2) reviewed the family leave policies for postdocs, a particularly important group in the research institute where Columbia's ADVANCE IT project was headquartered.

Efforts to diversify the pool of future faculty starting at the undergraduate level most often took the form of support for undergraduate research students in STEM fields. New Mexico State University (Cohort 1) and University of Puerto Rico at Humacao (Cohort 1) supported undergraduate research assistants as a form of research support for their women STEM faculty. The ACES (Academic Careers in Engineering and Science) project at Case Western Reserve (Cohort 2) provided support for summer ACES fellows from minority-serving institutions to conduct research with Case faculty.

The University of Montana (Cohort 2) directed ADVANCE support toward Native American students on its campus and toward building statewide connections among Native American women scientists. And New Mexico State (Cohort 1) scheduled its visiting scholars to interact with local K–12 classrooms.

The NSF's solicitation for the ADVANCE program eventually excluded funding for pool-building efforts that directly supported students, specifying that ADVANCE work should focus on faculty (see Laursen & De Welde, 2019, for a discussion of changes in the ADVANCE solicitation over time). Many other NSF-supported programs and projects continue to support efforts to diversify the pool of future faculty applicants. Readers interested in strategies for diversifying the future faculty are encouraged to consult sources such as Building Engineering and Science Talent, or BEST (2004); Espinosa, McGuire, and Jackson (2019); Estrada and coauthors (2016); Mack, Winter, and Soto (2019); and National Research Council (2011).

Examples

The University of Michigan's (Cohort 1) STRIDE (Strategies and Tactics for Recruiting to Improve Diversity and Excellence) committee has served as a prototype for many other institutions. Committee members were senior faculty who first educated themselves about implicit bias by reading and discussing the literature, and then carried this information to departments. They offered an interactive, data-based presentation to departments and worked with search committees to maximize the chances that well-qualified women and other minority candidates would be identified and, if selected for job offers, recruited, retained, and promoted. Crucially, STRIDE involved distinguished scholars and campus thought leaders with the legitimacy and power to generate urgency, mobilize allies, and build leadership networks as "organizational catalysts" (Sturm, 2007).

The Women in Science & Engineering Leadership Institute (WISELI) at the University of Wisconsin–Madison (Cohort 1) developed a workshop called Searching for Excellence and Diversity and offered it widely across departments and schools. WISELI has made this workshop, as well as its handbooks and brochures on hiring, available to other institutions (e.g., Fine & Handelsman, 2012a, 2012b). WISELI materials identify the essential elements of this workshop as the following:

- *Peer teaching.* The workshop involves faculty from the unit to deliver short presentations and serve as discussion facilitators.
- *Active learning.* Most time is spent in discussing workshop material and in sharing practices from different departments, while lecture-style presentation is kept to a minimum.
- *Unconscious biases and assumptions.* Participants are introduced to the social psychological literature on unconscious biases and learn how these tendencies might affect the hiring process.
- *Accountability.* Participants report on their success in recruiting diverse applicants to their pools.

Evaluation reports show that the workshops have been useful to the participants and that departments who sent at least one faculty member to a hiring workshop made more offers to and hired more women applicants. People who attended the workshops were much more likely than others to disagree that "the climate for faculty of color in my department is good," a finding felt by WISELI leaders to indicate greater awareness of the actual climate experienced by faculty of color. Later studies showed that several months after the workshop, participants showed ongoing bias awareness and reported behaviors that reflected that heightened awareness. These changes and self-reported actions were greater in departments that received the intervention and where at least 25% of faculty had participated. Most important, these departments hired 18% more women following the intervention (Carnes et al., 2012; Carnes et al., 2015; Devine et al., 2017).

Evaluation

Many institutions used field-specific data on current faculty composition versus national averages and national hiring pools as a tool to identify successes and opportunities and to raise awareness in individual departments and colleges. Such data can also be used to monitor the net impact of hiring initiatives by tracking the demographics of applicants and of candidates named to the short list, brought to campus, receiving offers, and ultimately hired. Because women's representation varies notably across different STEM fields, it is generally useful to compare local data with national statistics on the demographics of faculty in the specific discipline and, as a proxy for the diversity of the national hiring pool, on PhDs awarded in that field. Sources of comparative data include the NSF's National Center for Science and Engineering Statistics (NCSES) (www.nsf.gov/statistics), the American Association of University Professors (www.aaup.org/our-work/research), and some disciplinary societies that gather field-specific data.

Several campuses strengthened their processes for gathering data on applicant demographics, generally by working with the AA/EO officer or human resources office so that data could be gathered—but not inappropriately used—in decision-making. Some also tracked search committee composition and its relation to the demographics of applicant and candidate groups. The flux charts made popular by Hunter College (Cohort 1) are a visual way to document combined progress in hiring and promoting women; they highlight changes in faculty composition at each rank due to hiring, promotion, or departure. Ideally, such tracking is put in place in such a way that it can be sustained after the grant. Many ADVANCE leaders found it important to build a constituency for these data among institutional leaders, so that the effort to gather and report them could be sustained.

Whether or not such data show any change in the net percentage of women faculty will depend on both faculty size and opportunities to hire during the monitoring period. In our study sample, the greatest growth was observed at smaller institutions and for periods when hiring was not hampered by economic downturns. For example, New Mexico State (Cohort 1) was able to double its hiring of women in tenure-track faculty positions in STEM from 17% to 35% over seven years, creating a net increase in STEM women faculty of more than 40%. In contrast, other ADVANCE institutions faced budget constraints that prevented any hiring, so they focused on retention and advancement.

Because change in faculty composition is slow (Marschke et al., 2007), extended data collection is required to tie quantitative changes in faculty composition directly to hiring practices. At the University of California, Irvine (Cohort 1), evaluators reported that the percentage of women among new hires was greatest in those schools in which the equity advisors reported the most involvement in searches—with deans, search committees, and department chairs—suggesting that the EA model can be effective. Chairs and faculty felt that interactions with the EA had raised search committees' awareness and changed faculty thinking by "putting the subject of equity on the table." Long-term studies do demonstrate meaningful change in the hiring of women in response to institutional interventions, including published studies from the University of Wisconsin–Madison and Montana State (Devine et al., 2017; Smith et al., 2015). At the University of Michigan, researchers were able to connect quantitative data that showed an increase in women's representation in certain STEM departments to qualitative data about enabling features of these departments, especially the leadership of senior department members who took responsibility for the problem and were proactive in pursuing a more diverse faculty (Stewart, Malley, & Herzog, 2016). Conversely, these enabling features were missing in departments where hiring patterns had not changed.

ADVANCE projects' evaluation of their educational programs on implicit bias and recruitment often involved the use of self-reported measures of individuals' satisfaction and learning. Some of these measures can be tracked over time to connect them to training interventions (e.g., Sekaquaptewa et al., 2019). As a measure of the reach of such efforts, it is also useful to track who attends from which departments and what positions of influence they hold (e.g., chairs, search committee members). Over time, what percentage of all faculty or of a given target group has participated?

The University of Alabama at Birmingham (Cohort 2) used climate survey data to make arguments about the impact of its training for search committees. Survey items useful for this purpose focused, for example, on changes over time in respondents' awareness of initiatives to increase the number of women faculty, perceptions that their department made a concerted effort to invite qualified women to apply or interview and that qualified women did apply, and perceptions of fairness in the hiring process.

A study at Case Western Reserve (Cohort 2) examined the relationship of candidate pools to hiring for nearly 200 STEM searches in a six-year period. The researchers found that the proportion of women on the short list was significantly related to the likelihood of hiring a woman, and the proportion on the short list of other candidates from underrepresented groups was significantly related to the likelihood of selecting a candidate from a minority group (https://case.edu/aces /sites/case.edu.aces/files/2018-04/Candidate_Pool_Study-_Final_Report_6-26 -08.pdf).

Affordances and Limitations

Affordances of interventions that focus on hiring include the following:

- Hiring offers an obvious means to increase compositional diversity, especially if institutions have opportunities to grow a program or a school or to make cluster hires.
- Hiring in their department or college is important to faculty, and they take it seriously. Search processes may thus be a good place to reach sizable numbers of faculty with training and consciousness raising.
- The institution already invests substantial faculty time in any search; adding a diversity focus does not add much cost. Some activities are not expensive, such as extra funds for recruitment travel or interviews of candidates who would enhance diversity.
- What search committee members learn about implicit bias can be usefully applied in multiple domains in addition to hiring, including tenure and promotion decisions, recommendation letters, faculty recognition, and graduate admissions. Some institutions reported an informal trickle-over of these ideas into other domains, and some formalized the application of implicit bias ideas in additional domains. For example, Texas A&M University (Cohort 5) adapted its implicit bias workshop for search committees to prepare committees making decisions about college-wide and institutional awards.
- One institution found that search training customized for the department helped to avoid a one-size-fits-all mentality that could generate resistance to implementing proposed changes. The team also found that a customized approach helped to clarify department chairs' perceptions of relationships and climate in their department.

Limitations include the following:

- The opportunity to hire is limited in smaller departments and in times of economic cutbacks—which was the case for many institutions of higher education during the period of our study. Departments can't make progress on diversity through hiring if they can't hire; instead, they must focus on success and retention, which tend to show less rapid influence on quantitative indicators, such as compositional diversity.
- Resistance may arise if faculty perceive that their autonomy to make hiring decisions is compromised or if they feel they are being asked to

lower the bar for excellence. Training seen as pro forma and compliance-oriented can backfire and lead to negative outcomes (Caleo & Heilman, 2019; Dobbin & Kalev, 2018). Messaging must link equity and excellence.

- Simply hiring new faculty colleagues from underrepresented groups does not change the context and climate for their work and success. Hiring initiatives must be coupled with efforts to ensure that the new hires survive and thrive.

- For educational interventions, interactive training models have been more successful than assigned readings alone. However, sustaining and refreshing these workshops over time, especially at a large institution that conducts many searches each year, requires substantial effort and personnel who can commit the needed time. If this work is initially funded by a grant, thought must be given as to how it will be sustained, and resources must be committed to this work.

- Activities that seek to diversify the pool of future faculty applicants address the general issue of women's representation but may not provide a direct payoff in terms of faculty hiring at the institution itself. Moreover, the roles of pipeline building and outreach in ADVANCE projects have evolved over time as grant specifications have changed (Laursen & De Welde, 2019).

Summary

Hiring has high importance, both real and symbolic, as a venue for institutions to address equity. The evidence shows that well-designed initiatives to educate faculty and empower them to identify and counter implicit bias have been effective elements of change projects, often playing a cornerstone role. Discussing bias in the context of hiring seems to have several advantages. It may be less sensitive to consider bias in evaluating still-unknown job applicants rather than known faculty colleagues who are candidates for advancement or awards. Faculty take hiring seriously, and administrators have leverage they can apply to encourage participation and strengthen accountability. Because addressing bias can have ramifications well beyond the hiring context, well-designed bias education can be a good step toward culture changes that make the academy more inclusive. To have these effects, implicit bias education should be led and attended by respected faculty; it should incorporate active learning approaches and peer-to-peer discussion and should make use of current scholarly literature. Bias education will have more impact when it is coupled with proactive efforts to diversify the pool of applicants for faculty positions and with accountability for search processes and outcomes. However, hiring alone will not yield rapid or profound changes in faculty composition, so hiring initiatives must be coupled with other efforts that enable women and other faculty from minoritized groups to succeed and persist.

FURTHER READING

Isaac, C., Lee, B., & Carnes, M. (2009). Interventions that affect gender bias in hiring: A systematic review. *Academic Medicine: Journal of the Association of American Medical Colleges,* *84*(10), 1440–1446.

Moody, J. (2010). *Rising above cognitive errors: Guidelines for search, tenure review, and other evaluation committees* (rev. ed.). Kindle Direct Publishing.

Moody, J. (2012). *Faculty diversity: Removing the barriers.* New York: Routledge.

Yong, D., & Pendakur, S. (2017). Advocating for diversity and inclusion in faculty hiring. *Notices of the AMS, 64*(8), 897–902.

Strategy 2. Equitable Processes of Tenure and Promotion

Interventions of this type address institutional processes and procedures for faculty advancement through promotion and tenure (P&T). Because candidates' understanding of and attitudes about these evaluative processes are as important as those of their evaluators, we include interventions that inform and advise faculty as they go through these processes.

We do not cover here interventions that seek to develop individual faculty members' professional qualifications, skills, and capacities that may be needed to obtain tenure or promotion (Strategies 10 and 11). See Strategy 8 for policies that adjust criteria and timelines for P&T to accommodate faculty responsibilities in both personal and professional domains.

Rationale

As formal mechanisms for evaluating faculty members, P&T processes seek to maintain the intellectual excellence, creativity, and scholarly reputation of the faculty as a whole. When these processes are biased in subtle and often invisible ways, or when they fail to provide equal protection and transparency for all faculty, they may result in inequity that serves to uphold the status quo. As Marschke and coauthors (2007) pointed out, increased efforts to hire women do not lead to growth in women's overall representation unless attention is also paid to their advancement through the ranks. Relatively few ADVANCE IT projects have focused directly on gender equity in institutional P&T processes, but many institutions have addressed more generally the ways in which evaluation of faculty may be biased, as discussed under Strategy 1.

Careful analysis of institutional data is required to determine whether and where there are gendered differences in the rates of tenure or promotion from assistant to associate professor and associate to full professor, or in time at rank. For example, at one institution, Marschke and coauthors (2007) found that women and men who applied for tenure were awarded tenure at equal rates, but women were somewhat more likely to leave the institution prior to a tenure review. They were also substantially more likely to depart at mid-career. Fuzzy criteria for advancement and unspoken departmental expectations may impede a faculty member's success (Fox & Colatrella, 2006; Gardner & Blackstone, 2013; Lennartz & O'Meara, 2018), and this may be exacerbated if women are excluded from informal networks where advice and information are shared. Thus, attention to transparency and equity in preparing for tenure or promotion can help to ensure that candidates of all genders are well prepared for and well advised through each advancement process and that candidates feel confident in facing these professional hurdles (Stewart & Valian, 2018).

When considering the work of those evaluating P&T dossiers, research in cognitive science has identified the importance of subconscious or implicit mental processes in making decisions. Though we may like to think of ourselves as guided by explicit beliefs and rational thinking, research shows that people often hold unconscious assumptions that influence their judgments, including assumptions about physical or social characteristics associated with race, gender, and ethnicity, as well as stereotypes or expectations of certain disciplines, institutions, and job descriptions (Valian, 1999). Research also shows that implicit biases are pervasive; many studies find, for example, that men and women hold similar gender stereotypes. Thus, establishing equitable P&T processes requires that people in evaluative roles know how to identify these unreasoned distortions of judgment, how to guard against applying them, and how to respond when their own or others' biases arise during deliberations—that is, people need to have concrete strategies to reduce biased behaviors and actions.

Other issues in tenure and promotion arise due to gendered differences in the professional interests and activities of scholars. Women scholars may be more likely to pursue applied, interdisciplinary, or community-based scholarship; they may use nontraditional research methods or publish in different outlets; they may publish fewer but more significant papers compared to male peers (Demb & Wade, 2012; Duch et al., 2012; Rhoten & Pfirman, 2007). When scholarship that falls outside the traditional bounds of a discipline is devalued or delegitimated, faculty may experience epistemic exclusion, which may surface both in colleagues' informal communications and in biased formal evaluation based on productivity metrics derived from traditional knowledge production (Settles, Buchanan, & Dotson, 2019).

Moreover, women in departments with low numbers of women often face high formal and informal advising loads because women students seek them out for mentoring or choose them as advisors; this is especially the case for women of color. They may be asked to serve on multiple committees in well-intended but burdensome efforts to broaden committee representation, and they may receive more invitations to do outreach to members of underrepresented groups. All of these opportunities and invitations may be attractive to women scholars but also shape their use of time in ways that are different from men (Social Sciences Feminist Network Research Interest Group, 2017). These challenges are similar in nature but even more keen for faculty of color (Bellas & Toutkoushian, 1999). All of these factors may affect the number, nature, and authorship of scholarly publications that faculty produce, as well as the nature and number of other activities they present in their advancement portfolios. These variations in faculty work must be recognized by departments that seek to value diversity and uphold fair standards of excellence across a wide range of faculty activities.

Because the pre-tenure phase often overlaps with the years during which faculty members are starting families and raising young children, work/life issues are especially relevant to the tenure process and concomitant transition from assistant to associate professor (Mason & Goulden, 2002). While women's attrition or failure to advance is often explained as a matter of choice around work/family balance, such explanations tend to ignore gendered constraints in academic systems and structures (Beddoes & Pawley, 2014). Thus, work/life policies that allow for flexibility in individuals' job duties over time are highly relevant to equity in advancement. Due to their importance, such policies are discussed separately in Strategy 8—but any consideration of equity in P&T processes should also attend to work/life issues so that across the institution, policies and practices are mutually supportive and not in conflict or negatively reinforcing.

Promotion from associate to full professor may be a second bottleneck for women's advancement. Data often show that women's time at the associate rank is longer. Work/life concerns may be relevant here too, for example for women who take care of older children or ill or aging family members. Other issues raised in the literature include women's tendency to take on significant service roles that may not be valued in advancement decisions (Misra et al., 2011) and perceptions of vagueness, subjectivity, and lack of clarity about the timeline and criteria for promotion (Fox & Colatrella, 2006; Gardner & Blackstone, 2013; Lennartz & O'Meara, 2018). One of our interviewees hypothesized, "Women wait for the fairy to tap them on the shoulder and tell them it's time to go up for full professor."

Purpose

Broadly speaking, ADVANCE projects sought to improve equity in promotion and tenure through several approaches. Efforts to increase the transparency of advancement processes sought to inform all participants about formal P&T review processes and criteria. Changes to policy and procedure might set up checks and balances to ensure that these formal processes are equitably applied. Goals of transparency about P&T processes targeted both applicants and reviewers, although different interventions were used to engage the early-career faculty who were candidates for tenure and the senior faculty who would review their cases.

In some cases, formal processes of P&T required adjustments to mesh with other institutional changes intended to address gender equity. For instance, enhanced institutional policies for flexible work arrangements, such as a policy on tenure-clock stoppage for a faculty member with a new baby (see Strategy 8), might also necessitate refinements to review procedures, such as developing standardized language for communicating a tenure-clock change to external reviewers.

A few ADVANCE projects targeted women's advancement from associate to full professor, using workshops or coaching that guided associate professors to reflect on whether and when to apply for promotion and advised them on preparing the portfolio. Such workshops also supported the career planning needed for those who decided they were not yet ready to apply for promotion but wanted to do so in the future.

While some institutions addressed bias related to formal P&T processes, rather more common among ADVANCE IT projects was explicit attention to informal sources of bias in evaluation more generally, including bias in hiring, awards, and recommendation letters. Many projects made use of a growing body of literature on the psychological reasons for implicit bias and ways to combat it.

Audience

Educational efforts about implicit bias and how to detect and combat it in evaluating faculty portfolios were targeted at various groups of influential faculty, such as deans, chairs and heads, and members of committees involved in hiring or selection for institutional awards. In a few cases, P&T committees were explicitly targeted with such education. More often, promotion and tenure processes were not directly addressed; rather, because training (e.g., for hiring committees) was expected to reach many members of the institution over time, it was imagined that individual faculty members might transfer and apply their knowledge of implicit bias in their evaluation of P&T cases. We hypothesize that project leaders found it easier to present and discuss implicit bias in contexts where it was more hypothetical—considering unknown candidates for faculty positions—than in the context of tenure or promotion, where the candidates are specific individuals already known to the reviewers.

Efforts to ensure that people approaching a tenure decision were well informed about the tenure process and criteria were generally targeted to all pre-tenure faculty as a group or by cohorts (e.g., all those preparing for a third-year review), depending on the size of the group. Some projects made special efforts to encourage women in STEM to participate.

Models

A variety of approaches was used to address equity in P&T processes. Broadly speaking, interventions were either structural, making adjustments to policies and formal procedures around P&T, or educational, seeking to influence the knowledge, skills, beliefs, and self-awareness of individuals about their P&T roles.

Structural interventions are designed to increase the fairness of formal advancement processes by establishing clear procedures, formalizing them across units, and ensuring that all candidates receive comparable advice and preparation. Policies and procedural guidelines may set in place checks and balances, assign oversight roles, or build in a standard timeline for initiating review processes so that faculty members are not left out and so that they receive accurate signals about their progress prior to major reviews. By clarifying and standardizing aspects of advancement processes that can vary from unit to unit or person to person, such interventions can increase both real and perceived transparency and accountability in the P&T process. Another type of structural intervention—policies that affect faculty duties (such as tenure-clock stoppage)—is discussed in Strategy 8 on flexible work arrangements. Overall, structural interventions addressing P&T were less common among the ADVANCE IT projects we studied than were educational activities.

Educational interventions seek to ensure that all participants in P&T proceedings are well informed about the process and their own role. They aim to influence the culture, behaviors, and norms around advancement decisions by informing candidates of requirements and expectations so that procedures can be applied equitably, by educating members of P&T review committees about potential sources of bias in evaluating candidates for advancement, and by providing structures in which deliberations can take place and questions or concerns can be raised.

Structural and educational interventions were occasionally combined in ADVANCE projects, for example, when certain types of training or preparation for P&T committees were required as a condition of committee service.

Examples of Structural Interventions

Georgia Institute of Technology (Georgia Tech, Cohort 1) established the Office of Faculty Career Development Services, which was charged with processing all personnel transactions for academic faculty, including appointments, reappointments, promotions, tenure, post-tenure reviews, leaves of absence, and salary adjustments. Centralizing these activities was intended to reduce disparities from college to college and ensure that procedures were equitably applied.

Utah State University (Cohort 2) established a position of ombudsperson for each college and provided training to help those chosen to carry out the ombudsperson duties. As nonvoting members of each P&T committee, the ombudspeople monitor P&T activities and ensure that policies and procedures are uniformly applied. They use a checklist to document that committee members are present and procedures are followed, and they have the power to stop a meeting if due process is violated. As a record of this process, a signed copy of the checklist is included with the committee's final decision letter. Utah State's policy was moved through the faculty senate and incorporated into the faculty code (the academic handbook defining faculty governance procedures). ADVANCE leaders observed that the ombudsperson process helped to catch and avoid procedural errors, dispel rumors of procedural abuse, and reduce the number of grievances filed.

Utah State also instituted a policy that a promotion committee be established for each faculty member three years after their promotion to associate professor, thus ensuring that faculty members and their departments consider and periodically review each person's progress toward promotion to full professor.

The University of Texas at El Paso (UTEP, Cohort 2) instituted a third-year review, requiring all colleges to carry out a formal evaluation of the progress made by untenured tenure-track faculty toward tenure and promotion no later than the fall semester of their fourth year at UTEP. This policy sought to provide assistant professors with a clear picture of their progress toward successfully achieving P&T

and to give departments a chance to review accomplishments and provide assistance to untenured faculty members prior to the tenure review.

Kansas State (Cohort 2) included a review of P&T documents for clarity and transparency as one requirement for departments that were funded in its ADVANCE initiative. Consistent with Kansas State's highly decentralized institutional setting, no attempt was made to standardize documents across departments. Instead, they were reviewed by the ADVANCE team for areas of potential bias, and advice was given to departments as to how they could improve their P&T processes and communications. Project leaders reported that once given guidance, faculty could look at their policy documents and identify potential issues and ways to improve them. This can be viewed as a process of both education and improvement to formal P&T structures.

Examples of Educational Interventions

Here we separate examples of educational interventions by the audience and purpose of the activities. Recommended practices for all types of education include engaging faculty in active learning through a mix of teaching strategies, such as role playing, analysis of problem-based scenarios, panel discussions, small-group tasks, topical breakout sessions, or whole-group discussions. Providing food and beverages helps to attract participants and foster informal conversation.

EDUCATION AND TRAINING ABOUT IMPLICIT BIAS

At Georgia Tech (Cohort 1), the ADVANCE program developed an interactive online tool for preparing P&T committees for their work. The Awareness of Decisions in Evaluating Promotion and Tenure (ADEPT) tool includes case studies, games, and an extensive bibliography that are together intended to help users learn to identify forms of bias in evaluation and thus achieve more fair and objective reviews. Modules are targeted both to candidates preparing a record for evaluation and to members of P&T committees who will review such records. After piloting and testing, review of this online material was required of all members of P&T committees, and often committees were also required to discuss best practices and analyze fictional cases with their peers. Leaders reported that committees that discussed the hypothetical cases and consulted the games found they had less contentious deliberations. Review of the cases also helped committees to establish some shared understanding about criteria before they addressed the merits of specific tenure cases. The ADEPT resources are available online (http:/adept.gatech .edu; see also Rosser, 2007).

Several other institutions developed implicit bias training for other purposes, which was offered to various campus constituencies, including department chairs, deans, and hiring committees. Anecdotal reports indicated some trickle-over effect of this training into P&T committee deliberations. These efforts are discussed above in Strategy 1 on recruitment and hiring, because implicit bias training was often used as an intervention to influence hiring processes.

EDUCATION AND TRAINING FOR INSTITUTIONAL LEADERS

Several institutions offered workshops or seminar series to department heads that addressed their dual responsibilities for mentoring colleagues through P&T and carrying out evaluation processes fairly (see also Strategy 4 on development of institutional leaders). Workshop topics included:

- implementing flexible work policies, such as opportunities for faculty to stop the tenure clock or take on modified duties (Strategy 8), especially if these policies were new or revised
- carrying out tenure review (for new chairs or after a new process was implemented)
- mentoring early-career faculty through tenure
- conducting annual performance evaluations and awarding merit raises
- evaluating the scholarship of engagement (O'Meara, Eatman, & Petersen, 2015).

In addition to workshops, a variety of other educational strategies for unit leaders was developed.

The University of Michigan (Cohort 1) ADVANCE program worked with an on-campus theater group, the CRLT Players (based at the Center for Research on Learning and Teaching), to develop and disseminate an interactive theater presentation called *The Faculty Meeting*, which depicted faculty discussions on important topics, such as faculty searches and P&T decisions. Drawing on "forum theater" techniques that ask the audience to determine the course of the scenario, the skit showed how gender dynamics and faculty rank influence these conversations and affect the people involved (Kumagai et al., 2007; LaVaque-Manty, Steiger, & Stewart, 2007; Stewart & Valian, 2018). The CRLT Players have developed other skits related to bias in STEM, and their popular approach has been adopted by other institutions.

At Virginia Tech (Cohort 2), results from the Collaborative on Academic Careers in Higher Education (COACHE) survey of pre-tenure faculty were used to educate department heads and P&T committees on how pre-tenure colleagues experience life in their departments and the tenure process.

At Georgia Tech, the Promotion and Tenure ADVANCE Committee surveyed the faculty to examine their perceptions of advancement processes, faculty development, and evaluation. The committee also identified best practices in unit P&T practices and generated a report that was shared with all deans and chairs and made available on the ADVANCE website.

The PACE program at the University of Montana (Cohort 2) developed a retention guidebook intended to support chairs and other senior faculty in providing a supportive work environment and thus helping to retain a diverse and excellent faculty. The guidebook includes information on policies, mentoring, departmental climate, and everyday interactions (www.umt.edu/provost/faculty/faculty -development-office/chairs/docs/RetentionGuideBook.pdf).

EDUCATION OF PRE-TENURE FACULTY

Numerous ADVANCE institutions offered periodic short workshops or information sessions to apprise pre-tenure faculty of the tenure and promotion process, discuss preparation of the dossier, and address questions. Common formats for these sessions included working lunches, presentations or panels of senior administrators and P&T committee members, and panels of recently tenured associate professors. New faculty orientations offered an opportunity to share information needed early in a faculty career, while workshops offered later in the career timeline were more detailed and more focused. In addition to stand-alone events, P&T topics were often incorporated as sessions into other, more comprehensive faculty development programs for early-career faculty (see Strategy 10). Basic topics for these sessions included the departmental, college, and university review process and timeline, and the rights and responsibilities of tenure candidates. More extended programs included one-on-one consultation about dossier preparation, long-term career planning, or peer mentoring on issues of concern to faculty. Some projects constructed websites and produced documents that detailed processes and gathered resources.

At the University of Maryland, Baltimore County (Cohort 2), procedures were formalized to ensure that by the end of their first semester, all newly hired faculty members will have worked with their department chairs to develop a personal career development plan. The plan identifies major milestones that must be met in order to prepare successfully for a third-year review and tenure decision. The design of this intervention has an educational emphasis but includes a structural element due to its formalization across departments.

Many ADVANCE projects noted that tenure-related concerns and questions were frequently addressed in their mentoring programs (Strategy 12). At Case Western Reserve (Cohort 2), speed mentoring enabled individuals to gather feedback and advice on their CVs from senior faculty from other fields, particularly on how their CV might be viewed by someone outside the discipline. Likewise, the University of Colorado Boulder (Cohort 1) found that a coach from a different department could dispel myths about P&T and reduce anxiety among pre-tenure faculty members. Occasionally, more serious concerns could be identified and solutions sought proactively before they became barriers to a successful tenure bid.

EDUCATION FOR PROMOTION TO FULL PROFESSOR

A few institutions offered occasional workshops or informational brown-bag sessions for associate professors who were considering whether and when to apply for full professor rank. Topics included setting career priorities, making and implementing a career plan, and preparing a promotion dossier. Sessions provided opportunities for participants to reflect on and clarify their own goals and to compare notes with others. In some cases, these resources were targeted at women (and men) who had remained in the associate rank longer than average. ADVANCE leaders at one campus noticed a surge of applications—and several promotions to full professor—in the year following such a session.

Evaluation

Quantitative data on faculty composition by gender and rank, drawn from institutional records, are often used to identify issues and monitor institutional or departmental progress on women's advancement through faculty ranks. Interpreting these data can be challenging when the number of women in a field is small, and thus trends over time are hard to detect or to separate from the merits of specific advancement cases. However, such data, especially when set in a national disciplinary context, can be useful in helping departments to identify opportunities to improve and in monitoring progress on institutional goals.

Flux charts popularized by Hunter College's (Cohort 1) Gender Equity Project have been a useful tool at some institutions to communicate broad changes over time in women's status by rank within or across departments. They can be a visually effective way to portray trends in individuals' movement between ranks, showing, for instance, whether a decline in the number of women assistant professors is due to their promotion to associate professor or to their departure from the institution. Examples and instructions for preparing flux charts can be found at the Gender Equity Project's website (http://www.hunter.cuny.edu/genderequity /initiatives/benchmarks).

For educational interventions, standard approaches to evaluating workshops, such as short post-surveys or focus groups, can be used to probe the extent to which participants feel more knowledgeable and find the information useful, and to refine the delivery of workshops and info sessions (see also Strategy 10). Because P&T decisions are so individual, it is hard to measure or monitor the actual impact of educational approaches on P&T preparation, committee deliberations, or outcomes. Climate surveys may be useful to identify process and perception issues that need to be addressed and to monitor progress on them. For this purpose, many institutions have used the survey on faculty job satisfaction that is offered by the Collaborative on Academic Careers in Higher Education; a newer COACHE survey explicitly addresses faculty retention and exit.

Affordances and Limitations

Several affordances and limitations to addressing P&T were observed in the context of ADVANCE IT projects in our sample. Affordances of structural approaches include the following:

- Policy solutions are likely to be lasting and sustainable. Guidelines can be used to define in detail how a policy will be carried out and by whom. Institutional officers have responsibility and oversight for faculty advancement, and thus lines of accountability are generally clear.
- Policies apply to everyone; thus, they can reduce the impact of informal processes, which can be unfair, and can also address perceptions of inequality.

Their limitations may include the following:

- Aspects of campus culture—especially around centralization and hierarchy—may make it difficult or impossible to standardize P&T processes across all schools, colleges, or departments.
- Some resistance may be encountered if new procedures or policies are seen as infringing on faculty autonomy and leadership in defining standards of excellence for tenure and promotion.

Affordances of educational approaches include the following:

- Learning about implicit bias can be useful to faculty in multiple professional contexts, including evaluation for hiring, P&T, awards, admissions, recommendation letters, and undergraduate instruction.

- Because tenure and promotion are important to faculty, education on these issues is likely to be taken seriously.
- Over time, education on this topic can reach many faculty and influence a cultural change in how advancement processes are carried out and dossiers reviewed—helping to "push the needle," as one leader described it.

Limitations of these approaches include the following:

- Not all faculty participate in P&T deliberations, or they may not do so until well along in their careers. It may take a long time for new knowledge and behaviors to spread. Conversely, at some point, the training will reach saturation, and new approaches will be required.
- It is difficult to measure the impact of educational approaches on P&T outcomes.

Summary

Initiatives focused on tenure and promotion may be helpful in an institutional change portfolio to advance faculty equity. Demystifying the P&T process is important for all faculty, but especially for women and members of other groups who may have less access to informal knowledge networks. Support for those preparing for promotion to full professor is often neglected on campuses and therefore may be particularly influential.

Viewed from the institutional side, there is less evidence from ADVANCE projects about the impact of bias education for P&T evaluators than there is for hiring-related evaluation (Strategy 1). Such approaches may be most helpful when they are embedded in wider efforts to standardize P&T processes and broaden evaluation criteria (see O'Meara & Rice, 2005). One strategy that deserves more attention, in our view, is Utah State's ombudsperson approach to ensuring that appropriate processes are followed. In some institutions, equity advisors (Strategies 1 and 3) may be able to play this role.

FURTHER READING

Awareness of Decisions in Evaluating Promotion and Tenure [ADEPT] Library, Georgia Tech. (n.d.). Bibliography of Bias in Evaluation. Retrieved from https://adept.gatech.edu/library/bibliography.

Collaborative on Academic Careers in Higher Education [COACHE]. (2020). Cambridge, MA: Harvard Graduate School of Education. A growing library of reports and publications includes many examples of how institutions have used COACHE survey data to address inequities among faculty groups. Retrieved from https://coache.gse.harvard.edu/research.

Moody, J. (2010). *Rising above cognitive errors: Guidelines for search, tenure review, and other evaluation committees* (rev. ed.). Kindle Direct Publishing.

Strategy 3. Strengthened Accountability Structures

These interventions seek to establish or enhance accountability for gender equity and diversity in the institution. While initiatives that target improved workplace climates may increase individuals' sense of personal accountability for creating an equitable and supportive environment in their own workplace, here we focus on structural interventions, particularly institutional processes or functions that assign responsibility for actions, policies, and reporting on gender equity. Department chairs or heads, deans, and other institutional leaders have important accountability roles, which are discussed here; general leadership development for people in these key roles is discussed in Strategy 4. Communications strategies can play a role in enhancing accountability by informing and engaging stakeholders, and these are discussed in Strategy 6.

Rationale

The need for new accountability structures arises as institutions implement other interventions to advance women in STEM. Many examples from our research show that when no one is made accountable, backsliding follows, even where there is the best of intentions. People return to previous practices; well-designed programs are diluted or weakened; and processes are followed irregularly, leading to inequity in treatment or in access to benefits. Thus, a lack of accountability is a serious risk to the sustainability and consistency of equity efforts over time.

While some activities offered by ADVANCE projects have been voluntary and individual, such as faculty development (Strategy 10), other activities address processes and policies that apply across a college or the entire institution. In these cases it must be clear who is responsible for implementing and monitoring the new processes or policies. For instance, if departments are expected to follow new procedures and guidelines for recruitment and hiring (Strategy 1), then someone must ensure that these guidelines are followed and must have the power to apply appropriate consequences if they are not. Likewise, accountability needs emerge when changes are made to processes of tenure and promotion (Strategy 2) or to policies on flexible work arrangements that accommodate faculty members' changing personal circumstances over time (Strategy 8). To sustain mentoring and faculty development programs may also require assigning responsibility to specific individuals for offering the program and monitoring its continued quality and responsiveness to faculty needs. Other accountability structures, particularly those involving the gathering and review of data, may be required to benchmark the institution's general progress on gender equity.

Assigning accountability can also be viewed as a measure to increase the transparency of processes. Because women may be excluded from informal networks where valuable professional information is shared (Cullen & Perez-Truglia, 2019; De Welde & Laursen, 2011; Sonnert & Holton, 1995), increased accountability benefits women and others who are not included in typically white and male networks by making information about policies and practices equally available to all. So does formalizing accountability: research shows that if women faculty assume informal accountability roles (e.g., in departments) because they value the outcomes of equity initiatives, the work may be viewed as service and devalued as "institutional housekeeping" when they are reviewed for promotion (Misra et al., 2011). Furthermore, if accountability for gender equity and inclusion is managed informally and is handled only by individuals from marginalized groups, sustainable organizational change may not actually be occurring. In contrast, formal accountability structures affect the institution as a system in ways that contribute to deep, sustainable organizational change.

Purpose and Audience

In general, ADVANCE institutions developed accountability structures to assign responsibility for programs, policies, and reports related to institutional progress on gender equity, and to define consequences if procedures were not followed or if programs and policies were not administered fairly. Designating formal accountability for specific elements of an institutional transformation effort could also increase awareness of the issues and signal the importance of equity and diversity among institutional goals (see Strategy 6).

Because these were college- or institution-wide functions, active participation of administrators was essential. ADVANCE leaders took on roles of researching, proposing, and advocating for accountability structures as they developed policies and procedures to enhance gender equity and made wise use of their allies who held formal and informal leadership roles. Monroe and coauthors (2014) list several types of accountability measures related to data use, procedural checks, and oversight in their recommendations for institutional policies to improve gender equality.

Models

Not all ADVANCE institutions in the first two cohorts were explicit in address-ing accountability structures, although some likely built these into their activi-ties without fanfare. Institutions' reports showed that some created new admin-istrative positions to oversee equity issues or assigned specific oversight and reporting functions to existing roles. Some defined new procedures; others stan-dardized or enhanced existing processes, such as department- or college-level requirements for plans or reports about diversity. Others institutionalized the gathering, reporting, and review of data by campus leaders.

NEW OR REORGANIZED POSITIONS

Some institutions identified several accountability functions and defined new positions to oversee and implement this set of functions. A distinctive example is the equity advisor model developed at the University of California, Irvine (Cohort 1), in which designated faculty members based in each college oversaw and pro-moted best practices in recruitment and hiring for faculty positions and provided support for mentoring and career advancement for existing faculty in the college. At Michigan State (Cohort 4), people in these positions were called faculty excel-lence advocates. In other models, institutions designated an associate or assistant dean—in a new or existing position—to oversee searches and lead faculty devel-opment. These roles were housed in colleges, under the provost, or in offices re-sponsible for diversity or faculty affairs.

ACCOUNTABILITY PROCEDURES

Some institutions defined points of oversight as they modified specific proce-dures, especially those involving faculty hiring and advancement. For example, each search committee was required to report data on the composition of the ap-plicant pool and the steps it had taken to diversify that pool. Then the dean, provost, or equity advisor had responsibility to review and sign off on the commit-tee report before the search could move forward. In other cases, broad account-ability for equity was assigned to unit leaders. For example, colleges or depart-ments were required to prepare a plan for improving diversity, inclusion, and equity in their unit; review criteria for the reappointment of department chairs or deans then included progress on this plan as a measure of their success in this arena.

COMMUNICATION OF DATA

Institutions collected a variety of data to report to the NSF ADVANCE program on specific program-wide metrics (Frehill, Jeser-Cannavale, & Malley, 2007). Some ADVANCE projects built an internal clientele for these data among institutional leaders and then regularized data gathering and reporting on these metrics so that the analyses could be used for routine monitoring of progress on gender equity. Typical measures included faculty composition and salaries by gender and by rank; composition of applicant pools for faculty positions; and demographics of those receiving promotions and awards. Some projects carried out climate surveys or salary equity studies at regular intervals, while others tracked faculty job satisfaction and engagement using the COACHE faculty surveys. Various campuses reported sharing data with their provosts, faculty senates, campus commissions on the status of women, ADVANCE advisory boards, and/or deans and chairs at retreats or workshops. Others used specific disciplinary data on institutional and national faculty composition as a tool in working with departments and search committees.

Examples

The University of California, Irvine (Cohort 1), appointed one or two equity advisors in each school to provide local assistance in recruitment and retention. The equity advisors' main efforts focused on hiring: they met with search committees to educate them about expectations and best practices for searches, reviewed and approved search and recruitment activities, offered recruitment support, met with candidates to answer questions, and assisted with dual-career hiring opportunities. They held signature authority at several stages of the search process. For continuing faculty, equity advisors offered advice and troubleshooting of problems and nominated faculty for awards; they worked with deans on other equity issues, such as salary equity reviews. Some organized mentoring and faculty development activities tailored to their colleges, especially for pre-tenure faculty. The equity advisor role addressed accountability in two ways: search committees were accountable to them, and they, in turn, were accountable for providing several types of support, such as education of search committees on strategies for inclusion (Strategy 1) and assisting with dual-career hiring situations (Strategy 7).

Case Western Reserve University (Cohort 2) developed criteria for accountability of deans that addressed recruitment, advancement and retention, institutional climate, and faculty development, as well as overall progress on the representation of STEM women. Deans were given authority to sign off on search committees' short lists before candidates could be invited to campus for interviews.

Georgia Tech (Cohort 1) reviewed faculty handbooks for clarity, consistency, and independence of evaluation procedures and established the Office of Faculty Career Development Services, seeking to standardize faculty appointment procedures across colleges. These activities were institutionalized through the Office of the Vice President of Institute Diversity.

At Hunter College (Cohort 1), required annual reports held departments accountable for equity in distributing resources to faculty. Strong performance was rewarded by extra funding from the provost.

At the University of Maryland, Baltimore County (Cohort 2), departments were required to commit to a diversity plan before they could open a new faculty search. Periodic evaluation of chairs and deans incorporated progress on departmental diversity plans and was tied to departmental resources.

Utah State University (Cohort 2) instituted the role of ombudsperson for each promotion and tenure (P&T) case. These nonvoting members of the P&T committee monitored the committee's work to ensure that policies were followed and procedures uniformly applied. Strategy 2 provides additional details about this role, which was felt to reduce procedural errors and dispel perceptions of inequity.

The University of Rhode Island (Cohort 2) established IDEA (Institutional Data Enhancing Academics), a university-wide committee, to improve and institutionalize the mechanisms by which benchmark data are collected. The committee worked to identify the data needs of all IDEA members, to consider possibilities for aggregating these needs, and to transfer benchmarking activities permanently to the Institutional Research Office following the grant period.

The University of Maryland, College Park (Cohort 5), developed and institutionalized a faculty dashboard with the goal to increase the availability, accessibility, and transparency of data about faculty careers in each college. Data about faculty diversity, salary ranges, service, and median time to promotion from associate to full professor were collected, aggregated at department or college levels, and made available to all tenured and tenure-track faculty, department chairs, and deans. Drawn from institutional sources and presented in cumulative form, these indicators balanced the need to distinguish units from the need to protect individuals' privacy: for example, salaries were reported as median, twenty-fifth, and seventy-fifth percentiles aggregated by rank and by college. The goal was to foster conversations about faculty workload that were informed by data rather than myths and to empower women to initiate conversations about their own workloads and preferences.

Evaluation

There are few examples where accountability structures were evaluated as stand-alone efforts. Stepan-Norris (with Lind, 2007) evaluated the impact of equity advisors on hiring at the University of California, Irvine (Cohort 1), and concluded that their presence had a positive effect on the hiring of women. The equity advisors' interaction with the dual-career hiring program was also positively associated with hiring women. The report recommended that equity advisors have clear job expectations and procedures, and they should participate in collaborative professional development sessions to share challenges and good ideas. Interview data indicate that there was some variation in the effectiveness of individual advisors, suggesting that selection, preparation, departmental backing, and ongoing support are all important. A follow-up analysis showed that the equity advisor system did not improve retention of women, a failure the authors attributed to the initiative's focus on hiring and to a lack of institutional accountability for retention (Stepan-Norris & Kerissey, 2016).

Affordances and Limitations

Affordances of accountability structures include the following:

- Structures that hold departments accountable (e.g., signature authority over searches, required diversity plans, inclusion of diversity criteria in review of chairs) were perceived as sending a clear message that diversity was valued and taken seriously by the upper administration. We observed these measures more often in smaller and more centralized institutions and less often in institutions where departments held strong autonomy over faculty-related processes.
- Gathering and communicating data to institutional leaders and stakeholders helped to raise awareness of issues and thus to increase their felt responsibility for progress on the issues.
- Accountability for new or enhanced programs and processes operated best when the need was anticipated and built into the program or process design, rather than added on later. In this way, the thoughtful design of accountability can help to ensure the sustainability of these processes after a grant. Moreover, including accountability plans from the start of a

project conveys the point that accountability is a normal part of business rather than an extra to be addressed only if there is time or interest.

- New or reorganized positions were used creatively to combine a number of functions related to diversity and faculty support, thus potentially contributing to improvements in workplace climate and the success and retention of all faculty, not only women. Such positions also served a symbolic purpose in signaling strong organizational support for diversity and a long-term commitment to an institutional agenda of inclusiveness.

Our research did not document any limitations of accountability structures, but we can readily imagine accountability processes that are burdensome and inauthentic to the goals they are intended to serve. In designing accountability processes, care should be taken to build them organically into existing procedures wherever possible and to periodically review their effectiveness in relation to the effort involved.

Summary

In general, accountability structures serve to enhance other ADVANCE efforts and do not function as stand-alone measures. However, they are important in reinforcing those strategies and making expected practices and behaviors routine. Increased accountability must be coupled with appropriate support and resources for the accountable party to do the job. For example, if search committees are held accountable for increasing diversity in their applicant pools and ensuring equity in evaluating candidates, they must receive education and help for how to do this. Like other strategies, accountability should be responsive to the institutional context and matched to the particular intervention. Along with evaluation measures, accountability should be built into an intervention's design and implementation from the beginning.

FURTHER READING

Granberry Russell, P., & McDaniels, M. (2015). Aligning actions with core values: Reflections of a chief diversity officer and National Science Foundation ADVANCE director on advancing faculty diversity. In S. K. Watt (Ed.), *Designing transformative multicultural initiatives: Theoretical foundations, practical applications, and facilitator considerations* (pp. 119–135). Sterling, VA: Stylus.

Stanley, C. A., et al. (2018). Organizational change and the chief diversity officer: A case study of institutionalizing a diversity plan. *Journal of Diversity in Higher Education, 12*(3), 255–265.

Valian, V. (2009a). *Accountability: Principles and actions for deans, provosts, and presidents.* Retrieved from http://www.hunter.cuny.edu/genderequity/repository/files/equity-materials /deanacc0.909.pdf.

Valian, V. (2009b). *Accountability: Principles and actions for chairs and unit heads.* Retrieved from http://www.hunter.cuny.edu/genderequity/repository/files/equity-materials /chairacc.909.pdf.

Chapter Four

Reboot Workplaces

Both formal structures, such as policies, procedures, and leadership roles, and informal norms, including cultures, symbols, and messages, shape the everyday experiences of women scientists and engineers—in either supportive or constraining ways. The following strategies focus on improving work environments at scales from the department to the institution.

FACULTY MEMBERS' EXPERIENCES of the workplace climate are directly connected to their job satisfaction; their productivity and performance as scholars, teachers, and contributors to the institution; and ultimately their decision to pursue their careers inside or outside of the institution. Research shows that workplace climate is particularly important for women faculty, especially in STEM units, where they are often underrepresented. Research also documents more negative climates for women and higher frequencies of negative experiences, such as bullying, harassment, incivility, microaggressions, and exclusion from networking and decision-making. Thus, efforts to improve climate, particularly at the departmental level where faculty spend most of their work time and invest in relationships with others, have significant potential to help retain women and enable them to be productive and valued members of the department.

More broadly, across the institution, women's visibility sends positive messages to everyone about institutional values and priorities for inclusion. Women who are prominent as talented scholars and leaders can serve as role models and inspire students and colleagues from underrepresented groups. Educating everyone—faculty, staff, students, and the community—about women's achievements and challenges can counter stereotypes and empower people to speak up about bias and injustice.

Another approach to addressing institutional cultures and climates is to strengthen leadership at the departmental, college, and institutional levels. Leaders are important because they acquire and distribute resources, set the tone for decision-making and collegiality, and communicate expectations to the faculty in their unit (Laursen & Rocque, 2009; Stewart & Valian, 2018). Improving leaders' skills, knowledge, and abilities to solve problems and resolve conflicts thus has the potential to improve the work environment for everyone. Indeed, research has shown that departments where formal and informal leaders took responsibility and formulated concrete actions to diversify faculty hiring were successful in doing so (Stewart, Malley, & Herzog, 2016; see also McClelland & Holland, 2015). Leadership development is thus effective for improving workplace environments and diversifying the faculty, independent of who the leaders are.

But women are particularly underrepresented in senior administrative and leadership roles, holding only 25% of leadership positions in higher education (Lennon, Spotts, & Mitchell, 2013). This imbalance suggests a lack of recognition of women's leadership talent and biased processes of evaluating leadership potential or tapping people for formal leadership roles. Women leaders also face extra challenges that arise from conflicting societal gender schemas of women and leadership, including constraints on their ability to contribute their expertise and be taken seriously as leaders; interactions that discount their leadership and thereby reduce their effectiveness in the organization; and personal behaviors, attitudes, and responsibilities that add extra burdens for women leaders (Diehl & Dzubinski, 2016). Yet because women tend to have different and more effective leadership styles, increasing the presence of women in academic leadership may yield practical benefits to the institution (Eagly & Carli, 2003; Rosser, 2003). For example, the presence of women in the roles of provost, president, or trustee is connected to greater diversity throughout the institution, perhaps because it signals a welcoming environment for women (Ehrenberg et al., 2012). Thus, a potentially important approach is formal leadership development that engages women as potential leaders, shows them the nature of the role so they understand it and can decide whether it is a good fit, and prepares them with the needed skills, capacities, and relationships.

ADVANCE institutions developed a variety of approaches to improve departmental and institutional climates for women and to develop the leaders who can shape these. In this chapter we discuss three strategies that target work environments at multiple levels:

- development of institutional leaders, both to improve existing leaders' institutional knowledge, management, interpersonal and problem-solving skills, and their understanding of the challenges faced by women and faculty from other marginalized groups, and to recruit excellent women faculty into such roles (Strategy 4)
- approaches to enhancing departmental climate to improve communication, inclusion, collaboration, work/life practices, and intellectual exchange that contribute to faculty job satisfaction (Strategy 5)
- institution-wide efforts to raise the visibility of women scholars, women's achievements, and issues that face women in the academy (Strategy 6)

Strategy 4. Development of Institutional Leaders

More than half of the ADVANCE IT projects in Cohorts 1 and 2 included some form of development activities for institutional leaders or people who may become institutional leaders. This strategy addresses various approaches to leadership development, highlighting the wide array of audiences, types of programs, and topics addressed in ADVANCE leadership development efforts. Related approaches include Strategy 10 on faculty professional development, which may incorporate components of leadership development, and Strategy 12 on mentoring and networking as an approach to leadership development. Strategy 5 examines programs that can help department chairs to improve the experiences faculty have in the department.

Rationale

In the ADVANCE projects of Cohorts 1 and 2, leadership development interventions were implemented for several reasons: as a means to advance individual women in STEM fields, as a tool to change the culture of the institution, and as a lever for long-range and broad institutional change. A key rationale was that leadership—in combination with institutional policies, structures, and processes—is a central and arguably essential tool for effecting major organizational change (Kezar, 2014). Most department chairs receive little training, and it tends to be "woefully inadequate" (Flaherty, 2016), focused on the nuts and bolts of procedures rather than on developing knowledge and interpersonal skills that can fruitfully shape a departmental climate. Higher education institutions today need leaders of all genders who understand the importance of a supportive, inclusive environment; recognize the barriers to creating and sustaining such an environment; and know how to guide their institutions to create change that results in wide benefits for all. Leaders who take responsibility for these issues can make a difference (McClelland & Holland, 2015; Stewart, Malley, & Herzog, 2016).

Historically, most higher education institutions have had a majority of men among those serving in leadership roles at the unit, department, college, and central administrative levels. One way that colleges and universities can become more inclusive environments is by taking steps to ensure that people of all genders are well represented in leadership roles: their work can demonstrate the benefits of a diverse leadership group, and they can serve as models for other women and for people from other groups underrepresented in leadership positions.

Purpose

The leadership development programs designed by ADVANCE projects were typically intended to address one or more of the goals listed below:

- Develop the capacity of institutional leaders to understand and effectively carry out their roles at the department, college, or institution level and help them to acquire the specific skills and abilities to do so. Those already in leadership positions may gain knowledge and skills, and others may be encouraged to consider shaping their careers to include formal leadership responsibilities.
- Foster in institutional leaders a sense of agency to implement change in their units and the broader institution. Unit-level change, such as creating a more supportive and inclusive environment for all faculty members, is difficult to effect without the direct support and involvement of department chairs, deans, and other leaders.
- Empower women leaders specifically by strengthening their capacity as leaders. Women often have had fewer opportunities to learn leadership skills and to assume leadership positions. Thus, some leadership development programs were designed to help women see themselves as leaders and to expose them to career options involving leadership that they may not have considered.
- Build relationships and a sense of common purpose among colleagues across units, which will benefit leaders as individuals and influence the institution as a whole. Leadership programs specifically for women in STEM fields were often designed to help women meet others in similar roles and feel part of a like-minded community of leaders in the institution.

- Encourage leaders' commitment to the recruitment, retention, and success of women scholars. Leaders can be helped to see the issues and challenges facing women scholars, the importance of diversity to institutional quality and excellence, and the role of implicit bias and other barriers requiring explicit attention.

Audience

Institutions varied in how they defined the target audience for their leadership development programs. Some programs were open to all genders—for example, offering all department chairs the chance to develop the skills needed to lead and manage their departments. These programs ensured that all had opportunities to learn about the challenges confronting women faculty and the appropriate interventions and strategies to create inclusive departments. At least as frequently, however, ADVANCE projects offered leadership development opportunities specifically for women.

Programs also varied in the level of the leadership role addressed. Some programs targeted department chairs, recognizing that chairs occupy a pivotal place: they support their faculty colleagues and interpret university policies and priorities while also representing the interests of their department to more senior administrators. Other programs included both deans and department chairs, and some focused on women interested in exploring senior-level administration. Some also included faculty seen as having the potential for leadership responsibilities in the future, and some included other people, such as research team leaders or those in nondepartmental units, such as administrative leaders in grant development offices. A later wave of ADVANCE programs engaged men to act as allies and advocates for women when they were in positions of influence, whether formal or informal.

Models

Leadership development was designed and implemented in a variety of ways. Programs varied along the following dimensions:

- *Focus.* The possible topics addressed in leadership development are many. Some programs focused on tools that department chairs need to help their units to function well and their faculty members to feel supported, such as budgeting strategies, conflict resolution, approaches to mentoring faculty at different career stages, strategic planning, and managing difficult people. Other programs, especially those seeking specifically to foster women's interest in pursuing leadership careers, focused on topics such as the kinds of leadership careers available to women, balancing faculty commitments with leadership roles, the challenges that women may encounter, and communicating in ways that are effective with a wide range of people.

- *Preparation.* Strategies related to diversity, equity, and inclusion and to recognizing the specific issues confronted by women, especially those in STEM fields, were addressed differently across programs. Some projects addressed diversity through explicit programming while others wove diversity issues into the various topics they addressed.

- *Use of peers versus experts.* Some programs used peers as the central resources while others invited "experts" from inside or outside the university. Experienced department chairs, for example, facilitated leadership development for newer chairs. The use of peers as resource people had a variety of advantages, since participants could identify with institutional colleagues and knew they were well aware of the particular local context. Participants met people with whom they wished to cultivate longer-term mentoring or collegial relationships; seeing diverse models of leadership in the institution sometimes encouraged new leaders to see their own potential leadership roles. Peer presenters benefited too through the opportunity to reflect on their experiences, which helped their own leadership development and thereby enriched the institution. And sharing responsibilities meant that no single person needed to prepare all the materials for a leadership development program. On the other hand, the use of local or outside experts on leadership issues was sometimes seen to elevate the status of the leadership development program. An expert who studies leadership could offer expertise and research knowledge not already present on a campus.

- *Collaborative or top-down.* Some leadership development programs were designed as collaborative activities in which people worked together to identify and then discuss or solve problems. For example, peer-led programs that gathered chairs to discuss common challenges confronted by those in the role and the kinds of strategies they find useful were seen to create collegiality and extend the reach of good ideas. Top-down programs led by individuals with specific knowledge about a topic brought new resources and research to participants. For example, a

provost or president was invited to speak to participants about institutional directions, a higher education scholar discussed with department
chairs the literature on early-career faculty, or a psychologist or scholar of
gender studies discussed implicit bias. Both approaches have advantages,
and some programs combined the two.

Leadership development programs also varied in format and duration. Some
common formats used by ADVANCE institutions are listed below; some projects
used multiple formats.

- *Leadership workshop series for chairs.* Many institutions convened regular
  workshops, meeting a few times per term, for their department chairs
  (and, often, deans) to discuss important topics in institutional leadership.
  Since chairs are key in shaping departmental climate and play a central
  role in faculty recruitment, workshops can provide an effective way to
  disseminate information and highlight important institutional issues.
  Examples of topics addressed are budgeting, tenure and promotion, grants
  and contracts, team building, strategies for recruiting faculty from
  underrepresented groups, and family-friendly policies and leave policies.
  Such workshops enabled participants to meet and network with other
  leaders from across the institution and to gain institutional perspectives.
  Some ADVANCE institutions held regular workshops only for women
  leaders in these roles, thus providing a safer space to discuss their specific
  issues and questions and create connections with other women leaders on
  campus.
- *Leadership training for new chairs.* Some institutions offered a training
  workshop for those starting in department chair positions. These boot
  camps helped new chairs gain essential skills and knowledge of key
  institutional resources.
- *Events for women considering leadership roles.* Some ADVANCE projects
  offered workshops or lunch discussions for women who were considering
  leadership opportunities or beginning their leadership careers. These
  provided a safe setting to explore questions and concerns about such a
  career step, and they often involved more senior women who shared their
  own leadership experiences.
- *Executive coaching.* This form of leadership development provided leaders
  with individualized and focused support through sessions with experienced professional coaches (see also Strategy 12). One variation was to

provide coaching for individual faculty women interested in moving into leadership roles.

- *Executive leadership shadowing and internships.* Women considering moving into senior-level administration can benefit from the opportunity to try out the role of a senior leader for a defined period. Some programs arranged for women to shadow a senior leader for part of each week or in a more intensive regular arrangement. In others, a woman scholar took on an internship or fellowship in senior leadership for an academic term or year in order to explore her interest and skills in this arena. Some of these internships involved a specific project that the woman leader carried out during this period.
- *Occasional symposia.* A major institutional event can highlight a visit from a well-known scholar or higher education leader who discusses topics such as careers of women leaders, barriers (e.g., implicit bias), or how women overcome challenges as they pursue leadership opportunities. At some institutions, ADVANCE projects organized major symposia to bring key issues to the attention of the whole university community and to gather women from across campus for networking (see also Strategy 6).
- *National workshops.* The University of Washington's (Cohort 1) leadership workshops have enabled people from many campuses to take new leadership knowledge and skills back to their own institutions. Other long-standing national programs specifically target women's preparation for senior-level leadership, including workshops and conferences from the American Council on Education (ACE), the Higher Education Resource Services (HERS) institutes, and Drexel University's programs ELAM (Executive Leadership in Academic Medicine) and ELATES (Executive Leadership in Academic Technology, Engineering and Science) for women in academic medicine and in STEM fields. Some ADVANCE projects supported individual leaders to attend these national programs.
- *Male allies and advocates programs.* The ADVANCE FORWARD (Focus on Resources for Women's Advancement, Recruitment/Retention, and Development) program at North Dakota State University (Cohort 4) initiated the first of these peer education programs for men. ADVANCE provided space and support for senior men to work together to develop their knowledge and skills to serve as advocates and allies for women and to engage other men in supportive behaviors.

Examples

The examples below illustrate approaches to leadership development at various ADVANCE institutions. Laursen and Austin (2018) discussed further examples of leadership development targeted to women.

Case Western Reserve University's (Cohort 2) executive coaching program drew on expertise available in the university's Weatherhead School of Management to offer specially trained coaches to work with deans and chairs or with faculty women to support them in achieving personal and organizational goals and in undertaking productive change in their work. Coaching for deans and chairs involved eight to ten sessions, and the women faculty received six to eight sessions. Evaluation surveys showed very high satisfaction with the program. Hotline coaching provided trained coaches who could answer time-sensitive questions from women faculty and administrators about issues such as negotiating salary, moving from non-tenure-track to tenure-track positions, handling budgets, integrating work and home life, and overcoming challenges around collaboration and interpersonal relations.

Case also holds the Provost's Leadership Retreat each year to build collegiality and common purpose among department chairs and senior administrators. Speakers have included well-known national leaders involved in supporting women STEM faculty and in creating organizational change. Participants have the opportunity to network, review institutional data, discuss the climate for women on campus, and identify best practices in recruitment and retention. Evaluations have been very positive, and the event is well institutionalized.

At New Mexico State University (Cohort 1), the Advancing Leaders program offered monthly luncheons and a two-day retreat for faculty members interested in developing leadership skills. Participants from all six colleges and the library met regularly over lunch with an array of institutional leaders who discussed issues of importance in the university and in academic careers. While people of all genders were invited, the majority of participants were women.

The department chair series at the University of Alabama at Birmingham (UAB, Cohort 2) included monthly meetings, each focused on a topic of relevance to the chair role: administrative and personal skills needed to be an effective leader, case studies of difficult situations, strategic budgeting, family-friendly policies and leave policies, and tenure and promotion processes. In addition, UAB offered new chairs a half-day orientation and follow-up seminars. Topics included clarifying the roles and responsibilities of chairs, managing expectations and evaluating performance of faculty, developing programs, and working with the Office of Human Relations.

The University of Maryland, Baltimore County (UMBC, Cohort 2), offered the Presidential Leadership Fellowship for a woman scholar to be released from teaching responsibilities to intern as a senior administrator, but the institution found that few women applied. Instead, the ADVANCE program developed a cohort-based leadership initiative that was very successful. Each year, a small group of tenured women professors met regularly to identify leadership topics that they wished to investigate through reading, discussion, and interactions with senior leaders. Participants explored their career aspirations and leadership styles, developed plans for intentional career and leadership development, and met with women who were university presidents. Evaluations indicated that participants found the experience to be very valuable. Some went on to institutional leadership roles, and one woman also participated in advanced leadership development through the HERS Institute for Women Leaders in Higher Education.

ADVANCE at the University of Washington (UW, Cohort 1) has offered quarterly half-day workshops designed to help chairs to be more effective in running their departments and in creating better departmental climates for all faculty. Diversity and inclusion are woven into the workshop topics. UW has also offered quarterly mentoring-for-leadership lunches, designed to enable women attendees to hear the personal stories of invited leaders and to envision themselves in leadership roles. Designed with the feel of a "dinner party," according to UW reports, these events have reduced the sense of isolation and increased the sense of belonging among the women attending, thus contributing to a stronger pipeline of potential institutional leaders. While UW ADVANCE initially developed the workshops for their own campus leaders, they now open these to participants from throughout the country. Evaluations of these activities show enthusiastic responses.

North Dakota State University (Cohort 4) crafted a distinctive form of leadership development that engaged senior male faculty as allies and advocates for gender equity. Its approach acknowledges the role of men and masculinities in shaping institutional culture, and it seeks to educate, inspire, and support members of the dominant group to participate and hold each other accountable. The initial team, known as FORWARD Advocates, read the research literature and developed training materials for subsequent groups of men. They set the goal to place at least one ally or advocate in each university department, and by 2015, FORWARD Advocates had conducted 12 gender-equity ally training sessions with more than

165 men faculty. The program has continued at North Dakota State and has been adapted at several other institutions, with modifications that reflect differences in institutional contexts (Anicha, Burnett, & Bilen-Green, 2015; Bilen-Green et al., 2015; Laursen & Austin, 2014b).

Evaluation

The simplest form of evaluation records participation in leadership development since attendance suggests that the program is responding to faculty interests and needs. As an example of the formative use of such data, some institutions found that few women faculty were interested in executive shadowing or internships and thus discontinued these programs or modified them (see the discussion of UMBC above). In another example, at Lehigh University (Cohort 5) interviews conducted with mid-career women helped to shape the institution's leadership development program. Women did not equate leadership to institutional administrative roles, however, but thought rather more broadly about leadership as developing prominence in research, scholarship, teaching, and service in their discipline. As a result, Lehigh reshaped its program into a more individualized one that offered mid-career women funding and mentoring that would together support their proposed career development plans (see Laursen & Austin, 2014c).

Most programs also have been evaluated with simple surveys that participants complete after the event (e.g., a workshop or seminar) or at the conclusion of a longer program (e.g., a year-long series). These evaluations typically indicate whether participants found the program a good investment of their time and offer formative feedback to improve it. For some programs, interviews were conducted to learn about participants' experiences, but this more time-consuming form of assessment seems to have been infrequent.

We are unaware of evaluation efforts that have tracked participants' use of new leadership skills or knowledge over time, but anecdotal observations from some institutions suggest positive repercussions in departments where heads have participated in leadership development and training on gender equity. For example, Bilen-Green and coauthors (2015) offered several methods of measuring the impact of advocates and allies programs that engage men.

Because the number of women engaging in these programs is often small, it is not hard to document their movement into leadership roles, and many institutions have reported these individual successes as a summative evaluation measure. Indeed, participants' moving to a leadership role even in another institution should be considered a positive outcome of leadership development programs, evidence that women see themselves as leaders and can present themselves as such effectively.

Affordances and Limitations

Strong and skilled leadership has been assessed as particularly important in any effective institutional change strategy, and thus leadership development is a worthwhile investment to support change efforts. Important affordances overall include the following:

- *Individual career development.* Participants in leadership development reported gaining specific knowledge and skills that helped them achieve career goals or consider new goals previously unexplored or deemed unattainable. In this way, individual possibilities were encouraged, and institutional human capital was expanded.
- *New levers for institutional change.* Most programs included some attention to challenges confronting STEM women and people from other groups that are marginalized in the academy, and they addressed strategies to advance organizational change in support of more inclusive environments.
- *Wide institutional impact.* Leadership development programs promoted an overall understanding of institutional priorities, plans, and issues and enabled the development of cross-institutional connections. These in turn paved the way for collaborative and productive working relationships, which benefit the institution.
- *Relatively affordable.* While the financial costs associated with leadership development varied depending on the particular project design, many programs were organized as discussion groups or workshops. In many cases, food and speakers were the main costs. Released time so that individuals could intern involved higher costs but typically for only a few people at a time.

The limitations of leadership development emerged largely as issues of the fit between program design and institutional context. Each university must assess which leadership development approaches are appropriate for its goals, context, and needs, and it also must match the approaches to the interests and purposes of the participants. What is successful in one situation may be less appealing to those working elsewhere. For example, the executive coaching that has been so successful at Case Western Reserve University did not attract much interest at other ADVANCE institutions. The leadership program at Lehigh University was received more warmly after it was adapted to include informal leadership in the discipline or community organizations as well as formal institutional leadership roles (for more on this, see Laursen & Austin, 2014c). In several institutions, executive shadowing was not popular, but Texas A&M's (Cohort 5) fellowship program was well received and ultimately institutionalized. The particular reasons for such variability of interest in programs among potential participants are not always evident, so it is generally worth doing some advance investigation of faculty needs and interests.

Summary

Because leaders are central in shaping smooth-functioning and supportive higher education environments, leadership development is key to institutional change efforts. Because our mental schemas of leaders are often associated with men, it is important to be inclusive—not just invite the usual suspects—and to portray leadership as a capacity that can be developed, not as an "innate" or "natural" talent. For those already in formal leadership roles, equity and climate issues can be infused into existing programs (where they exist) or can be the basis of stand-alone workshops. These offer side benefits, such as peer networking and collegial support. Compared to some other interventions, development of existing leaders is a relatively quiet strategy: even when participants benefit greatly, others in the institution may not be aware. Given the more general benefits to the institution, such programs often find a logical, long-term home in faculty affairs or in the provost's office. Programs targeting women as leaders may be more visible and may serve as positive professional development for tenured women faculty, whether or not they pursue formal leadership roles.

PROGRAM RESOURCES

Several national programs offer leadership development for new or potential academic leaders.

The American Council on Education (ACE) offers several programs, including the ACE fellows, ACE Women's Network, and regional summits. https://www.acenet.edu/leadership/Pages/default.aspx.

Drexel University offers ELAM (Executive Leadership in Academic Medicine), https://drexel.edu/medicine/academics/womens-health-and-leadership/elam; and ELATES (Executive Leadership in Academic Technology, Engineering and Science), https://drexel.edu/provost/initiatives/elates.

Higher Education Resource Services (HERS) offers summer academies and other resources for women leaders. http://hersnet.org.

FURTHER READING

American Association of University Professors [AAUP]. (2008). *Gender equity guidelines for department chairs.* Retrieved from https://www.aaup.org/issues/women-higher-education /gender-equity-guidelines-department-chairs.

Baker, V. L., et al. (Eds.). (2018). *Success after tenure: Supporting mid-career faculty.* Sterling, VA: Stylus.

Diehl, A. B., & Dzubinski, L. M. (2016). Making the invisible visible: A cross-sector analysis of gender-based leadership barriers. *Human Resource Development Quarterly, 27*(2), 181–206.

Hecht, I. W., et al. (1999). *The department chair as academic leader.* Phoenix, AZ: Oryx.

Leaming, D. R. (2007). *Academic leadership: A practical guide to chairing the department.* Bolton, MA: Anker.

Lucas, A. F. (2000). *Leading academic change: Essential roles for department chairs.* San Francisco, CA: Jossey-Bass.

Ward, K., & Eddy, P. L. (2013). Women and academic leadership: Leaning out. *Chronicle of Higher Education.* Retrieved from http://chronicle.com/article/WomenAcademic -Leadership-/143503.

Wolverton, M., Bower, B. L., & Hyle, A. E. (2009). *Women at the top: What women university and college presidents say about effective leadership.* Sterling, VA: Stylus.

Strategy 5. Approaches to Improving Departmental Climate

Programs to foster individual women's career success were fairly common in ADVANCE IT institutions, but efforts to address the climate and working conditions in their departments were less so. Here we highlight initiatives that directly targeted departmental climate and culture. In decentralized institutions where departments have significant autonomy, policies and procedures for faculty hiring, advancement, and enabling work/life flexibility may be strongly department-based, but we discuss these separately (Strategies 1, 2, and 8) rather than as primarily departmental concerns. Likewise, we do not focus here on initiatives that were delivered through departments as a means of reaching faculty if they did not target the department itself as the unit of change.

Rationale

The department is the home base for most faculty, the environment in which they spend most of their daily working hours. Departmental climate and conditions thus have an outsized impact on faculty job satisfaction (Archie, Kogan, & Laursen, 2015), and faculty perceptions of them may be quite distinct from their sense of the institutional climate as a whole. Several studies have suggested that collegiality and climate are particularly important to women faculty and to faculty of color and are critical factors in their decisions to leave the institution. Thus, initiatives to address climate at the departmental level may help to retain a diverse faculty (Archie, Kogan, & Laursen, 2015; Bilimoria et al., 2006; Britton et al., 2012; Callister, 2006; Hardcastle et al., 2019; Laursen & Rocque, 2009). As Britton and coauthors (2012) pointed out, despite differences in how various groups perceive work and contextual factors, the factors that predict satisfaction are broadly similar across all faculty. Thus, efforts to improve departmental climate benefit all faculty, not just women and not just in STEM departments.

Purpose

Most departmentally targeted initiatives sought to enhance department climate through improved collegiality, communication, and sense of joint purpose. The specific issues to be addressed varied depending on the department, and indeed identifying needs and concerns was an important first step for many department-focused initiatives. For example, in some departments, improved communication and greater transparency in departmental decision-making were key objectives. In other cases, it was important to increase faculty members' understanding of each other's intellectual interests and thus enhance everyone's sense of being valued and supported by their department.

The history of the department and the field more broadly were often important in understanding the origins of department-level dynamics. For example, in some cases generational divides had arisen when differences in hiring rates over time left gaps in faculty ages and career stages. In others, intellectual divides had emerged when disparate departments were merged, or as new research methods and interests arose in a field over time and were represented in the scholarship of newer hires. Sometimes tensions occurred when some but not all faculty had obligations to other disciplinary units or to externally funded research centers. Such differences can lead to factionalism, isolation of some individuals, or discomfort and uncertainty for newer hires asked to take sides; faculty members and chairs might not have all the interpersonal skills needed to manage these challenges. The department climate initiatives we reviewed sought to help departments reduce conflict and find ways of working that are less emotionally demanding and more productive for everyone.

Audience

A defining characteristic of these initiatives was their targeting of the department as a whole. Some approaches involved all members, engaging them in department-wide discussions at workshops or retreats. In other cases, the main target was the department chair or head, whose skills, knowledge, and leadership capacities were recognized as crucial in setting a tone and managing department operations.

Models

Four models appeared in the data we collected from ADVANCE IT institutions. Two models placed responsibility for the nature of the initiative in the department's hands: they empowered the department to identify its own problems and propose its own solutions while providing some support for enacting these solutions. The other two models placed more emphasis on engaging departments to implement changes that were identified and recommended by ADVANCE as effective for improving climate. These two types of models may be contrasted as bottom-up and top-down approaches, but in practice the observed differences were less stark. Faculty buy-in was important for each of these approaches, and guidance from ADVANCE and other institutional leaders was influential in shaping the most successful ones.

DEPARTMENT-INITIATED APPROACHES

Grants offered support for departments to pursue a strategy of their own design that addressed a climate-related problem that they had identified. Often, these were awarded in a competitive proposal process that required evidence of faculty buy-in to the project and/or their active involvement at some level. Several institutions used this approach. In the programs we reviewed, awards of $10,000–$20,000 were large enough to motivate departments to apply for funding and to support a project of substance.

Departmental consultation was a more intensive approach that involved close work with faculty to identify issues and to develop and institute collaborative solutions. Some departments were invited to apply or were selected based on administrators' recommendations. Often, a first step was data collection through faculty surveys, interviews, or focus groups about areas of concern, perhaps augmented by input from chairs and deans. Using these data to identify particular concerns and assets perceived in the departmental work environment, facilitators worked with faculty members to prioritize issues and to devise and implement solutions, drawing on ADVANCE for ideas and material support when needed.

INSTITUTIONALLY DESIGNED APPROACHES

Work with department chairs or heads targeted these leaders in their interpersonal role of setting a tone for departmental interactions and in their professional roles of hiring, mentoring, and promoting faculty; allocating resources; and making work assignments. Through workshops, retreats, panels, or lunches, many institutions sought to help chairs develop the knowledge and skills to do their jobs effectively, to generate awareness of policies and procedures (e.g., work/life policies), and to inform them about ways that bias can arise in evaluating job applicants or faculty candidates for promotion. Strategy 4 focuses on leadership development in detail, and Strategies 1 and 2 address implicit bias education, including trainings targeted at chairs or heads. As with other forms of education and training, the use of interactive teaching approaches was important. Peer-to-peer models, such as panel discussions or presentations by chairs with a campus reputation for effectiveness, were seen to be particularly useful. Peer-to-peer engagement also fostered connections among chairs.

Quid pro quo models were used at some institutions whereby departments gained access to ADVANCE resources in return for taking part in specific activities. Some departments were self-identified, but more often departments were recommended by administrators as being likely to benefit from assistance. For example, the University of Rhode Island (Cohort 2) expected departments that had received support for a faculty fellow to participate in a departmental climate workshop. At Kansas State University (Cohort 2), each ADVANCE-designated department received funds it could use for faculty support and in turn took part in activities such as gender equity workshops, reviews of departmental tenure and promotion procedures and documents, and reviews of the departmental website.

Examples

The University of Michigan (Cohort 1) ADVANCE project offered departmental transformation grants in a range of sizes: smaller grants for self-study and larger ones to support self-initiated projects. For example, the chemistry department used its grant to enhance faculty recruiting and mentoring; foster the success of current women faculty; and improve the general departmental climate. The department invited women scholars to give talks, awarded travel funds to women faculty and graduate students, organized forums for all pre-tenure faculty and especially for women, supported summer salary for women faculty, and administered a departmental climate survey. The department credited its strong growth in women assistant professors (from 10% to 41% of assistant professors over the grant period) to these initiatives. Faculty leaders noted positive ripple effects that carried over into the environment for graduate students, and data on the increase in the number of women in Michigan's PhD program offer corroborative evidence (Laursen & Weston, 2014).

At the University of Rhode Island (Cohort 2), climate workshops using an appreciative inquiry framework were provided to all STEM departments. During the initial three-hour workshop, faculty identified features of an excellent working environment and explored ways to achieve these features in their department. Departments identified their own goals, for example:

- plan for people to get together to decrease isolation
- create a positive and constructive review process
- encourage active recognition
- protect junior faculty from department politics
- celebrate how well we do with the resources we have
- communicate with the administration better

During follow-up sessions, departments met for 90 minutes to review the goals set in the first session and to develop action plans that identified specific steps, the responsible people, and timelines.

At Utah State University (Cohort 2), nine departments were identified through climate survey data and through the recommendations of faculty, deans, and the provost, and they were invited to participate in a departmental transformation process. This process sought to help the departments become more productive by identifying and ameliorating dysfunctional behaviors that interfered with a positive work environment for all. Utah State's approach included extensive data collection and customization:

- The ADVANCE PI, the co-PI, or an outside consultant interviewed all department members to assess climate concerns across the faculty and among subgroups.
- The interview data were analyzed, and themes from this analysis were presented to department members in a facilitated retreat.
- As a group, department members drew on the data to identify the issues they wanted to address and then brainstormed solutions, set goals, and developed a plan of action.
- The department then wrote a proposal to ADVANCE to fund these initiatives and received funds to implement them.

- ADVANCE leaders checked in and worked with the department as desired along the way, although the department was empowered to pursue a course of action of its own choice.

Various departments undertook actions around recruiting faculty, strengthening research support and collaboration, increasing interaction and informal networking, improving the effectiveness of department meetings, bridging generation gaps, and/or supporting particular women faculty members. For example, one department furnished a space to enhance collegial interactions and established a regular coffee hour and seminar series to learn more about each other's research. Members of another department were surprised to discover through the climate review process that their habits of sports-related socializing excluded some faculty from informal exchanges of useful, work-related information; in response they initiated new activities that emphasized common intellectual interests. In a third case, institutional leaders became aware of how bias entered the faculty hiring process, and they took active steps toward improvement.

The Utah State ADVANCE team reported some significant successes, which were corroborated by improvements in departmental climate survey data. Even in cases where the departmental consultation process was seen to be less successful, the effort drew administrators' attention to intractable problems that required their intervention, such as removing specific individuals from decision-making roles. Active involvement of the department head was essential. Unfortunately, the ADVANCE team found this highly customized approach to be labor-intensive and thus unsustainable in the long run.

The University of Texas at El Paso (Cohort 2) applied a collaborative leadership model to engage department chairs in "chair chats" or focus group discussions to brainstorm ideas for how to establish a positive climate that facilitates women's retention and promotion.

ADVANCE at the University of Washington (Cohort 1) emphasized developing leadership skills in its department chairs and potential future leaders. Departmental grants coupled with UW's workshops and "chair school" were used to craft a multipronged strategy for addressing departmental quality of life.

Iowa State University's (Cohort 3) ADVANCE project developed an intensive intervention around department climate, which was based on action research and known as collaborative transformation. The process began with focus groups and interviews to probe each department's culture, practices, and structure, the results of which were shared back to the department and used to initiate collaborative problem-solving. Departments made both small-scale and large changes to their governance documents, and they addressed issues such as promotion and tenure policies, work/life balance, recruitment and hiring, the use of departmental resources, and the number of women full professors. Leaders saw the process as having a "civilizing" effect on department cultures. The work was time-intensive but valuable enough that elements of collaborative transformation were sustained as part of the institution's regular departmental review process, which is conducted every 5–7 years and applies to all colleges (Bird & Latimer, 2019).

A signature innovation at West Virginia University (Cohort 5) was a dialogical change process for departments to increase unit members' collective engagement in institutional transformation to achieve gender equity and diversity goals. Seeing this as essential to improve the everyday work environments for women, trained faculty facilitators engaged each department in a series of structured conversations aimed toward planning for the department's future and making decisions about its strategic directions, a dual agenda that linked diversity directly to the institution's strategic plan (Bird & Latimer, 2019). Meetings were structured to disrupt everyday exclusion and maximize transparency, and a written product summarized the work and built toward the final plan. Pre- and post-surveys of participating units documented reduced conflict, increased collective efficacy, and more realistic views of the efforts needed to attain gender equity (Latimer et al., 2014; Laursen & Austin, 2014d).

Evaluation

ADVANCE leaders reported that it was difficult to directly measure the impact of department-targeted climate initiatives, yet they often cited anecdotal and experiential evidence that these efforts had a positive impact on work relationships, job satisfaction, and interpersonal dynamics. They drew on interviews and self-report surveys to show evidence of changing perceptions and relationships in participating departments and documented accomplishments that the departments themselves had selected. The impact of some department-level initiatives could be tracked in numerical indicators, such as hiring, but in other cases the time lag between departmental actions and opportunities to recruit or retain women faculty meant that quantitative indicators did not show rapid change.

At Utah State University (Cohort 2), the ADVANCE team monitored outcomes that had been targeted in departments' action plans. For example, in one department, faculty reported more interaction around the office, more involvement in department meetings, and broad participation in newly instituted brown-bag seminars. In some cases, climate survey data showed improvements over time in departmental means for items such as intrinsic task motivation, perceived access to resources, reduced isolation, and satisfaction with promotion processes. In other cases, possible improvements in climate indicators at the department level were masked by general university-wide declines in morale attributed to faculty concerns about institutional budget cutting.

At the University of Colorado Boulder (Cohort 1), department enhancement grants were initiated in response to data that identified faculty needs for improved department collegiality and climate (Laursen & Rocque, 2009). Units that received awards provided short reports, and a simple qualitative analysis of outcomes described in these reports showed that departments had implemented activities to target collegiality, mentoring, and effective departmental function—issues aligned with research on departmental climate—and that these activities had a high return on investment (Laursen, 2008). Annual receptions to honor grant recipients celebrated success and thereby elevated the grants' symbolic importance.

At Texas A&M (Cohort 5), evaluators were able to link department-level data from climate surveys to participation of one or more department members in the ADVANCE planning and implementation process. A statistical analysis was possible because the ADVANCE team had intentionally involved a large number of faculty in its work and because the institution has a large number of departments. Using a difference-in-difference approach, the evaluators showed that ADVANCE participation had spillover or "contagion" effects, improving job satisfaction of women faculty and reducing turnover of women full professors (Taylor et al., 2017). They concluded that "the evidence suggests that exposure to the design and implementation of the ADVANCE activities . . . was an effective treatment in and of itself" (Taylor et al., 2017, p. 401). While this was not an evaluation of a department-based approach, it was a clever evaluation strategy for detecting signs of department-level impact of engagement with ADVANCE, and the same strategy could be applied by considering other interventions as the "treatment."

Affordances and Limitations

Advantages of a focus on departments include the following:

- *High importance.* Departments are a crucial locus of faculty job satisfaction. Interventions targeted here have the potential to make a very big and lasting difference for faculty in the unit.
- *Manageable scale.* As a unit of change, the department operates at a scale where interventions can be more readily implemented and observed,

compared to the institution-wide scale. Working with a few departments at a time is a practical way to divide up a large campus or to pilot new ADVANCE initiatives with early adopters. For example, at Case Western Reserve University (Cohort 2), ADVANCE made certain forms of faculty support available to new sets of departments each year, thus distributing this resource equitably over time without overburdening ADVANCE personnel and resources.

- *Opportunities for strategic choices.* Department-focused initiatives may seek to engage well-functioning departments that want to improve their diversity track record and that can serve as models for others. Alternatively, they may target units with known problems in need of solution.
- *Enhanced relationships.* Several ADVANCE leaders noted the importance of building helpful and collaborative relationships with department chairs, from whom they learned much and upon whom they drew as advisors, allies, and sounding boards for other ADVANCE efforts.

Limitations of department-focused climate initiatives include the following:

- *High degree of difficulty.* ADVANCE leaders who undertook significant work on departmental climate reported that this work was slow and required excellent interpersonal and facilitation skills. It was challenging to offer feedback to departments on dysfunctional behaviors and have it be well received and taken seriously. Not all efforts at departmental change were successful.
- *Measuring impact.* Campus-wide climate surveys were often felt to be blunt instruments for measuring effectiveness at the departmental level. Response rates were not always high enough for data to be sensitive to change over time or to differences by department. Quantitative measures of women's representation may not reflect changes in department climate on the time scale of the grant-funded project.

Different models offer different affordances and limitations:

- A focus on department chairs targets individuals with high influence and important roles. Some campuses found chairs to be receptive to ADVANCE resources that helped them do their job, while others reported difficulty in getting chairs to attend events and participate actively. The chair's role and influence on departmental colleagues may vary widely depending on each campus's structure and culture.

- A focus on departmental grants or consultations empowers departments to take steps they self-identify as needed in their unit. However, some departments had trouble identifying actions that would truly improve climate, proposing instead actions to help individual women. Some ADVANCE teams debated whether to support a proposal that was less than "transformational" but might build good will and provide opportunities to work further with the department. One interviewee reported that perceptions that ADVANCE "beat up on" some departments deterred other units from participating.
- The quid pro quo model offers resources to carry out specific changes that are evidence-based and that could be transformational. However, departments may resist changes that they perceive as undermining their autonomy.

Summary

Because departments have high influence on workplace satisfaction, department climate initiatives have high potential to make positive changes for women in STEM while also offering benefits to other department members. They are not for the faint of heart, but good models do exist from ADVANCE initiatives that have demonstrated their effectiveness and documented how they worked with departments. In department-initiated models, change leaders should not assume that departments will have the expertise to plan activities that affect climate in transformative ways. They will need to educate and guide departments toward actions that will make a difference in overall climate and to steer them away from approaches that tend toward "fixing" women, such as directing resources to women as individuals.

FURTHER READING

Finney, J., et al. (2008). Creating a positive departmental climate at Virginia Tech: A compendium of successful strategies. Retrieved from https://vtechworks.lib.vt.edu/handle /10919/72135.

Kezar, A. (2014). *How colleges change: Understanding, leading, and enacting change.* New York: Routledge.

Strategy 6. Enhanced Visibility for Women and Gender Issues

Here we discuss interventions that seek to enhance the visibility of women as scholars, teachers, and leaders in STEM disciplines and to elevate the issues that impede women in their advancement in the academy. Taking a wide variety of forms, these interventions all seek to raise awareness by celebrating women's accomplishments, sharing research on the state of women's representation in STEM and the reasons for it, or drawing attention to the work of the campus ADVANCE project in reducing barriers to women's full participation in the academy. Education on implicit bias serves to increase awareness of bias, the body of research behind it, and its impacts on equity in the academy. Targeted education for specific groups (e.g., search committees) to achieve specific institutional goals (e.g., diversifying faculty hiring) is discussed in Strategies 1 and 2.

Rationale

Numerous studies show that women's scientific contributions are devalued compared to those of men (Goldin & Rouse, 2000; Lincoln et al., 2012; Long & Fox, 1995; Wennerås & Wold, 1997). Both men and women evaluate men more favorably than they do women, even when they have identical credentials (Correll, Benard, & Paik, 2007; Moss-Racusin et al., 2012; Steinpreis, Anders, & Ritzke, 1999). Moreover, self-assessment of ability is influenced by cultural beliefs about differences in men's and women's capabilities (Correll, 2001); as a result, women are less likely to apply for awards or ask to be nominated (Rudman, 1998). Women use less self-promoting language in their research publications (Lerchenmueller, Sorenson, & Jena, 2019). They are also less likely to receive awards for their scholarly work (Lincoln et al., 2012) compared to winning awards for teaching or service. Both the language of award criteria (Carnes et al., 2005) and the language of recommendation letters (Trix & Psenka, 2003) may be biased by gender schemas that do not portray women as intellectual leaders. The net outcome is that women's accomplishments are less visible and less valued than men's. ADVANCE projects sought to counter this pattern by highlighting and promoting women's accomplishments.

ADVANCE projects also found value in communicating the barriers that STEM women face in the academy and the institutional work required to remove or reduce these barriers. To achieve transformation that was truly institutional, ADVANCE IT projects had to broadly affect many campus systems and many local, unit-based cultures; to do this required engaging the active support of a wide array of constituencies on campus. Thus, communications about a campus ADVANCE project and its goals aimed to educate and engage a wide range of on- and off-campus audiences, seeking to generate interest, inform discussion, draw participants into the programs, and enlist allies and partners. These activities not only were important as outreach but also benefited the project by helping team members to hone their language, identify needs, solve problems collaboratively, develop partnerships, and become aware of where and why they might meet with resistance.

Purpose and Audience

Different communication efforts targeted different audiences. Informational materials and meetings were used to make individuals aware of opportunities and to inform departments about activities they could join. Reports to particular stakeholder groups—such as deans, chairs, or administrators at certain levels—were used to update and engage people at their regular convenings or in special topical sessions. Websites were used to honor women scholars, celebrate awards and accomplishments, disseminate resource collections, provide information on upcoming events, and share information with other ADVANCE efforts. Well-organized websites also served to document the project's activities, accomplishments, and outcomes when the award period ended.

About half of the ADVANCE IT projects in Cohorts 1 and 2 organized visiting scholar programs designed to provide benefits both to women STEM scholars and to the broader university community. These scholars were often senior STEM women whose work is highly respected or senior researchers with expertise on gender in STEM. Their presence on a campus symbolically highlighted the ADVANCE project and raised the visibility of successful women STEM scholars. Events with visiting scholars provided both public occasions and private conversations for discussing critical factors and institutional issues relevant to the recruitment and success of women STEM faculty. Institutional movement toward significant cultural and policy changes can sometimes be aided by examples of what other institutions are doing. As one institutional leader asserted, visiting scholar programs offer considerable benefits for low cost and are "win-win across the board for everybody." We thus give particular attention to this approach to elevating the visibility of women and gender in STEM.

Models

Interventions to enhance visibility necessarily overlap in both substance and function. We distinguish them by three main purposes: to celebrate women's professional accomplishments, to highlight the status of women in STEM and offer research-based explanations for this status, and to draw attention to the work of the ADVANCE project itself. A well-designed and comprehensive communication plan will make use of several of these approaches and will repeat, revise, and strengthen them over time.

CELEBRATING WOMEN'S ACHIEVEMENTS

Collectively, these approaches seek to highlight and publicize the accomplishments of women on campus. Such publicity may help to dispel myths about women's productivity or merit, and it may help individual women to claim due credit for their successes or to recognize opportunities for appropriate self-promotion. Making senior STEM women more visible on campus may help to remedy inequities in recognition at the top levels where women are most under-represented, such as distinguished professorships or named chairs. Other approaches include highlighting women's contributions to science more broadly and ensuring that women are nominated for campus, regional, and national awards.

Many projects featured the achievements and leadership of their own institution's women faculty on their website or in their newsletter, recognizing awards for research, teaching, or service; tenure and promotions; professional society roles; major grants and papers; and other notable achievements. Some projects highlighted the scholarly work of specific women through a spotlight article or video. Some hosted celebrations to acknowledge women's accomplishments, often jointly sponsored with other women's networks or centers on campus, or held a reception for grantees in their faculty grants programs (see Strategy 11). Others drew attention to senior women scholars on their campus through special designations as scholars or ADVANCE advocates (e.g., the Lamont-Doherty Earth Observatory Research Professors at the Columbia ADVANCE project, Cohort 2) or through a colloquium series featuring women scientists.

Events featuring distinguished women from other institutions as visiting scholars offered opportunities to showcase women's accomplishments and contributions to progress in science, to model successful career paths, and to inspire women scholars at all career stages. Such visits often included public talks, colloquia, presentations, or lectures to the university community at large or to specific departments. To reach multiple audiences, visiting scholars sometimes interacted one-on-one with STEM women faculty, met with students, visited local K–12 schools or teachers, or talked with key institutional leaders about supportive and inclusive institutional cultures that are conducive to the success of women STEM faculty.

Finally, studies show that women are less often nominated for and less often awarded professional awards for their research (Lincoln et al., 2012), and this applies to institutions as well as professional societies. Some institutions documented gender differences in awards given at the campus level and then compiled and publicized information about these awards to encourage nominations of women. Some projects helped departments to identify external awards in their disciplines for which faculty could be encouraged to apply or be nominated. Hunter College (Cohort 1) worked with its provost to add questions to departments' annual diversity reports about departmental nominations of faculty for awards, enhancing data collection as well as reminding departments of their nominating role.

DRAWING ATTENTION TO THE STATUS OF WOMEN IN STEM

Effective use of social science research on gender and diversity as a tool for change has been a hallmark of the ADVANCE program as a whole. Local data on women's representation and advancement can also be powerful for communicating the need and urgency for institutional change, and theater and visual media can be used to prompt reflection on research-based messages.

ADVANCE projects found a variety of ways to communicate evidence about the status of women in STEM and its causes, such as gender bias in evaluation. Visiting scholars were often invited to address these topics, as well as give a science research seminar and meet with faculty, students, and administrators. Public presentations can frame the work, challenges, and successes of women STEM scholars in ways that help to open new conversations on a campus. Behind the scenes, external scholars' visits can further institutional momentum for change through frank conversations with senior leaders about the importance of institutional commitment, strategies for moving forward this agenda, and examples from other institutions.

Some projects featured their own institution's gender scholars in talks, panels, discussions, and symposia. As team members developed expertise in these topics, they incorporated this research into brochures, videos, and presentations and shared the bibliographies they created. They also made use of indicator data, such as those requested by the NSF from institutions receiving ADVANCE grants, to localize the issues in their own institutional context (Frehill, Jeser-Cannavale, & Malley, 2007). Strategies 1 and 2 note some useful references on implicit bias in particular.

The University of Michigan's (Cohort 1) CRLT Players pioneered the use of theatrical performances to dramatize issues about the status of women faculty. ADVANCE supported the troupe to develop and perform humorous, research-based performances that portrayed situations such as a faculty meeting dominated by a bully or the deliberations of a tenure committee in which faculty expressed and tried to respond to implicit bias. In this model, actors followed each performance with a facilitated discussion of the issues raised. The group has performed at other campuses and led workshops for other troupes that wished to develop their own shows. Other institutions have developed similar programs (e.g., Shea et al., 2019).

Popular media can also be used to elevate discussion about these issues. For example, Georgia Tech (Cohort 1) hosted a Women in Science film festival.

PUBLICIZING THE ADVANCE PROJECT

Efforts to raise awareness of women's accomplishments and the barriers they face provided some opportunities to make stakeholders aware of how the ADVANCE project was tackling these challenges. Beyond this, ADVANCE projects found it important to very actively communicate the goals and substance of their work in order to enlist participation and support at all levels and to establish their team as a trusted resource on diversity, equity, and inclusion.

New ADVANCE projects had to establish an identity and name recognition. Nearly all developed logos and websites and created a consistent look for newsletters, brochures, and slide sets. Small branded gifts (pens, notepads, sticky notes, tote bags, portfolios, water bottles, mugs, coasters, magnets, mouse pads) to speakers, workshop leaders, and participants helped to spread the project's name and logo around campus and beyond. Furnishing and labeling a dedicated ADVANCE office raised the project's visibility and fulfilled practical needs for meeting and work spaces. At Texas A&M (Cohort 5), the ADVANCE Center included staff offices, a meeting space, and a play area to engage a child while a parent participated in a meeting; baskets of snacks and a refrigerator stocked with refreshing beverages contributed to its welcoming feel.

ADVANCE leaders described the need to "maintain a drumbeat" of communication about ADVANCE to campus constituencies. Media commonly used included the project website; online or print newsletters; brochures, flyers, postcards, and business cards; bulk and targeted email; and videos. Some customized materials provided specific groups with relevant information (e.g., programs available to assistant professors).

Project teams attended meetings to provide information to and gather input from individual academic departments, professional units relevant to ADVANCE work (e.g., human resources, campus communications, institutional research), faculty governance bodies, committees involved in faculty issues, and special task forces (e.g., a committee on the status of women, a strategic planning group). They sought out invitations to present their work to the university regents, trustees, chairs, deans, students, and alumni.

As their expertise developed and awareness grew, ADVANCE personnel were sometimes asked by the provost or president to take an advisory role in specific projects or to provide information on particular issues, for example, to prepare a background paper on childcare needs or gather data on work/life policies at comparable institutions. Across campuses, ADVANCE leaders used and further developed their personal and professional relationships to gain allies, generate ideas, and solve problems.

Communication to off-campus constituencies centered on institutions' ADVANCE websites, which often included event calendars and sign-up systems, brochures, workshop handouts, presentation slides and posters, research manuscripts, resource collections, evaluation reports, NSF proposals and annual reports (edited where needed to protect confidential data), information about the project team, data about evaluators and advisors, and opportunities for people to get involved. Press releases and advertisements in local papers and other media outlets helped to inform the broader community and invite the public to open events.

Some ADVANCE projects compiled lists of campus or community resources for faculty (e.g., work/life policies, faculty development opportunities) and publicized them through brochures or websites. Some developed short videos as informational tools. For example, the University of Wisconsin–Madison (Cohort 1) made videos about three of its popular programs: Life/Cycle Grants, Department Chair Climate Workshop, and Searching for Excellence and Diversity. Projects generously shared online their intellectual products—evaluation findings, research activities, bibliographies, and manuscripts—and presented their models, findings, and experiences at the annual ADVANCE investigators meetings, at professional meetings, and through regional consortia. The web portal developed at Virginia Tech (Cohort 2) collected resources from all ADVANCE projects and was a valuable resource for many years.

Examples

The University of Rhode Island (Cohort 2) formed the Internal Advisory Action Council of university leaders to discuss issues surrounding institutional climate change and held the Administrators Breakfast Summit to put work/life issues at the forefront.

At Case Western Reserve University (Cohort 2), ADVANCE cohosted a yearly celebration with the campus women's center to recognize all of the honors received by women faculty over the preceding year. The annual Women of Achievement luncheon became a popular and well-attended event. A new award for an outstanding woman scholar in each school was also established, and the recipient was announced at the luncheon.

At the University of Texas at Rio Grande Valley (Cohort 6), the ADVANCE project convened women from across departments for a *merienda* (high tea). As a result, women recognized a shared experience of relative isolation in their departments, identified shared concerns, and took action to formalize the Women's Faculty Network (WFN) with bylaws and standing committees. They sought and obtained representation on key institutional committees where they could contribute faculty women's perspectives and interact with the president and provost, thus elevating women's concerns and interest in decision-making. Large percentages of faculty women have participated in WFN talks, workshops, and social events, and the WFN has become a source of empowerment as well as a useful means of sharing important and timely information (see Laursen & Austin, 2014f).

New Mexico State University (Cohort 1) intentionally organized its visiting scholar program to have an impact on the university's women STEM scholars, graduate students, and undergraduates, as well as on K–12 students. The program aimed to enhance the visibility of women scholars and to affect the pipeline of women in STEM fields. To achieve these goals, every ADVANCE visiting professor interacted with K–12 classes or educators in order to be a role model and affirm the place of women in science. The visits lasted several days and also involved public seminars, research colloquia, and luncheon talks.

Following the great success of a visit in 2003 by author Virginia Valian, WISELI at the University of Wisconsin–Madison (Cohort 1) hosted a major event and talk by a high-profile speaker each year, rather than multiple smaller events. Each occasion was designed to bring together women faculty from throughout campus to promote cross-departmental networking.

Utah State University (Cohort 2) built relationships with a wide range of campus offices that yielded new and creative ideas for supporting women faculty and staff. Human resources personnel were crucial in sustaining the training of search committees and monitoring search data after the grant ended. Staff in facilities management helped to develop and furnish lactation spaces; people in parking management offered pregnant people a parking permit in their third trimester; and the women's basketball coach helped to raise funds for a campus childcare facility.

A few institutions experimented with efforts to raise students' awareness of gender issues in STEM. The team at Case Western Reserve (Cohort 2) found that classroom presentations were not well received, but results were improved when the session was career-focused, held outside of class, promoted by student organizations, and involved graduate students as leaders.

Georgia Tech (Cohort 1) held a town hall to discuss sustaining and institutionalizing its ADVANCE activities.

Montana State University (Cohort 6) pioneered the strategy of a "data charrette," sharing presentations and posters at an open house to frame institutional challenges around diversity and equity, share the work being done, and communicate evaluation and research results.

The University of Puerto Rico at Humacao (Cohort 1) supported the production (and a DVD recording) of a play written by a faculty member about mathematician Emmy Noether. Noether's struggles to obtain a faculty position in the early twentieth century were linked in the play to the current situation of women in the sciences. Some 800 people attended the performances, which included a special showing for administrators and department chairs.

The Earth Institute at Columbia University (Cohort 2) convened a symposium, The Science of Diversity, which featured scholars from social science and law who discussed research that sheds light on gender issues. Topics included cognitive bias, judgment, and decision-making; the effects on individuals of subtle environmental changes; structuring inclusive environments; and translating research into action. The symposium was featured in a highly visible medium in the geosciences, which was relevant for stakeholders at this research institute (Laird et al., 2007). The visibility and prestige of the event conveyed a strong message to the research community and the university about the critical importance of the issues addressed.

The ACES (Academic Careers in Engineering and Science) project at Case Western Reserve (Cohort 2) developed a comprehensive communication strategy. Team members met with each department as it was scheduled to receive the ACES interventions. Faculty received packets with general information about ADVANCE and the ACES initiatives, as well as readings and resources customized for faculty women and men and for department chairs. Packets were updated every summer to reflect the expansion of services and the current offerings.

All chairs, faculty, and department assistants of the 32 ACES departments received regular email updates and flyers about activities, visiting lecturers, networking events, and application deadlines. The PI gave presentations and updates about ACES at meetings of the board of trustees, the faculty senate, and the dean's council and handed out the ACES progress report at events and meetings. The project director led workshops on search guidelines and procedures for business managers and department assistants university-wide, and provided other bias and diversity training and meeting facilitation by request. The ACES newsletter was distributed twice a year.

Evaluation

Examples of formal evaluation of communication strategies were rare. Attendance at events was documented, and web analytics were used to track the use of online resources. Projects should have a robust system to track the team's outreach efforts to departments, committees, and other campus groups since this information is helpful both in reporting and as formative feedback for recognizing additional opportunities. But team members' time may be better invested in doing the communicating than in evaluating it systematically.

Some climate survey items indicated how well the project penetrated the campus consciousness. For example, the final climate survey at the University of Colorado Boulder (Cohort 1) showed that 91% of tenure-stream faculty who responded were aware of the ADVANCE project by name, and 38% of this group had participated in one or more events (Laursen, 2009). Both awareness and participation were higher among women than men and were lower among teaching- and research-focused faculty, who had only partial access to project activities compared with tenure-stream faculty.

Projects offered somewhat more detail in their assessment of visiting scholar programs. For the scholars themselves, participating in such events offered an opportunity to be generative while also being honored; enriched their knowledge of other institutions' programs; and expanded their collegial networks. Benefits to the institution included:

- enhanced intellectual vibrancy
- heightened visibility of women in science and of gender issues in the workplace
- a reputation for addressing equity that may attract future applicants for faculty positions
- widened national visibility of the institution
- visiting scholars may recommend the university to their undergraduates for graduate study

We discuss the outcomes for faculty of mentoring and networking with visiting scholars in Strategy 12.

Affordances and Limitations

These visibility-enhancing strategies offered several affordances:

- Strong communication strategies were important for raising awareness of ADVANCE early in the project. As team members practiced and received feedback on their public messages, they gained clarity about how to best reach various audiences and refined their theories of change.
- Use of social science research on gender was widely felt to be effective in persuading stakeholders that the problem was real, persistent, and often grounded in widely held, unconscious psychological schemas (Valian, 1999). Leaders found empirical evidence to be necessary (though not sufficient) for persuading STEM faculty since data "speak scientists' language."
- Online resources were readily accessed by individuals on and off campus, while in-person events, such as colloquia and panels, often doubled as opportunities for networking (see Strategy 12).
- Most communication strategies were relatively low in production cost, although the time investment to develop messages and materials could be significant. The campus communications office or colleagues who specialize in marketing could provide advice. Some logos and materials needed to be vetted by campus communications officials. Sponsoring a visiting scholar incurred costs for travel, lodging, food, and an honorarium (typically $400–$500 at the time the projects in our sample were active), which were seen as a modest investment relative to the benefits received.
- Early actions also served as means to get the word out. For example, some projects found that distributing funds through small grant programs (Strategy 11) was an effective way to draw faculty attention and alert department chairs to how ADVANCE might benefit their faculty.

Project leaders also noted some limitations:

- Consistent support for web development and updating was a recurring issue. If this expertise was not available on the project team, it was important to negotiate technical support, including who would provide it and what priority it would have. It was also important to build in staff time and create a schedule for steadily generating website or newsletter content.
- Not all audiences were favorable to ADVANCE. Team members needed to develop good listening skills, but also thick skins. They had to prepare to

respond thoughtfully to critics yet avoid becoming discouraged when resistance emerged. It was important to recognize that the pace of change varied in different units and thus to be patient and "cheerfully relentless," as one leader put it.

- As the ADVANCE office became more visible, it often became a go-to resource for individual women seeking advice about difficulties in their personal lives or departments. ADVANCE leaders took on support, advocacy, and ombudsperson roles that they had not anticipated; as senior and well-connected people, they could often serve as intermediaries or discreetly alert colleagues to a problem. While these activities were important, valued, and clearly needed, they could be time-consuming and emotionally draining. And absent a formal role in a unit's tenure process, ADVANCE leaders could find such work to be politically tricky, for example, when advocating for fairness in a tenure appeal without seeming to advocate directly for a particular tenure candidate. We list this as a limitation to alert project teams to the likelihood that these issues will arise so that they can consider in advance how they might respond.

Summary

The possible strategies to elevate women's visibility are manifold, offering opportunities to be creative and to devise positive coupling with other project activities. On their own, visibility strategies will not change the institution, but public events can generate enthusiasm, enhance receptivity, and thus prepare the way for other strategies that go deeper. Celebrations of women's accomplishments have high symbolic value and offer opportunities for networking and support. And unsung though they may be, we observed that effective and wide-reaching communication channels were a hallmark of the most successful ADVANCE projects. Many of them had a skilled project manager or coordinator who could take on these duties with substantial independence and, in the process, develop useful relationships campus-wide.

FURTHER READING

Cadwalader, E. L., Herbers, J. M., & Popejoy, A. B. (2014). Disproportionate awards for women in disciplinary societies. In V. P. Demos, C. W. Berheide, & M. T.Segal (Eds.), *Gender transformation in the academy: Advances in gender research* (pp. 243–263). Bingley, England: Emerald Group.

Collaborative on Academic Careers in Higher Education [COACHE]. (2014). Benchmark best practices: Appreciation and recognition. Cambridge, MA: Harvard Graduate School of Education. Retrieved from https://coache.gse.harvard.edu/files/gse-coache/files/coache _appreciation-and-recognition.pdf.

Stewart, A. J., & Valian, V. (2018). Recognizing faculty accomplishments. In their *An inclusive academy: Achieving diversity and excellence* (pp. 373–414). Cambridge, MA: MIT Press.

Chapter Five

Support the Whole Person

Both the biological realities of childbirth and gendered societal expectations mean that women bear more of the load for family responsibilities. Institutions can take concrete steps in policies and practices to enable women to thrive as academic scientists and engineers.

EFFORTS TO STOP bias (Strategies 1–3) deal with gendered perceptions of faculty and their work. However, there are real factors in the lives of women faculty that are different from what men experience and have effects on their careers. Women have a specific biological role in childbearing, and research shows that women in heterosexual couples tend to have different and more demanding family roles while their children are young, even in egalitarian partnerships. In US society, women's family responsibilities continue at a higher level on average than those of men, even after children are of school age. These personal and family roles conflict with academic life because academe is an up-or-out profession that requires substantial commitment and productivity during a fixed probationary period. This puts people at a disadvantage who "experience large, temporary negative productivity shocks, such as having children" (Antecol, Bedard, & Stearns, 2018, p. 2423). Academic institutions are often described as "greedy institutions," affording substantial autonomy but also requiring high commitment and time—a demand that is challenging at certain times of life, such as when a child is young or a partner is ill (Ward & Wolf-Wendel, 2012).

The impact of family responsibilities can be seen in data on faculty career paths: women are less likely to have children before tenure than are men, and they are less likely to get tenure if they do have children (Mason & Goulden, 2002, 2004). However, if they delay having children until after tenure, they will also be older

and may experience more difficulties with fertility and pregnancy. This is not specific to faculty careers and seems to be exacerbated in STEM fields. The attrition
of new mothers from STEM is very high: 43% of women leave full-time STEM
work after their first child (Cech & Blair-Loy, 2019). Nor is it just a problem for
mothers: 23% of new fathers also leave STEM work after their first child. Women
postdocs are more likely than men to shift away from academia, especially if they
have children, and they are more likely than men to cite children as a reason for
changing career goals (Mason & Goulden, 2002). These shifts result in the con-
centration of women in less prestigious academic roles. Finally, women who do not
have children before tenure are less likely to have them at all, suggesting that they
are making a deliberate decision not to combine a family with an academic career
(Mason & Goulden, 2002).

For these reasons, policies and practices that enable a faculty member to have
a family and maintain an academic career are important strategies for ensuring
women's full participation on STEM faculties. The approaches in this chapter recognize that considerations for a partner or family are often important in women's
decision-making to take a job at a particular institution, that personal and family
events may temporarily interfere with faculty members' ability to fulfill all of their
duties (yet should not derail their careers in the long term), and that arrangements
for childcare and lactation may be important to faculty members' decision to take
a job and to their productivity once they do. While these issues are often salient
for women, they are important to faculty of all genders, and practices and policies must be designed to include people with all types of personal and family
arrangements.

Several resources on the landscape of family-friendly policies in higher education may help readers compare common practices to their own institution's offerings. Tower and Dilks (2015) compiled work/life policies from ADVANCE institutions; these offer generally progressive benchmarks. Morgan and coauthors (n.d.)
created a searchable database of leave policies from some 200 North American
institutions. A guidebook from the University of Michigan's Center for the Education of Women remains useful as a conceptual organizer for those developing
policies (Smith & Waltman, 2006); although some of the guidebook's examples of
specific policy language are now dated, many of the same institutions continue as
policy leaders. The American Association of University Professors (AAUP) offers
data, position statements, and guidebooks on the legal aspects of family-friendly
policies (http://www.aaup.org). The Center for WorkLife Law at the University of
California's Hastings College of the Law offers resources on best practices and

model policies for avoiding gender and family discrimination (https://worklifelaw
.org; https://toolsforchangeinstem.org).

In this chapter we describe three major types of programs that ADVANCE institutions have developed to support faculty as whole people throughout the life
course:

- strategies that enable hiring two well-qualified faculty who are partners (a
  dual-career couple), which helps women, who are more likely to be
  partnered with another academic (Strategy 7)
- flexible work arrangements that allow temporary or long-term adjustment
  of faculty duties in response to life events (Strategy 8)
- practical, family-friendly accommodations that support faculty through
  physical and logistical challenges related to family formation and caregiving (Strategy 9)

Strategy 7. Support for Dual-Career Couples

Meeting the needs of dual-career couples is critical to recruiting and retaining highly qualified women faculty in STEM and other fields. Institutions with
ADVANCE IT projects in Cohorts 1 and 2 were keenly aware of this issue; nearly
all (80%) of these projects addressed dual-career hires in some capacity.

Rationale

More than 70% of academics have partners who also work, and of these, about
half have academic partners (Astin & Milem, 1997; Schiebinger, Davies Henderson, & Gilmartin, 2008). Moreover, women are more likely than men to have academic partners. These women report that job opportunities for their partner or
spouse are important to their own career choices, and they will actively refuse job
offers if their partner cannot find satisfactory employment (Schiebinger, Davies
Henderson, & Gilmartin, 2008). Therefore, to attract and retain excellent women
in STEM fields, institutions found it important to address the needs of dual-career
couples.

Research is beginning to show that these policies do work. In a study of the
impact of work/life policies on women's representation and promotion in university economics departments, Juraqulova, McCluskey, and Mittelhammer (2019)
found that the presence of an institutional dual-career hiring policy was positively
associated with women's representation at assistant and associate professor ranks.

Research also suggests that both members of a dual-career couple become productive academics. Woolstenhulme and coauthors (2011, 2015) showed that compared to peers, the initial or "primary" hire was more productive and the accompanying or "secondary" hire was equally productive, as measured by publications. Thus, jointly hired couples generally outperform their peers and are also more likely to receive tenure. These authors argued that dual-career policies afford rural institutions the opportunity to hire and retain talented scholars who might otherwise go to higher-ranked institutions. Similarly, Morton and Kmec (2018) found that candidates who revealed their dual-career intentions during the job hunt experienced more positive later career outcomes than did those who did not reveal their status. Together, these studies suggest that dual-career policies help individuals achieve professional goals at the same time as they help institutions attract and retain excellent and more diverse scholars.

Purpose

Dual-career initiatives seek to positively influence the decision of a preferred candidate to accept a faculty position and to attract both members of a talented couple to enrich the community. Successful placement of a partner may increase the job satisfaction of new hires and thus help to retain them at the institution. Finally, making job applicants aware of possibilities for dual-career hiring during the recruiting process is felt to signal an institution's family friendliness, thus helping to attract interest from talented people for whom the availability of opportunities for a partner is a strong consideration. By broadening the pool of talented applicants for faculty positions and by making the institution and its community an attractive place for professional couples to work and live, dual-career initiatives seek to enhance universities' ability to hire and hold onto excellent faculty.

Audience

While ADVANCE projects directed their efforts toward attracting STEM women, policies were generally written to apply to all genders and to include same-sex partners where this was not otherwise legally prohibited. Institutions most commonly targeted dual-career accommodations to early-career faculty considering tenure-track offers, but sometimes they used the same approaches to hire a senior woman or to retain a current faculty member. A few institutions used their dual-career policies or practices to recruit or retain senior-level administrators or non-tenure-track faculty.

Compared to institutions in urban areas with greater numbers and variety of employers, institutions in rural locations reported partner hiring to be a more salient issue—a "fundamental fact of faculty hiring [in our context]," as one interviewee put it.

Models

We identified three major types of interventions from the data. Some projects worked to develop and implement an institutional policy on dual-career hiring where this did not exist, or to strengthen and/or publicize an existing policy. Formal policy approaches were chosen to address the hiring of two academics due to the substantial financial and institutional commitment that this represents and to the lengthy formal hiring process for academic faculty. Such policies typically stated the institution's willingness to pursue dual-career hires while asserting units' autonomy in making hiring decisions. Practical details defined processes for proposing and pursuing a dual-career hire, specified language for advertising, identified roles in the recruiting process, and spelled out funding mechanisms and commitments.

Another approach was to provide partners with assistance in finding positions on campus or in the community by working to develop and formalize linkages with potential employers. Tactics included working through the human resources office to connect partners to non-academic campus jobs, building connections with other academic institutions and employers in the community or region, and providing the partner with access to the services of an outside firm specializing in placement and relocation.

Finally, many ADVANCE leaders provided informal assistance to job candidates during the recruitment process. Most often, this meant participating in campus interviews as a neutral party who was well connected but outside the hiring committee. The ADVANCE liaison could confidentially ask candidates if they wished to share their family situation and needs and then could provide information and make personal connections to assist with partner placement or initiate a dual-career hiring effort. At some institutions, this liaison role was formalized as the point person for dual-career assistance. Because this method can operate in combination with either or both of the other interventions mentioned above, it was sometimes used as an initial approach to address dual-career needs and opportunities while more formal processes and relationships were worked out.

STRENGTHENING POLICY

Some institutions that had dual-career hiring policies already in place reviewed and reevaluated them. In some cases, this review revealed that while strong policies existed, chairs and faculty members did not know of them or were reluctant to use them. These projects worked to ensure that policies were refined, expanded, or simply implemented more fully, taking one or more of the following steps:

- updating language, procedures, and protocols to make the policy more clear, easier to use, and more effective because it was better aligned with what worked in practice
- identifying funds that could be used to enable a dual-career hire
- disseminating the policy to deans, heads or chairs, and faculty through workshops, guidebooks, brochures, meetings, websites, or presentations to change their understandings, perceptions, and attitudes about the policy

To create a new dual-career policy, institutions typically took the following steps:

- engaging stakeholders to study issues, assess needs, build buy-in, and investigate options, such as examining policies at comparable institutions
- drafting a policy and perhaps revising it in response to stakeholder feedback
- using local governance procedures to propose, approve, and implement the new policy

The resulting policies typically identified

- mechanisms for inquiring about a candidate's dual-career needs and interest without introducing inappropriate information into decision-making processes
- processes for opening partner-hiring negotiations with other departments
- procedures for waiving a search or expediting an application
- sources of bridge funding to support a partner hire, and procedures for requesting funds
- incentives for departments to consider a partner hire
- pathways for converting a partner from an initial soft-money or non-tenure-track position to a tenure-track position

The most common cost-sharing arrangement reported by the ADVANCE projects was division by thirds, with a third of the salary for the second position covered by the hiring department, a third covered by the partner's department, and a third covered by the dean or provost. Typically, this arrangement lasted two or three years, giving the secondary hiring department time to reallocate funds to cover the partner's salary for the long term.

BUILDING INSTITUTIONAL LINKAGES

Several institutions offered job placement assistance to spouses or partners, connecting individuals to institutionally maintained networks. Project leaders described engaging support from the university's human resources office, drawing on alumni networks, participating in the local chamber of commerce and other civic networks, and contracting with a local firm to assist with placement. At Utah State University (Cohort 2), for example, partners seeking university staff positions were referred to relevant units, and their applications were given priority when appropriate positions became available.

Other institutions were already members of their regional HERC (Higher Education Recruitment Consortium) and made a practice of referring candidates to this resource. HERC is a nonprofit coalition of academic employers that supports member institutions in hiring and retaining outstanding and diverse employees.

OFFERING CASE-BY-CASE INFORMAL ASSISTANCE

Making personal contact with faculty candidates during their campus visit was an approach that could be implemented right away while more formal policy or networking efforts proceeded. ADVANCE team members who were not on the search committee met with the candidate to find out whether dual-career issues would affect the candidate's interest in taking the position if offered, to answer questions, and to serve as a resource for any other work/life issues. Departments could often be more responsive if they obtained earlier knowledge about the influence of a dual-career situation on a favored candidate's response to a potential offer.

Examples

A review of policies at the University of Washington (UW, Cohort 1) showed that the university had many policies in place that provided flexibility for faculty, including dual-career hiring, but department chairs and faculty either were reluctant to use these policies or did not know that they existed. UW ADVANCE thus focused on changing the attitudes, knowledge, and perspectives of faculty and department chairs by reviewing policies at its quarterly leadership workshops and by focusing one workshop session on dual-career hiring. UW ADVANCE also proactively highlighted these institutional policies when meeting with women faculty candidates. Here, the role of ADVANCE was to increase understanding of the need for and rationale behind these policies within the institution.

The ADVANCE program at the University of Alabama at Birmingham (UAB, Cohort 2) worked with UAB's human resources department to assist spouses and partners interested in university employment. An external consulting group was contracted to assist with job searches and relocation for partners and spouses of faculty and senior administrators who sought employment outside the university. UAB planned to continue working with the external firm beyond the life of its grant.

New Mexico State University (Cohort 1) worked to establish a regional hiring consortium with other academic and technical institutions located within commuting distance.

At the University of Montana (Cohort 2), PACE (Partnership for Comprehensive Equity) team members were instrumental in developing a new policy by working through a presidential task force. They first gathered qualitative data to identify issues around recruiting and retaining faculty in their rural and geographically isolated setting, and then brought these concerns to the attention of university leaders. The task force examined a suite of issues related to work/life flexibility, developed policies where they were needed, and moved them through the university's policy approval process. PACE also helped to build a new website to share information about the new policies and other work/life resources.

Texas A&M University's (TAMU, Cohort 5) ADVANCE project included both a formal dual-career hiring process for academic couples and a support service for partners seeking non-academic positions inside or outside the university. Both approaches had been previously used with success at TAMU; these efforts were centralized, reinvigorated, and institutionalized under ADVANCE in response to increasing need. Kaunas, Tomaszewski, and Yennello (2018) described the role and activities of the dual-career program coordinator, who assists partners in finding non-academic employment in the community. This position was sustained in the dean of faculties' office when the grant ended.

Evaluation

Projects commonly reported the number of successful hires in which assistance had been provided or dual-career policies applied. Comparing such data to periods prior to the ADVANCE grant may show how awareness and use of the policy changed. For example, Virginia Tech (Cohort 2) revised its dual-career policy and reported 39 recruitment and 18 retention cases over the life of its ADVANCE grant.

The University of Texas at El Paso (Cohort 2) created a policy and also worked on a case-by-case basis. It reported assisting 12 dual-career couples, which enabled UTEP to hire 12 STEM women and also to hire 4 men of color.

New Mexico State University (Cohort 1) reported assisting 5 dual-career couples on a case-by-case basis, and Case Western Reserve (Cohort 2) successfully assisted 13 recruitment and retention cases after adopting a formal dual-career policy.

Montana State's (Cohort 6) family advocates helped with partner accommodation cases as well as other family needs (see Strategy 8). During the five-year ADVANCE grant, Montana State documented work on more than 70 partner accommodation cases, resulting in 33 faculty accepting tenure-track positions in 21 different departments (ADVANCE Project TRACS, 2017). Of these, 63% were women; partners were accommodated in tenure-track (53%) and non-tenure-track (47%) academic positions.

The University of Nebraska–Lincoln (Cohort 4) carefully documented its work on dual-career situations at each stage (Anderson-Knott, Wonch Hill, & Watanabe, 2013). Out of 61 STEM faculty searches, its efforts yielded 8 successful hires of STEM women with a partner placement, plus 6 additional women hired through opportunity hires and retention situations, far exceeding the project's initial goals.

At Texas A&M (Cohort 5), tracking a set of metrics related to partner referrals, job-hunting activity, job placement, and department and partner satisfaction helped to improve the program and make a case for its institutionalization (Kaunas, Tomaszewski, & Yennello, 2018). Climate survey data also helped to make the case for addressing dual-career couples' needs.

Together, these data from varied institutions show that the magnitude of impact may depend on the approach used, as well as on the size of the faculty, the degree of need in the particular local context, and the availability of new positions in any measurement period.

After a policy has been in place for some time, institutional samples may be large enough that it is possible to compare productivity, advancement, and retention for dual-career and solo hires; for example, see the studies by Woolstenhulme and colleagues (2011, 2015), which were based on data from Washington State University (Cohort 4). It may also be useful to monitor faculty attitudes about dual-career placement. Some observations have suggested that animosity toward partners gaining "unearned" positions diminishes when institutions have five to eight years of experience of the practice. Over time, dual-career hiring becomes understood as an asset for attracting strong faculty and an accepted element of institutional culture (Rice, Wolf-Wendel, & Twombly, 2007).

Affordances and Limitations

Dual-career initiatives were most often emphasized by institutions in rural or isolated locations, where alternative employment for partners was less readily available in the community. In our sample, institutions in or near urban centers with multiple academic and other employers found dual-career issues to be less of a barrier in their ability to hire STEM women faculty. This pattern is, of course, sensitive to local geography and economic factors.

As several interviewees noted, it is important not only to have a policy and inform faculty about it, but to mitigate any stigma associated with the hiring of a partner. This includes avoiding language that labels one person as a "trailing" spouse (alternatives in the literature include "accompanying" or "opportunity" hire). One ADVANCE project made a point to publicize to chairs the success of both partners in the institution's initial dual-career hires, showing how this approach could be very positive for a department. Members of dual-career couples also noted ways in which they helped to dispel stereotypes, for example, pointing out examples to minimize the concern that partners would "vote as a bloc."

Policy interventions—especially where a new policy was developed or an existing policy was significantly revised—were seen as slow and time-consuming but having staying power. In some cases, newly drafted documents did not rise to the level of formal policy because administrators were concerned about permanently committing to financial support for dual-career hires. Nonetheless, the drafts were circulated to department chairs, recommended as institutional practice, and put into action. While this approach provided fiscal flexibility, it also risked fostering inequity among departments, especially some years after the initial policy draft was circulated, when experienced chairs were aware of this informal dual-career practice and newer chairs were not. This highlights the need for institutional transparency about policies and practices around dual-career hiring.

In addition to helping to attract and retain strong faculty candidates, a number of interviewees noted positive side effects of their dual-career programs:

- It sets a supportive tone and demonstrates institutional commitment to supporting faculty around their work/life issues. Newly hired faculty reported that even failed efforts to place their partners created good will and a sense that the institution cared about their success and happiness.

- It helps to diminish inequity by standardizing the path through which partners may be accommodated.
- Use of the policy over time helps to diminish stigma as growing experience on campus begins to dispel negative beliefs about hiring couples.

We do not have an evidence base by which to compare the relative effectiveness of the strategies noted above, but several affordances and limitations were noted in interviews:

- A policy enabling dual-career hires and expressing institutional support was seen as a necessary baseline in order to remain competitive with other institutions. Policies are sustainable changes.
- Assisting with placement by working through the networks of a designated liaison was low in cost and could be powerful. However, this approach relied on one individual's personal and professional connections, continued interest and ability to maintain these contacts, and willingness to participate in multiple searches in this capacity. While initially this approach may have demonstrated the merit of providing case-by-case support, it was sustained long term only when it was designated as a work role in an appropriate office (typically under human resources or the provost). Campuses varied substantially as to whether placement assistance was seen as within the purview and capacities of the human resources office.
- Hiring an external agency can provide needed expertise and does not add to the workload of campus offices. However, such a firm may not be locally available, and paying the cost must be sustained beyond the award funding.
- The idea of a regional network to support couples in finding positions at institutions within a reasonable commute is appealing, but we did not see examples of success in establishing *new* regional consortia among the first 19 institutions. Building these relationships is time-consuming and—since it takes time to bear fruit—may be less prioritized by busy ADVANCE personnel. Some ADVANCE institutions have access to regional HERCs, and most of these are located in well-populated regions.

Finally, it is important to be sensitive to gender dynamics when applying such policies. A few studies have explored potential risks to candidates who reveal that they are part of a dual-career couple. Allen, Smith, and Ransdell (2019) designed experimental studies to explore institutional biases in offers to dual-career couples.

They found that department chairs did not evaluate initial candidates differently due to their dual-career or solo hiring status, suggesting there was no negative impact for candidates in self-disclosing their partner accommodation needs. However, chairs proposed different salaries and start-up packages for the initial candidate compared to those for the partner presented as an "opportunity hire," and these proposals depended on the chair's gender. The authors concluded, "Although a candidate was not penalized for requesting a partner accommodation, support and resources for the opportunity candidates depended on if the evaluator was male or female. This means that while it might be fine for a woman to disclose a dual-career need in her job application, her partner might not receive the resources needed to be successful" (p. 170).

From the candidate side, Morton (2018) found that women in heterosexual couples were less likely to initiate dual-career negotiations than were men, although this depended on their perceptions of the importance of their own career in relation to their partner's career. Morton and Kmec (2018) also reported some gender differences in how men and women approached these negotiations. Together, these studies show that dual-career negotiations are themselves freighted with gendered dynamics. While these policies are beneficial to women in many respects, care must be taken to make the process fair.

Summary

Dual-career hiring programs have been helpful for ADVANCE institutions, particularly where partner employment has historically been a negative factor in women's decisions to accept a faculty job offer. The availability of such programs is increasingly becoming the new normal for academic employers. Working one hire at a time does not generate rapid change in faculty demographics, but dual-career hires can be institutionally important in some cases: establishing a foothold for women in departments where they are severely underrepresented, recruiting a senior woman leader, generating opportunities to hire two excellent candidates, or strengthening retention of successful couples. The decision to include dual-career approaches in an institutional change portfolio or ADVANCE project is necessarily highly contextual. Through their experiments with this approach, ADVANCE institutions have notably enhanced the research basis about this practice.

FURTHER READING

Higher Education Recruitment Consortium [HERC]. (n.d.). Dual career resources for job seekers. Retrieved from https://www.hercjobs.org/dual-careers/dual-career-resources.

McMahon, M. R., Mora, M. T., & Qubbaj, A. R. (Eds.). (2018). *Advancing women in academic STEM fields through dual career policies and practices.* Charlotte, NC: Information Age.

University of Rhode Island ADVANCE. (2007). Rationale for a dual career hiring program. Retrieved from https://web.uri.edu/advance-women/work-life-support/dual_career_background.

Wolf-Wendel, L., Twombly, S. B., & Rice, S. (2004). *The two-body problem: Dual-career couple hiring practices in higher education.* Baltimore, MD: Johns Hopkins University Press.

Strategy 8. Flexible Work Arrangements

More than half of the ADVANCE IT projects in the first two cohorts developed policies to offer flexible work arrangements to faculty members whose personal responsibilities had the potential to interrupt their usual work activities or time allocations. These arrangements varied in detail but typically offered adjustments to the tenure clock or to the duties required as part of active service. Our discussion here addresses specific policies offering flexibility in the structure and expectations of work. Related topics are Strategy 2 on tenure and promotion policies and Strategy 9 on family-friendly initiatives.

Rationale

The recruitment, retention, and success of women are enhanced when formal policies accommodate both personal and professional responsibilities. While many men care for family members, women often handle a large part of family responsibilities. Thus, policies that offer flexible work arrangements are especially important for attracting and supporting women faculty.

Institutions also benefit from these approaches. The existence of visible, formal policies for flexible work arrangements enhances the institution's attractiveness to potential faculty candidates. Moreover, after making major investments to attract, hire, and provide start-up support for a new faculty member, an institution benefits when it makes modest adjustments to work arrangements to ensure that she can succeed and remain with the institution. Even if informal arrangements have been made fairly regularly or easily in the past, the presence of formal institutional policies ensures fairness for all and alleviates concerns that individual chairs or deans might not consistently apply informal norms.

Purpose

Policies typically focus on providing support to faculty members in situations where personal responsibilities are unusually demanding and may require rearranging or adjusting the time and energy allocated to professional work—in the short or longer term. Life events that may generate these circumstances include the birth, adoption, or fostering of a child; primary caregiving to a child, elder, or other family member; or illness, injury, or disability of the faculty member.

Some institutions created and implemented new policies to accommodate these needs; others revised existing policies. In still other cases, institutions developed better processes for implementing these policies or making them known. Typically, policy creation involves work by university committees and approval by governing bodies, such as a faculty senate.

Audience

Typically, policies supporting flexible work arrangements are available to faculty of any gender, although specific details vary by institution. Eligibility criteria may require the faculty member to be carrying out the relevant personal duties for a certain percentage of time. For example, some policies for parental leave require the faculty member taking leave to be engaged in caregiving for at least 50% of the time. This requirement is a way to offer caregiving benefits to people of any gender, while seeking to ensure that a nonprimary caregiver does not simply accrue more time to complete academic work by tapping into the policy.

Some research suggests, however, that it is not straightforward to design such policies equitably. For example, in a study of top economics departments, men who worked at institutions with gender-neutral policies to stop the tenure clock for new faculty parents experienced a boost in high-profile publications and higher tenure rates compared to women at the same institution (Antecol, Bedard, & Stearns, 2018). The authors concluded that "gender-neutral tenure clock stopping policies do not adequately account for the true gender-specific productivity losses associated with having children. As a result, gender-neutral policies actually increase the gender gap in economics at research-intensive universities" (pp. 2439–2440). Clock stoppage policies that applied to women only neither helped nor hurt women's tenure rates.

Flexible work policies must also account for the particulars of faculty responsibilities. For example, it may not be practical to take a teaching leave in the middle of a semester-long course; STEM faculty who run laboratories may need to continue some oversight of their research students and lab operations (e.g., Schimpf et al., 2013). Some researchers have suggested that localized, informal communication channels should be promoted to ensure that potential users of work/life policies understand and have full access to formal accommodations (Schimpf, Santiago, & Pawley, 2012).

Models

Policies for flexible work arrangements typically fall into three categories, and an institution may include several of them in its policy portfolio.

STOP-THE-CLOCK POLICIES AND TENURE CLOCK EXTENSIONS

These policies offer provisions for stopping or extending the tenure clock under certain conditions, including the birth, adoption, or fostering of a child; health issues faced by the faculty member or an immediate family member; or elder care needs.

Some policies add time automatically to the tenure clock in the event of a birth or adoption. These opt-out policies do not require the faculty member to wait additional time for tenure review, but do require them to actively request removal of the tenure-clock extension. Under opt-in policies, faculty may apply to stop or extend the tenure clock. Opt-out policies are thought to reduce any stigma around use of the policy.

Institutional policies vary as to how often this provision can be exercised. Once or twice in the career is typical, but in some cases the faculty member can enlist this provision as often as needed. In cases where the reason for extension is childcare, some institutions require faculty members to sign a statement that they provide 50% or more of the primary childcare duties.

ACTIVE SERVICE WITH MODIFIED DUTIES

These policies involve adjusting the responsibilities of a faculty member for a period of time due to birth or adoption, death of a spouse, or other family matters. Some institutions automatically arrange for a faculty member to be relieved of some or all teaching for a term immediately after a birth or adoption, and for those without teaching responsibilities to get equivalent release time. Arrangements in other situations, such as when a faculty member needs to provide elder care, are often made on a case-by-case basis involving consultations among the faculty member and others, such as the department chair, dean, and human resources department.

PART-TIME TENURE-TRACK APPOINTMENT POLICIES

These policies cover several situations, such as employing a tenure-track faculty member at 0.5 FTE (full-time equivalent), shifting a 1.0 FTE faculty member to 0.5 FTE for a period of time, or filling a single faculty line with two 0.5 FTE faculty members. These policies are less common than the first two types, but they offer options that may enable faculty members with significant personal responsibilities to engage in a full faculty life, including progressing toward tenure. These appointments usually involve adjustment of both regular duties and tenure timelines. Drago and Williams (2000); Herbers (2014); and Quinn, Lange, and Riskin (2004) discussed some considerations for individuals and institutions in making these arrangements.

Examples

While institutions may have similar objectives, the specific policies they develop usually reflect the particular cultures and circumstances of their particular organizational contexts, as these examples show.

At Case Western Reserve University (Cohort 2), stop-the-clock arrangements are automatic for the addition of a child; for other family matters, such as elder care responsibilities, they are available by request and then at the discretion of a dean. At Case, faculty members can stop the clock for family leave as many times as needed.

At Kansas State University (Cohort 2), a stop-the-clock policy covers situations of a new child, childcare duties, and health issues for the faculty member or an immediate family member. Faculty members may use this provision two times in their career.

The *Handbook of Operating Procedures* at the University of Texas at El Paso (Cohort 2) indicates that any faculty member can request a tenure review delay of one year for legitimate family matters, including becoming a new parent; becoming the primary caregiver for an elderly, ill, or disabled family member; or if a faculty member is experiencing serious illness, injury, or disability. A second year of delay may also be requested, but the tenure clock cannot be delayed more than two years in all. The process begins with the faculty member writing a request to the department chair; the chair makes a recommendation to the dean; and the dean applies to the provost, who makes the decision. Faculty members work closely with professionals in the human resources department to determine the appropriate request for their situation.

Utah State University (Cohort 2) established a practice that faculty may use the tenure-clock extension option up to two times for birth, serious health issues in the family, or responsibilities as a primary caregiver. Faculty couples can split the benefit, with one doing half-time teaching for one semester and the other teaching half time for the second semester. The faculty member's college pays a portion of the related costs; the provost underwrites a small portion of the financial burden; and the faculty member is paid 90% of their usual salary.

The University of Montana's (Cohort 2) modified duties policy enables any faculty member in a tenure-stream position who has caregiver responsibilities due to birth, adoption, or care for a primary family member to be released from teaching, research, and service for one semester, with the provost's office funding the teaching replacement costs. The policy also provides a one-year tenure-clock extension and delays the faculty member's annual evaluation by one year. The University of Montana also drafted policies to address part-time tenure-track options.

Montana State's (Cohort 6) ADVANCE project, known as TRACS (An Empirical Investigation of Transformation through Relatedness, Autonomy, and Competence Support), appointed family advocates who could help people learn about and navigate the university's policies and programs for flexible work and other family needs (see also Strategy 9). They served as a first stop to steer faculty, staff, and students to appropriate resources for their own situations. Faculty who held this role also provided information on family and dual-career resources to job candidates (see Strategy 7). The family advocate roles were institutionalized within the provost's office when ADVANCE funding ended.

In developing flexible work/life policies and practices, institutions have tended to work on several issues:

- Processes and deliberations to create policies usually involve senior-level administrators, faculty committees, and institutional governing boards. Institutional leaders reported that policies were more likely to be politically acceptable as they moved through institutional governance structures if they addressed the interests and needs of all genders and family situations.
- Creating policies is not sufficient. A communication and training plan should address deans and department chairs, human resources staff, and faculty members themselves, both as potential policy users and as colleagues of those who do. Deans and department chairs must be aware of and knowledgeable about the policies and often need support in making faculty aware of their options. Professionals in human resources and business units also must be well aware of all policy options and prepared to help individual faculty members assess their own situation and make appropriate decisions. They need to understand faculty workloads and how the policy can be implemented to meet varied

situations (see Schimpf et al., 2013; Schimpf, Santiago, & Pawley, 2012). Some institutions have developed special brochures or websites to spread the word about the policies that support flexible work arrangements.

- Just knowing about policies also is not enough. Faculty members must feel that it is risk-free to use such policies and that they are encouraged to do so. Thus, some institutions widely advertise their policies about flexible work arrangements and strive to normalize their use.

Evaluation

We know of no specific evaluation studies conducted by ADVANCE awardees on the impact of flexible work policies, but our interviews with institutional leaders, ADVANCE IT project leaders, and faculty members indicate that such policies are important signals of institutional commitment to the success of a diverse faculty. Faculty use of these policies can be tracked to document their popularity and costs and to look for any indicators that stigma or other factors are inhibiting use of the policy. Human resources officers may already undertake some institution-level documentation of usage and costs. However, in any evaluation design that uses information about people who access the policy, great care must be taken to preserve the confidentiality of individuals' private medical and family information.

Affordances and Limitations

Institutional leaders and faculty members have cited a number of benefits that emerge when institutions develop and implement policies that support flexibility in work arrangements. These affordances include:

- *Support for individual faculty members.* Institutional support in the form of policies for flexible work arrangements can enhance morale, institutional commitment, and energy for creativity and productivity (Gappa, Austin, & Trice, 2007). Such policies also may help individual faculty members choose to have the families they want (Mason & Goulden, 2002, 2004).
- *A more supportive campus.* Policies that support flexibility in work arrangements help to change the culture of an institution. One institutional leader explained that these policy changes are "more friendly and more reflective of what the needs of our female faculty are, and what the needs of our faculty are who are going through certain transitions" regardless of gender.
- *More attention to diversity and inclusion.* The process of developing and spreading the word about policies opens conversations that help to make

members of the campus community more aware of the diversity of circumstances of their colleagues. This can enhance understanding and recognition of ways to include everyone in the institutional culture.

- *Symbolic value outside the institution.* When an institution has specific policies in place that support the diverse professional and personal lives of the faculty, it sends a message about its values and culture. Such symbolic messages may enhance its attractiveness to prospective faculty members.

Limitations related to policies that support flexible work arrangements include the following:

- *Lack of use.* Policies may not be widely used if faculty members fear that using them carries the risk of appearing less than fully committed to their work responsibilities and careers. Explicit, widespread, and consistent messages about the policies and institutional support for their use are important steps to ensure that flexible work policies become normalized aspects of academic employment.
- *Concerns about overuse.* Worries about the abuse of flexible work policies are common, but institutional leaders reported that initial concerns that the presence of such policies would encourage inappropriate use have been unfounded.
- *External perceptions.* Outside reviewers of tenure and promotion dossiers sometimes are unfamiliar with how to evaluate the materials of faculty members who have extended their tenure clocks, arranged modified duties, or held part-time tenure-track positions. Institutions need to provide explicit information and instructions about how evaluators should understand such policies (see Kramer, n.d., for sample language).

Summary

Programs to enable flexible work arrangements acknowledge that family life is demanding for all caregivers, and they also accommodate life transitions that may interfere with career progress, especially as faculty members are approaching tenure or other milestones. Because they address the needs of a wide range of faculty members and across the life span, they contribute generally to faculty retention and success and, in specific cases, can reduce some practical work/life barriers for women. However, for tenure-clock extensions in particular, research suggests that these policies are not gender-neutral. While there are good reasons to have these policies in place, closing gender gaps may not be one of them.

FURTHER READING

American Council on Education. (2005). *An agenda for excellence: Creating flexibility in tenure-track faculty careers.* Washington, DC: American Council on Education.

Curtis, J. W. (Ed.). (2005). *The challenge of balancing faculty careers and family work.* San Francisco, CA: Jossey-Bass.

Pribbenow, C. M., et al. (2010). The tenure process and extending the tenure clock: The experience of faculty at one university. *Higher Education Policy, 23*(1), 17–38.

Strategy 9. Practical, Family-Friendly Accommodations

A majority of ADVANCE IT institutions included practical, family-friendly accommodations in their portfolio of interventions to support the recruitment and success of STEM women faculty. In this strategy we highlight and describe these accommodations, which address the daily lives and challenges facing many faculty women. Strategy 8 covers a set of related interventions that enable flexible work arrangements, including changes to appointments or to the tenure clock, while Strategy 11 includes grants that support faculty recovering from challenging personal circumstances. Together, these approaches provide an array of policy and programmatic initiatives to support faculty who are handling personal as well as professional responsibilities, showing how interventions to support individual circumstances can be implemented in diverse ways consistent with an institution's context, history, and goals.

Rationale

In US society, women often invest more time and have disproportionate responsibility for family matters than do men, even as many men take on more duties in households. Furthermore, research shows other ways in which the relationship between personal and professional responsibilities differs for academic women and men: compared to men, women report more spillover of family responsibilities into their work lives, and they are more likely than men to choose not to have children due to professional demands. When they do have children, the presence of babies in the household has more impact on their careers than it does for their male counterparts (Archie, Kogan, & Laursen, 2015; Bracken, Allen, & Dean, 2006; Gappa, Austin, & Trice, 2007; Mason & Goulden, 2002, 2004; Ward & Wolf-Wendel, 2004, 2012). For many ADVANCE institutions, these trends signal the importance of interventions that recognize the complex, multifaceted lives of faculty of all genders, as well as the particular pressures that often fall more heavily on women.

ADVANCE institutional leaders reasoned that a faculty member is a critically important institutional asset. The process of recruiting, hiring, and setting up a new faculty member, especially in STEM fields where start-up costs are often substantial, means that a university has invested much in a new faculty member and faces a major loss in terms of human and financial resources if the scholar leaves for any reason. By supporting faculty in managing aspects of their personal responsibilities, especially in circumstances where personal issues come up against their professional opportunities, institutions of higher education can help women scholars to thrive. Ensuring her success in research contributes to the likelihood that a woman scholar can achieve a positive tenure or promotion decision. Furthermore, interventions that support women faculty in managing their multiple responsibilities can help them see the feasibility of creating meaningful lives that include both personal and professional commitments, without a need to sacrifice one for the other. As some ADVANCE institutional leaders pointed out, a family-friendly environment gives a university a better chance to recruit and retain excellent faculty.

Offering and highlighting practical, family-friendly accommodations also has symbolic value that results in institutional benefits. The presence of such practices sends a powerful signal that an institution is attentive to both the personal and professional needs and interests of faculty, a message that attracts talented potential faculty colleagues. Indeed, ensuring that faculty women have support to handle both personal and professional responsibilities may even help to strengthen the flow of younger women into STEM careers. Women faculty who have varied and meaningful personal and professional lives are important role models for women students trying to envision a life as a STEM scholar (De Welde & Laursen, 2011). Some institutions also recognize that all students stand to lose when their teachers face difficult personal situations that divert their attention from teaching; thus, practical interventions to help faculty through such challenges also redound to students' benefit. One ADVANCE leader explained how offering family-friendly accommodations relates to institutional excellence: "We are showing that we want people to be at their best. . . . If that means being able to breastfeed your child, that is important."

Purpose

The purpose of family-friendly accommodations is to offer practical support for the range of life situations and challenges that confront many faculty members at some point in their careers. In ADVANCE institutions, family-friendly accommodations have included childcare resources, support and facilities for nursing parents, opportunities for family-related leave, and grants to help faculty members continue their scholarly and creative work during periods of major life transition. These are separate from the flexibility of work arrangements described in Strategy 8.

Audience

Institutions vary in whom they primarily intend to support with their family-friendly accommodations. An important consideration is whether and how to make accommodations available to all genders. For lactation rooms, the target audience is clearly lactating people, typically including staff and students as well as faculty. For family leave, institutions with explicit leave practices tend to offer this opportunity to faculty members who are doing the bulk of caregiving or managing a specific family need. Resources on childcare within or external to the institution address the needs of parents of any gender, although women especially may benefit if they handle more of the responsibility for childcare. In most cases, individual grants for people facing life transitions have been made officially available to faculty of any gender, although in practice a greater share of individual grants at ADVANCE institutions has gone to women.

Practices at Columbia and the University of Wisconsin illustrate two different rationales about eligibility. The Columbia University (Cohort 2) ADVANCE IT team chose to direct its Transition Support awards to women faculty, explaining that while many of its activities were open to men and women, some life events have a disproportionate impact on women. In contrast, at the University of Wisconsin–Madison (Cohort 1), the Vilas Life Cycle Professorship Program is open to all genders, with the rationale that success in advancing women cannot happen without everyone's support, and therefore such a program should be open to all.

Institutions also have varied in what career stage their programs target. Some institutions have organized their life transition grants to be available to all faculty; a few target their grants to early-career faculty with the goal to help pre-tenure faculty to achieve tenure success.

Models and Examples

Family-friendly accommodations took several forms in ADVANCE institutions, each targeting different aspects of personal life or offering different ways to accommodate faculty in times of heavy personal demands.

INDIVIDUAL FACULTY GRANTS IN SUPPORT OF LIFE TRANSITIONS

These grants were designed to help faculty members continue their scholarly work during periods of major life transformation (e.g., childbirth or adoption, illness or death of a family member; see also Strategy 11). Typically, faculty members could use these grants in the ways most useful for their own scholarly progress. Examples included taking a leave of absence; buying out a portion of teaching responsibilities; hiring a student assistant to help with research; supporting a technician to keep a lab operating while the faculty member is away; providing for childcare while the faculty member is doing fieldwork or attending a professional meeting; or hiring someone to assist with data analysis.

Grants varied in size across institutions, from a few hundred dollars to more than $50,000, but most programs offered $5,000 or less. At some institutions, the application process was formal, with a set award limit, application deadlines, formal requirements, review criteria, designated review committees, and a specified number of awardees per cycle. Such formal guidelines fit well in the academic culture where faculty members are often engaged in grant writing. Other institutions preferred less formal processes: applications could be submitted on a rolling basis, and details of an award were based on the specifics of the case.

For example, Case Western Reserve University (Cohort 2) offered ADVANCE opportunity grants to help women maximize their success at the institution. The grants were typically small (but ranged from a few hundred dollars to $25,000) to supplement other available support or to assist when funding was hard to get from other sources. Grants supported seed funding for research training or unusual research opportunities, travel to attend meetings on a new technology or research methods, time to write a book, or childcare while the scholar attended a professional meeting or conducted research. While these grants originally were offered to departments working directly with the ADVANCE program, they were later made available to faculty in all departments across the university.

The University of Michigan (Cohort 1) offered the Transitional Support Program for faculty facing major life changes. The purpose of the awards, which averaged $18,000, was to assuage problematic impacts of such transitions on academic careers. Grants provided special laboratory equipment, graduate student or postdoc support, conference or travel support, and release time.

The University of Wisconsin–Madison (Cohort 1) offers the Vilas Life Cycle Professorship Program, which was originally designated for women but is now open to people of any gender from any academic affiliation and any rank. This grant program supports faculty needs at critical junctures in their professional careers: childbirth or adoption, a family death, or a hiatus in grant funding. Recipients reported many positive effects on their personal and professional lives as a result of these grants.

The individual growth grants at the University of Colorado Boulder (Cohort 1) were aimed at tenured faculty members making career transitions, embarking on new scholarly or creative directions, or restarting scholarly work after a significant period of university service. While not limited to women in STEM, the majority of awards have gone to women whose careers had been affected by family and/or institutional service responsibilities. The results have been significant, with 90% of the recipients reporting that grant proposals, manuscripts, or artistic performances were under way or completed with the support of the grant. Awardee reports also noted the positive emotional impact of feeling supported and valued by the university. The program has continued under the Office of Faculty Affairs.

FAMILY LEAVE OPPORTUNITIES

A few ADVANCE institutions explored ways to offer a period of leave when significant family-related issues arose, even if formal policies were not available (see Strategy 8). The cost of formal family leave was mentioned as a barrier by several institutional leaders. In response, some departments made informal, internal departmental arrangements to relieve a faculty member of some or all teaching responsibilities for a term, with the course covered by colleagues. The arrangement was then reciprocated in a subsequent term, so that the needs of other faculty could be covered. In tight budget times, such informal arrangements help institutions move forward in supporting family needs, even when creating a formal policy seems politically insensitive or unwise—but they do not provide a long-term solution.

For example, at Kansas State University (Cohort 2), resources could not be allocated to family leave. However, recognizing the importance of such leave at specific times, department leaders arranged individually developed swaps, in which faculty members covered the teaching of a colleague after she gave birth, knowing that similar flexibility could be extended to them should the need arise. ADVANCE leaders made a point to share and highlight how these informal arrangements were handled.

At Utah State University (Cohort 2), the ADVANCE leaders worked with human resources officials to arrange faculty leave upon request. Each was treated on a case-by-case basis in consultation with the relevant chair and dean. Recognizing that in this institution's context, formal family leave after a birth would be difficult to provide in an official way, the university has an unofficial but widely known tradition of providing a term of reduced teaching responsibilities for women with new babies.

SUPPORT FOR PREGNANT OR NURSING PEOPLE

These measures recognized the physical demands on pregnant and nursing people. A number of institutions established lactation rooms for breastfeeding, which were accessible to faculty members or to all faculty, staff, and students of the institution. A few institutions publicized their commitment to comply with state laws addressing the needs of nursing parents and their infants. One institution provided parking permits to faculty in their third trimester of pregnancy. Several others established creative ways to publicize information about lactation spaces and support for nursing parents, for example, by appointing a breastfeeding advocate to meet with and support new mothers. And still others provided informational workshops or established websites or offices to share information about lactation support and other family-friendly practices. Providing lactation rooms was innovative at the time of early ADVANCE grants, but since 2010, US workplaces have been required to ensure that employees have a private space for breastfeeding. Initiatives to address these issues may find ready allies among facilities managers and administrators who oversee legal compliance.

For example, the University of Rhode Island (Cohort 2) made public its commitment to comply with Rhode Island law addressing the needs of nursing parents and their infants, including the right to breastfeed and bottle-feed in any place open to the public.

The University of Montana (Cohort 2) established a permanent university breastfeeding advocate to work with new mothers. Services included helping mothers find facilities for pumping, arranging the no-cost loan of refrigerators for storing expressed milk, and talking with parents to help solve their breastfeeding needs.

Georgia Tech (Cohort 1) held sessions to provide information about lactation facilities for faculty, staff, and students.

CHILDCARE RESOURCES

The availability of high-quality, easily accessed childcare is an important issue for many early-career faculty members, and this issue was tackled by a number of ADVANCE projects. Institutions typically addressed the need for childcare in one or more of the following ways: creating or expanding childcare facilities on campus; developing childcare spaces in the broader community; publicizing information about local childcare; and establishing a campus resource person or center tasked with compiling information and meeting with prospective and current faculty about childcare needs. Efforts to expand childcare options often were intended to benefit staff and students as well as faculty.

For example, Utah State (Cohort 2) took a comprehensive approach to childcare support. Institutional leaders invested much time in creating a new childcare facility on campus. Additionally, the institution developed the Aggie Care program, which identifies and offers referrals to childcare providers in the community. The program provides training and certification to providers, makes home visits as part of the certification process, and offers books and games for providers to borrow. The university also offers a monthly Family in Focus luncheon for those interested in discussing childcare.

At Virginia Tech (Cohort 2), childcare options were increased when each college dean and senior university administrators pledged five years of annual support from discretionary funds for a contract with a local daycare provider. The provider was able to expand the number of places available for children and guarantees 60% of the new slots to Virginia Tech families.

GENERAL PRACTICES FOR OFFERING FAMILY-FRIENDLY ACCOMMODATIONS

The availability of family-friendly accommodations does not guarantee their positive effect on the advancement, success, and retention of STEM women faculty. Potential users must know about available resources, programs, and policies, and they must feel that these options are acceptable and safe. Policies must then be equally available to different-sex and same-sex couples. Several strategies have emerged from ADVANCE institutions to ensure wide knowledge and to encourage acceptance of these policies, resources, and practices. These approaches include:

- creating, maintaining, and publicizing institutional websites dedicated to making full resource information available in one location
- identifying a person or an office with the responsibility to maintain information about all relevant policies, programs, and resources, and making this person known to all faculty
- training search committees so they are knowledgeable about resources and can provide relevant information, and designating a contact person who can respond confidentially to queries from all candidates for faculty positions

- including information about family-friendly accommodations in professional development for department chairs
- encouraging institutional leaders (including provosts, deans, and chairs) to emphasize frequently that the available resources, policies, and practices are intended for use

Montana State's (Cohort 6) ADVANCE project worked on many of these aspects of work/life for faculty and other campus community members and organized them succinctly for easy reference (see ADVANCE Project TRACS, 2017).

Evaluation

Assessment of the impact of these programs and accommodations generally is done through informal feedback, testimonies, and case examples of individuals whose lives and work have been affected in positive ways. For example, faculty members who used lactation facilities informally expressed appreciation for the support. A faculty member at one university with a grant program said the support "saved [her] life" during a difficult period, enabling her to continue being productive while coping with family problems. In some cases, the use of particular facilities or programs can be tracked, although great care must be taken to preserve individuals' privacy.

Institutions with grant programs often collected statements from recipients about the outcomes and benefits of the support. In some cases, evaluators interviewed faculty about family-friendly accommodations, and institutional climate surveys were used to monitor faculty perceptions of the need and the support that was available. Formal evaluation through self-reports by recipients of grants at the University of Colorado Boulder (Cohort 1) indicated specific scholarly products resulting from the individual growth grants.

The consensus among ADVANCE leaders is that informal evidence speaks to the important role of family-friendly accommodations in enabling faculty to manage personal and professional roles, which is a conclusion consistent with scholarly literature.

Affordances and Limitations

Institutional leaders and faculty members cited a number of benefits when institutions developed and implemented family-friendly practices. These affordances include the following:

- *Support for individual faculty members to manage multiple demands.* Family-friendly policies help faculty members handle their professional responsibilities, even when challenges arise in their personal lives. The result of such support is enhanced motivation, commitment to the institution, greater productivity, and a greater likelihood that the faculty member will remain at the institution (Gappa, Austin, & Trice, 2007). Furthermore, family-friendly practices and resources contribute to creating an academic environment in which all faculty can work productively while also creating the kinds of personal lives that they value (Mason & Goulden, 2002, 2004). Family-friendly resources make academic careers more attractive and feasible to today's young faculty, many of whom worry whether it is a life they can sustain (Rice, Sorcinelli, & Austin, 2000).
- *A more supportive and attractive campus.* Family-friendly resources and practices, along with flexible work/life policies, support and facilitate the flexibility that faculty need. They signal institutional cultures in which holistic and balanced lives are valued and in which faculty members are supported in creating such lives. In the words of one senior ADVANCE leader, such practices and resources "make an environment permissible so that people can enhance both [personal and professional roles] and keep them in balance."
- *Symbolic value inside and outside the institution.* An institution conveys its values when it ensures that practices and resources are in place to support the diverse professional and personal lives of its faculty. Such symbolic messages help enhance the institution's attractiveness to prospective faculty members.

Limitations of policies to support family-friendly accommodations include the following:

- *Concern about using such accommodations.* As with flexible work policies, faculty members may be reluctant to use some family-friendly accommodations if they fear that others will interpret their use as an indication of diminished ability or commitment to professional responsibilities (Drago et al., 2005, 2006). For example, grants to support life transitions should not suggest to others that a faculty member is not thriving. Thus, explicit support from senior leaders, wide advertising of opportunities for accommodations, and normalizing the use of family-friendly accommodations help signal that their use is routine and expected.

- *Unequal access to informal policies.* Informal policies were offered by institutions where it was seen as difficult to implement a formal policy or as a stopgap while a policy was under development. A risk of informal approaches is that not everyone who is eligible is aware of the policy, and informal approaches may be applied inequitably as different people interpret norms differently. Training and communication with key leaders, particularly department chairs or heads, are essential in these settings, and formal policies offer more equitable solutions in the long term.

Summary

In addition to flexibility in work responsibilities, a variety of practical accommodations can ease work/life conflicts and thereby help faculty members manage professional and personal commitments. Because not everyone needs these accommodations, and most need them only temporarily, they are not in general costly for institutions to provide, but they can offer high symbolic value. Mechanisms should be carefully examined to be sure they accommodate people with different job classifications, cis and trans people, same-sex couples and single parents as well as different-sex couples, and so on.

FURTHER READING

Anderson, E. K., & Solomon, C. R. (2015). *Family-friendly policies and practices in academe.* Lanham, MD: Lexington.

Bracken, S. J., Allen, J. K., & Dean, D. R. (Eds.). (2006). *The balancing act: Gendered perspectives in faculty roles and work lives.* Sterling, VA: Stylus.

Ward, K., & Wolf-Wendel, L. (2012). *Academic motherhood: How faculty manage work and family.* New Brunswick, NJ: Rutgers University Press.

Williams, J. (2000). *Unbending gender: Why family and work conflict and what to do about it.* New York: Oxford University Press.

Chapter Six

Foster Individual Success

Systemic change is slow and irregular. Since some parts of the academy change more slowly than others, it's crucial to continue to support individual women as they make their way through the system.

WOMEN WHO BECOME faculty members in STEM fields are very accomplished and have already faced and resolved many challenges, yet they still may not achieve the highest levels of success in the academy (Fox, 2008). As Fox and others have emphasized, the status of women in STEM fields is a function not only of the ability, background, and attitudes of individual women, but also of the nature of the work environment, including variations due to the availability of resources and the patterns of exclusion (Fox, 1991, 2001, 2008; Fox & Mohapatra, 2007; Sturm, 2006).

It is important to directly challenge these institutionalized patterns of exclusion by targeting institutional systems, using structural and cultural approaches such as those we discuss in chapters 3–5: recognize and counter bias in evaluation in hiring, rewarding, and promoting faculty; build more supportive workplace climates; and recognize and accommodate faculty members as whole people with needs and challenges outside work that evolve throughout the life course. However, these bigger cultural and structural changes are not quick to take hold. Indeed, studies from the University of Michigan ADVANCE team documented that change of this type is slow: it took 12 years before measures of institutional climate shifted notably and positively at Michigan, despite strong and persistent efforts based on work done under an ADVANCE Institutional Transformation project and then formalized with institutional funding to apply across the entire university

(UM ADVANCE, 2013). Similarly, significant changes in the proportion of women faculty in STEM departments required more than a decade to take hold, even in departments that embraced their responsibility and took proactive steps toward more inclusive hiring (Stewart, Malley, & Herzog, 2016). Moreover, there is no singular and universal change; change occurs unevenly across different departments, schools, or sectors of the institution (Morimoto et al., 2013).

Change that occurs unevenly and on a decadal time scale is not compatible with the needs of faculty whose career ladders include an up-or-out tenure decision just 6–7 years after hiring. Thus, efforts to support individual women are also important and appropriate as part of a change portfolio. Such efforts recognize the immediate needs and support the success of women working in the system now, at the same time as significant but slower efforts to change systems and structures are under way. Supporting individual women now is essential to ensure that women are well represented and visible in the institution. When they are enabled to acquire the credentials and readiness necessary for leadership, they can in turn assist in securing the longer-term changes needed to more completely achieve gender equity on STEM faculties.

It is important that these individual success programs are not the only change strategy deployed. Merely increasing the numbers of women in the institution is insufficient to change the forces that have led to women's low numbers and marginalization in the first place. Efforts to support the success of women in place must be coupled with broader structural and cultural change efforts that work on multiple fronts using multiple methods, with a proactive awareness of challenges that may arise along any path. As De Welde reminded us, "'Moving the needle' on equity and inclusion is not the work of any one office or committee" (2017, p. 206).

In this chapter, we discuss programs developed by ADVANCE IT institutions to foster the success of individual women scholars:

- faculty development to strengthen the skills and sense of agency needed to succeed in academic STEM careers (Strategy 10)
- grants to support scholarship or teaching innovation, or to mitigate life events and support work/life integration (Strategy 11)
- networking and mentoring activities that provide advice and foster connections that offer strategic, professional, and emotional support (Strategy 12)

Strategy 10. Faculty Professional Development Programs

Many ADVANCE IT projects in Cohorts 1 and 2 offered professional development in the form of workshops or trainings to improve faculty members' ability to effectively and efficiently perform their jobs and to manage the multiple demands on them. In this strategy, we distinguish performance-focused offerings from other interventions that may also share the goal of supporting faculty learning and professional growth: coaching and mentoring programs that offer individualized guidance or advice; networking events, lectures, and presentations; and individualized funding to faculty members to support their scholarly and creative work (see Strategies 11 and 12).

Rationale

Professional development activities addressed specific aspects of faculty members' research, teaching, and service duties, or offered general skills that are helpful in conducting these activities. While the need for these skills and capacities is not specific to women nor to STEM disciplines, effectiveness in multiple domains of faculty work is a prerequisite for advancement in the academy. Faculty development also helps the institution by building an effective faculty and developing future leaders. Some projects targeted STEM and non-STEM faculty of all genders, with the rationale that a rising tide raises all ships. These projects assumed that addressing the skills and attitudes of all colleagues can promote a better workplace climate and establish an atmosphere of support in which all can succeed, without singling women out as if they need remediation.

Other projects took the perspective that STEM women will benefit particularly from developing skills that are often absent from formal preparation for faculty careers and instead are commonly gained through informal socialization in networks from which women are more likely to be excluded. Bringing women together for faculty development can be a way to foster those supportive networks and to recognize that faculty development needs are gendered because of the multiple responsibilities that women may hold as professionals and caregivers (Laursen & Rocque, 2009).

Purpose

To identify needs that could be addressed through faculty development, ADVANCE projects often conducted a needs assessment using focus groups or campus-wide surveys. An extensive literature addresses the needs of new faculty

(Austin, 1992, 2003, 2010a, 2010b, 2011; Austin & Rice, 1998; Austin, Sorcinelli, & McDaniels, 2007; Beach et al., 2016; Boice, 1992; Sorcinelli & Austin, 1992; Sorcinelli et al., 2006), while knowledge about the needs of mid-career and senior faculty is less well developed (Baker et al., 2018; Baldwin et al., 2008; Laursen & Rocque, 2009).

Workshop topics in response to identified needs included the following:

- meeting tenure and promotion expectations
- balancing research, teaching, and service
- writing and public speaking (e.g., grant proposals, papers and books, responding to reviews, technical and public talks)
- managing time and stress (e.g., prioritizing writing, saying no, time management tactics)
- managing people (e.g., supervising students, managing a research group, dealing with conflict)
- gender, incivility, and bias
- managing money (e.g., budgeting a grant proposal, managing an award, university processes for spending and tracking funds, hiring research personnel)
- communicating effectively (e.g., negotiating, dealing with conflict, difficult conversations, personality differences that affect mentoring preferences, running effective meetings)
- promoting and presenting yourself (e.g., crafting a CV, preparing a tenure or promotion packet, promoting your work to colleagues)
- career planning (e.g., long-term strategic planning, strategies for work/life balance, using the summer wisely, developing a research agenda)

Teaching is an element of faculty work in which professional development may also be needed, but teaching skills were not generally a topic of ADVANCE-sponsored workshops, perhaps because other units already offered teaching support at many campuses or because most of the institutions in our sample are not teaching-focused. However, aspects of teaching were incorporated in many of the topics above, for example, public speaking, problem-solving about gender and incivility, career planning, and time management.

Audience

Many workshops targeted early-career faculty whose job skills were developing. Others addressed the needs of mid-career or senior faculty to hone new skills to advance professionally. Workshops were framed to appeal to different audiences, for example:

- a new faculty orientation
- a research life workshop for tenure-stream and research faculty who manage labs
- a writing retreat for mixed or disciplinary groups
- a grant-writing assistance program that included training, release time to write a grant proposal, and the expectation to submit a proposal
- a workshop series on planning for promotion to full professor

Models

In-depth programs included intensive, multiday offerings in a short course or retreat format, and extended offerings with multiple sessions spaced over a term, a year, or even longer. These formats typically enrolled a cohort of participants who continued together for the entire program.

Shorter, one-time offerings were often part of a series. Each session typically lasted one hour to half a day, with open enrollment or voluntary participation. Some individuals participated in several of these over a year, but they did not regularly meet with a continuing cohort.

Both models were common at ADVANCE campuses, and a few campuses provided offerings in both forms.

Across projects, planners emphasized the importance of engaging faculty in active learning with methods such as role playing, analysis of problem-based scenarios, panel discussions, small-group tasks, breakout sessions, and whole-group discussions. Offering food and beverages helped to attract participants and foster informal conversation. Other design considerations revealed in our examination of faculty development offerings in ADVANCE programs included the following:

- time and timing (summer or academic year, intensive or extended, one time or with follow-up, stand-alone or series)
- audience (general or targeted to a specific career stage, for women or open to all, targeted to a specific discipline or college or to all units)
- building an audience (the philosophical message or framing, practical incentives such as food or a monetary stipend)
- facilitation (internal or external facilitators, use of existing skills and knowledge on campus, building a menu of workshops that could easily be repeated)

- complementary programs (whether and what faculty development programs were available on campus already, how new programs would address unmet faculty needs)

Choices made in these areas not only influence how a workshop accomplishes its professional development objectives, but also shape its social or collegial side effects. For example, secondary objectives may be to build a collegial support group for individuals, to connect faculty across stages or disciplines, or to network faculty broadly across campus. Laursen and Austin (2018) described a variety of faculty development models for mid-career STEM women that emerged from ADVANCE IT projects.

Examples

Institutions created a variety of professional development offerings that addressed these issues in different combinations.

At the University of Colorado Boulder (Cohort 1), faculty professional development was a central and sustained activity for the ADVANCE project, which was known as LEAP (Leadership Education for Advancement and Promotion). Three-day introductory leadership workshops offered twice a year, during winter and summer breaks, drew groups of 12–15 assistant professors to learn about topics such as managing time and stress, working with research and thesis students, applying strategies to prioritize writing, and balancing research, teaching, and service.

Evidence from focus groups, immediate post-surveys, and follow-up interviews (Laursen, 2009, and reports cited therein) showed substantial benefits to early-career faculty—not only the targeted skills and knowledge but new professional and personal connections that proved to be supportive over the longer term. At the end of the project, the LEAP workshops were institutionalized in the faculty affairs office, and new faculty hires were given the opportunity to attend this workshop as part of their job offers.

At the University of Texas at El Paso (Cohort 2), IMPACT was a cohort-based program in which faculty worked together over the course of a year to construct an integrated plan for their own career success. Cohorts of about a dozen faculty—half early-career, half senior—met for a week in the first summer, monthly during the following academic year, and again for a final summer meeting. The goals were to build community; identify creative ways to integrate research, teaching, and service; develop leadership skills; and develop a habit of reflection.

Evaluation data gathered from participants' annual reports indicated that participants developed practical skills, such as managing their workload, and they reported strong affective outcomes that supported their work as faculty members, including greater self-awareness, positive attitude, and empowerment. The institution was perceived to benefit through development of future leaders, growth of collaboration and collegiality, and improved integration of new faculty as whole individuals into the fabric of the institution. The program was not sustained in the same form after the end of the ADVANCE grant, but elements were incorporated into leadership training for new chairs and into the mentoring program offered by the campus teaching and learning center.

The University of Rhode Island (Cohort 2) offered a year-long series of four or five career workshops targeting early-career faculty. Faculty were encouraged to attend the whole series but could sign up for single workshops. Topics were those relevant to building successful careers, such as teaching, grant writing, lab and project management, negotiation, and communication skills.

The University of Washington (Cohort 1) offered quarterly half-day workshops to department chairs and deans. Chairs were invited to bring a faculty member with emerging potential for leadership. These workshops have been sustained through the university's ADVANCE center. Typical topics include running effective faculty retreats, recruiting and hiring for inclusive excellence, navigating generational differences, and models for faculty workload and merit reviews (see http://advance.washington.edu/camps/leadershipworkshops.html for topics and sample agendas). UW's ADVANCE Resource Library contains an extensive set of materials used in these workshops (search for "leadership development" at http://advance.washington.edu/apps/resources).

Jackson State University (Cohort 5) developed a cohort-based summer writing retreat to bolster the publishing and grant-writing productivity of women STEM and SBS (social and behavioral sciences) faculty, especially those at the associate professor rank, where women were concentrated. Recognizing that mentoring, writing, and collegial connections were central to the success of Jackson State's male full professors, ADVANCE leaders sought to foster the same skills and relationships for women, thereby helping them advance to full professorship while also strategically supporting Jackson State's evolution into a research-intensive institution. By bringing women together off campus for a week of focused writing, the program elevated writing as an important faculty activity, increased grant activity at the institution, and generated supportive collegial networks and peer-to-peer accountability. Jackson State received additional grant support to expand this model to a network of other historically Black and Hispanic-serving institutions, thus further enhancing scholarly productivity and professional connections among STEM and SBS women of color (see Laursen & Austin, 2014e, 2018; Moore et al., 2016).

Evaluation

Approaches to evaluating professional development may include short pre- and post-surveys, post-only surveys, or focus groups to assess participants' satisfaction with the workshop, solicit advice for improving it, and document their immediate, self-reported gains. These data are most useful as formative feedback to improve and monitor the workshop and to determine whether participants' responses are aligned with the workshop's intended objectives. For one-off events, an "exit ticket"—a short reflection on a sticky note or index card—can record one idea that the participant is taking away. For longer-term events, follow-up surveys, written reports, or interviews can be used to probe whether and how participants used the workshop material and what challenges they faced in applying it (Guskey, 2000). Summative evaluation data may be used in making arguments to sustain or expand the program.

Evaluation of faculty development programming at the University of Colorado Boulder by Laursen and colleagues (2005) showed a combination of these approaches. The findings provided evidence that was used to make decisions to alter some programs and institutionalize others.

Affordances and Limitations

We observed both affordances and limitations in the context of ADVANCE IT projects in our sample. For more general issues, an extensive literature offers advice in designing, implementing, and evaluating faculty development activities, and most campuses have faculty and administrators with expertise in this area.

In the context of ADVANCE projects, cohort-based, in-depth models have some affordances, including:

- They build a supportive network for faculty alongside professional skills or knowledge.
- They mix participants from across departments and schools, which can address isolation and provide safe outlets for faculty to share concerns. This may be particularly helpful to women and other "solo status" faculty (Roberson et al., 2003).

These models also have some limitations:

- They reach a limited set of faculty, and thus have less net impact on large campuses.
- They may fail to engage the faculty who most need such support, who may be reluctant to make what appears to be a significant time commitment.

Advantages of one-off workshops include the following:

- They are relatively easy to get started. Most campuses have people who already have expertise on many topics useful for faculty career development.
- They can draw new participants into the ADVANCE community, thus raising the project's visibility on campus.
- They support faculty directly and thus build political capital for ADVANCE on campus. For this reason, it may be useful to inform department leaders and deans about how the project is supporting specific faculty in their units.

Limitations of the one-off workshop model include the following:

- It is often difficult to detect whether they are effective. While faculty development can be argued to build the effectiveness of the faculty over the long haul, it is harder to measure the outcomes of long-term investment when the intervention is delivered in small doses.
- Faculty development models have been critiqued as not directly addressing the systemic and structural issues that constrain women's advancement (Morimoto et al., 2013).

Using outside facilitators can be a good way to start a faculty development program, but this is likely to become expensive in the long run. Professional development models become most sustainable when expertise on certain topics is developed in-house and shared among multiple facilitators. Projects have been successful in sustaining faculty development activities through train-the-trainer approaches, such as inviting past participants to become leaders, involving faculty with relevant scholarly expertise, and building a portfolio of workshop activities and materials that can be used by various facilitators. After their ADVANCE awards ended, some projects housed these activities in the faculty affairs office or faculty development center.

Summary

When they are responsive to identified faculty needs, faculty development approaches can be supportive to individuals from underrepresented groups and to departments' goals for advancing and retaining diverse faculty. In offering opportunities for collaboration, conversation, reflection, and networking as well as useful knowledge and resources, they tend to be popular with participants. ADVANCE institutions have found faculty-led programs relatively easy to start and sustain, although this is not automatic: programs do need a permanent home and someone who is responsible for coordination and logistics. Importantly, these programs do not substitute for efforts to generate deeper, system-based change. Rather, they may support individuals to develop skills, capacities, and fruitful relationships while slower processes of systemic change get under way and begin to take root.

FURTHER READING

Baker, V. L., et al. (Eds.). (2018). *Success after tenure: Supporting mid-career faculty.* Sterling, VA: Stylus.

Beach, A. L., et al. (2016). *Faculty development in the age of evidence: Current practices, future imperatives.* Sterling, VA: Stylus.

Gappa, J. M., Austin, A. E., & Trice, A. G. (2007). *Rethinking faculty work: Higher education's strategic imperative.* San Francisco, CA: Jossey-Bass.

Gillespie, K. H., Robertson D. L., & Associates. (2010). *A guide to faculty development* (2nd ed.). San Francisco, CA: Jossey-Bass.

Professional and Organizational Development [POD] Network in Higher Education. (n.d.). http://podnetwork.org.

Strategy 11. Grants to Individual Faculty

A majority of ADVANCE IT projects in Cohorts 1 and 2 distributed resources to individual faculty members to catalyze their scholarly and creative work, support career development, or enhance work/life balance. Other types of faculty development, such as workshops and mentoring, and other uses of grants, such as departmental grants targeting climate, are analyzed separately in this book (see Strategies 5, 10, and 12). While individual grants to ameliorate work/life conflicts are discussed here, other types of work/life interventions are addressed in Strategies 8 and 9.

Rationale

Commonly, the rationale behind grants to individuals is to directly support STEM women's professional advancement with resources to enhance their scholarly work and career growth. If women then achieve tenure and thrive at the institution, they may increase the critical mass of women faculty and step into future leadership roles. Grants may redress inequities in access to research resources, for example, if women are less aware of resources due to exclusion from networks and lack of mentoring, less likely to press for them due to gendered differences in confidence and negotiation skills, or less successful in attracting funding due to gender bias in grant review.

Work/life grants seek to accommodate the dual roles of women who are caregivers, especially early in their careers when lab or field hours are long and children are young. These needs are often gendered because academic women are more likely than men to have partners who are in the same line of work; in such couples, both partners face high job demands.

Purpose

Grant programs typically targeted individuals or collaborative teams to cover research costs, to support career development activities, or to enhance work/life balance. Research awards sought to support individuals' scholarly and creative activities, while career development awards supported faculty to explore new career directions or develop new skills. Grants targeted at work/life sought to enable faculty to maintain or resume research productivity during critical life junctures. In our study, solicitations for faculty grant programs frequently listed a combination of these categories.

Audience

Most programs offered by Cohorts 1 and 2 ADVANCE IT institutions offered research and career grants to women faculty members only. A few were also open to other applicants who demonstrated commitment to the advancement of women in STEM (e.g., by pursuing research on gender issues). Work/life grants often invited proposals from faculty of any gender.

A few programs provided research funding in connection with structured collaborative or mentoring activities, such as Hunter College's (Cohort 1) sponsorship program and the University of Montana's (Cohort 2) visiting scholar/mentor program (see also Strategy 12). Finally, some programs targeted collaborative efforts that included women investigators and/or that addressed gender-related issues. The majority of institutions focused on STEM faculty only.

Some individual grant programs were open to faculty members at any career stage. Other programs focused on faculty at particular career stages. Programs for tenured faculty targeted those seeking to jump-start progress on a new career goal—whether restarting scholarly work after substantial university service or time away, pursuing a significant change in research direction, preparing for advancement to full professor, or moving into or out of an administrative role. Programs for pre-tenure faculty sought to support their scholarly growth and enhance their tenure prospects.

Models

ADVANCE small grant programs typically targeted one or more of three types of activities: career development, research, and work/life support. Research and career development were the most common targets for individual grants.

Career development grants provided:

- domestic and international travel funds to visit other laboratories, carry out fieldwork, collaborate with colleagues elsewhere, or attend professional conferences, training courses, or workshops
- seed money to initiate collaborative research across disciplines
- payment to a sponsor, such as a senior scientist in their research field, to provide early-career faculty with research and career advice

Research awards focused on covering research-related expenses, such as

- equipment, lab space or renovations, materials, and supplies
- support for student research assistants or postdocs to support faculty research activities
- expenses for site visits or fieldwork
- course release time to carry out scholarly work
- bridge support to enable continuance of research activities during gaps in grant funding
- seed money to support faculty to establish a collaboration or carry out a pilot project in order to develop a successful proposal for external funding

Work/life awards provided support for faculty during major life transitions or during critical times of need, including:

- release time to accommodate childbirth, adoption, care responsibilities (for children, elders, or ill family members), major family transitions, or death of a family member
- childcare expenses (e.g., babysitting, travel costs for a caregiver) to permit faculty parents to pursue research activities, attend professional meetings, or conduct fieldwork, site visits, or collaborative work

Individual grant amounts varied from a few hundred dollars to $54,000 at Columbia University.

Two forms of application process were common. The first was a competitive process with a set award limit and deadline. These programs set formal requirements for application materials to be reviewed by a committee. Because STEM faculty in particular are accustomed to grant writing, this model fits STEM academic cultures. The other was a less formal process of rolling applications reviewed on a case-by-case basis, with varied, often modest award amounts. This approach was more typical for travel grants and work/life awards, situations where individuals might not anticipate their needs far in advance.

Factors that influenced whether institutions used individual grant programs—and how they were designed—included the following:

- *Faculty needs.* For example, associate professors who have remained in rank for a number of years are often underserved and may benefit from this type of individualized support (Baldwin et al., 2008).
- *Number of faculty in the targeted group.* Can enough awards be made to make a difference for significant numbers of faculty?
- *Availability of other campus programs.* What options exist for supporting faculty scholarship or travel?
- *Desired positive side effects.* Beyond scholarly productivity, goals included reducing isolation, providing informal mentoring, and building cross-disciplinary collaborations.

A few institutions used individual grants as a means to target a particular problem. For example, the Research Assistantship Program for Current Faculty at the University of Maryland, Baltimore County (Cohort 2), provided funds to support a graduate research assistant for associate professors close to promotion. By compensating for high service loads or providing bridge money between grants, the program sought to ensure the success of women STEM faculty moving through promotion.

Examples

Institutions created small grant programs that targeted specific or broad groups for varied purposes.

The University of Michigan's (Cohort 1) Elizabeth Crosby Research Awards provided broad support to individual STEM faculty on tenure, research, or clinical tracks to meet career-relevant needs and enhance their prospects for retention or promotion. For example, grants provided support for women through difficult pregnancies, sponsored a speaker series on women in mathematics, and supported individual scholars' travel and childcare costs at professional conferences. The program has been institutionalized with a maximum award of $20,000, though most grants are smaller.

The University of Montana (Cohort 2) established a visiting scholar/mentor fund to support pre-tenure STEM faculty in building a relationship with a disciplinary mentor off campus by swapping visits. This provided faculty with the opportunity to build collaborative relationships with scientists from institutions outside Montana, thus alleviating isolation at their rural campus. While leaders described this as a small part of their overall program, they reported major outcomes for those who received the grants. Recipients established collaborations and valuable mentoring connections and made good progress on publications and experiments.

Flexibility was key to the University of Wisconsin–Madison's (Cohort 1) Vilas Life Cycle Professorship Program. This grant of up to $30,000 was available to faculty, regardless of divisional affiliation or rank, who encountered critical events that affected both their research and personal lives, such as a life-threatening illness and recuperation, caring for elderly parents or children with special needs, or disability of a family member.

Program evaluation identified many positive effects (and no negative ones) on recipients' personal and professional lives, as well as on the students and staff also at risk when a faculty member faces a life-changing event. Reports credited the Vilas Life Cycle Professorship Program with preserving faculty success, decreasing faculty attrition, supporting staff and students who assist in research activities, and fostering an innovative model for faculty career flexibility (Pribbenow & Benting, 2004). Initially serving women, the Vilas Life Cycle Professorship was extended to all genders, expanded to serve more awardees, and institutionalized with support from an external donor.

At Utah State University (Cohort 2), the Collaborative Grant Support Program provided 6–10 awards of $6,000–$8,000 each to conduct initial research on a collaborative project that would lead to submission of a grant proposal to a national funding agency. The program was intended to catalyze formation of interdisciplinary research teams led by STEM women faculty. This award was open to tenure-track and research faculty at all ranks.

Project reports noted success in bringing senior women engineers and scientists together with early-career STEM women faculty to create new ideas, build networks, and seed new research initiatives. Collaborations also helped to break down barriers, improve faculty communication across ranks and disciplines, and stimulate effective, informal peer mentoring. The program led to proposal submissions; leveraged diverse faculty skills, expertise, and experience; and netted a positive return on investment due to larger, external grants that were awarded based on work initiated under these seed monies.

At Columbia University's (Cohort 2) Lamont-Doherty Earth Observatory, research workshop awards enabled early- and mid-career women to convene research workshops with senior scientists from Columbia and elsewhere. The workshops sought to provide recognition to women as scientific leaders and to stimulate new research collaborations.

Kansas State University's (Cohort 2) Advanced Distinguished Lecturer Series (ADLS) was a signature feature of its ADVANCE IT project, lauded by institutional leaders and faculty members as the program's greatest success and a "huge return on investment." The program sought to support and advance the careers of pre-tenure STEM faculty. Early-career STEM faculty women could propose to host a distinguished nationally recognized scholar once a year for up to five years. The visitor spent time at the lab and discussing common research interests with the host and gave a talk open to the university community. Dinner with the host and her department chair and/or dean helped to make the early-career faculty member more visible and to highlight her research to institutional leaders.

To advertise the program, ADVANCE hosted a spring luncheon, funded by deans and departments, for eligible early-career faculty members and their department heads. The luncheon celebrated ADLS awards made the previous year and featured a panel of previous grant recipients, who discussed their experiences and lessons learned about effective visiting scholar activities. Since some early-career faculty are initially nervous about inviting a highly regarded senior scholar, the luncheon was intended to provide information about all aspects of the process and alleviate any concerns.

The program has documented significant long-term benefits for early-career faculty participants: ongoing and long-term collaborations, joint grant proposals, invitations to visit the senior scholars' campuses, the development of wide collegial networks, and publications (Dyer & Montelone, 2007). One institutional leader explained, "I just can't say enough about that program and the small amount of money it takes to make a huge impact on the individual faculty member and on the campus." The program has been institutionalized in Kansas State University's Office for the Advancement of Women in Science and Engineering.

Evaluation

Most small grant programs documented applications, awards, and awardee demographics. For evaluation of outcomes, most relied on reports from grant holders, using a standardized format so that grantees responded to a common set of questions.

At the University of Colorado Boulder (Cohort 1), a simple qualitative analysis of faculty outcomes of the individual growth grant program documented publications, presentations, grant proposals, and new courses or curriculum materials, as well as affective outcomes, such as faculty members' sense of being valued by the institution. The analysis demonstrated a high return on investment and thus was helpful in securing long-term funding for the program (Laursen, 2008, 2009). It remains in place as the university's associate professor growth grants program.

The University of Maryland, Baltimore County (Cohort 2), collected testimonials from women in its Research Assistantship Program for Current Faculty, which awarded support for a research assistant for associate professors preparing for tenure. These testimonials revealed that the funds were critical in successfully assisting several women to achieve tenure or promotion.

Evaluation of the Vilas Life Cycle Professorship Program at the University of Wisconsin–Madison (Cohort 1) has included accountings of grant expenditures, monitoring of applications and recipients, qualitative analysis of participant reports, and documentation of scholarly accomplishments attributed to the grant support.

Kansas State (Cohort 2) asked ADLS grant recipients to report how the grant had contributed to their careers, which resulted in reports of benefits to the early-career faculty. Surveys of those who served as visiting scholars provided useful insights about their views of the program. One finding was that the word "distinguished" in the name of the program was attractive to invited scholars.

Affordances and Limitations

Several pros and cons to offering funds to individual faculty members were observed in the context of ADVANCE IT projects and their equity goals. Affordances reported for various types of individual grant programs include the following:

- *Fast start-up.* Individual grant programs were reported to be fairly easy to establish. They can offer a quick start to a new ADVANCE project and make ADVANCE known widely across the faculty, and they are seen to benefit faculty immediately.
- *Good return on investment.* Small grants of $5,000–$10,000 were sufficient to buy out a course or to initiate a research project. Numerous ADVANCE PIs reported that these grants had a high return on investment, often leading to larger, externally funded projects.
- *Political good will.* Individual faculty grants fostered good will due to their popularity. PIs reported that faculty and especially department leaders appreciated that resources were shared with faculty.
- *Symbolic value.* For young faculty in particular, winning a competitive award can be career-enhancing. Some institutions hosted an annual celebration that recognized all grantees, celebrating their accomplishments and fostering collegiality.
- *Holistic benefits.* Work/life awards were typically highly valued for their recognition of faculty as whole people, not just worker bees. In program evaluations, recipients often cited the emotional benefits of feeling recognized and valued, and they consequently felt more loyal to the institution. Applicants could apply for support without feeling judged by authority figures in their home units.
- *Collaboration and mentoring.* Collaborative seed grant approaches in particular added value by fostering connections across departments, disciplines, and career stages, benefiting multiple faculty members at once. Programs that supported pre-tenure faculty to pursue specific collaborative or mentoring arrangements reported increased scientific productivity as well as positive mentoring in the discipline through interactions such as review of proposals and manuscripts, invitations to conferences, and recommendation letters for the tenure packet. Strategy 12 discusses these mentoring benefits in more detail.

Limitations of the small grant model include:

- *Modest circle of impact.* Particularly on a large campus, grant funds may not reach far.
- *Focus on individuals rather than systems.* Because grants benefit individuals, they may be seen as fixing the swimmer rather than draining the pool of inequity. Other programs are required to address wider-ranging issues faced by the larger faculty community.
- *Resistance.* A few institutions reported backlash from faculty who were ineligible for these awards.

Programs that offered fewer grants of larger dollar amounts reported smaller numbers of people affected, but a greater impact to each. Increased administrative attention was required to design and run a program that offered large sums and required more of participants. Smaller grant programs were reported to get off the ground quickly and were institutionalized more frequently.

Summary

Like the faculty development programs discussed in Strategy 10, small grants programs are relatively quick to start up and are readily tailored to target particular faculty audiences or needs. They are received well by participants and departments, which see them as supportive to faculty retention and success. Grants programs for early-career faculty are most effective when they incorporate elements of collaboration or mentoring with other faculty inside or outside the institution. Programs for mid-career faculty signal reinvestment in a faculty group that is too often overlooked; they offer strong symbolic value and the opportunity to celebrate faculty accomplishments. As with faculty development, individually targeted strategies do not substitute for deeper systemic change and must be coupled with other strategies.

FURTHER READING

Kalivoda, P., Sorrell, G. R., & Simpson, R. D. (1994). Nurturing faculty vitality by matching institutional interventions with career-stage needs. *Innovative Higher Education, 18*(4), 255–272.

Strategy 12. Mentoring and Networking Activities

Mentoring has been a popular strategy in many types of organizations to promote successful career advancement, especially for those in underrepresented groups (National Academies of Sciences, Engineering, and Medicine, 2019). Interest in mentoring has also been evident among ADVANCE institutions, with the great majority of institutions in Cohorts 1 and 2 offering some form of mentoring, coaching, or networking. Here we focus on the range of ways in which mentoring and networking programs have been conceptualized and organized, emphasizing programs to foster relationships that help faculty receive career-related advice and generate ideas for addressing problems.

Other strategies are related in various ways. Efforts to develop institutional leaders (Strategy 4) may include models that include mentoring opportunities for women preparing for leadership roles. Likewise, faculty development activities (Strategy 10) may include events that, in bringing together people from across the institution, provide occasions for mentoring and networking. Some of the strategies discussed here use visiting scholars to play a role in mentoring early-career scholars, and these campus visitors also contribute to raising the visibility of women scholars and gender issues in the academy, as discussed in Strategy 6.

Rationale

As a change strategy, mentoring and networking activities are intended to support women scholars' advancement within challenging institutional contexts, ensuring that they have the knowledge and problem-solving skills to navigate paths to success. While doctoral education generally provides scholars with the skills and values to be excellent researchers, it typically does not focus explicitly on the full range of skills that faculty need for career success, nor does it offer much preparation for institutional leadership roles (Austin & McDaniels, 2006). Furthermore, especially in fields dominated by men, women are often not included in the informal spaces where information is shared (Fox, 2001, 2008; Sturm, 2006). Thus, mentoring and networking opportunities provide avenues through which women can gain information and feel supported as they develop the array of skills, abilities, and problem-solving strategies that are needed for career success in their particular institutional contexts.

Mentoring and networking activities also address the isolation that women in STEM often feel, particularly if they are in fields heavily dominated by men. Specifically, such programs may foster collegial relationships that offer encouragement, guidance, and career development models and that provide structures of emotional and practical support when women encounter difficult situations. Opportunities to discuss their experiences can help women understand how their own challenges relate to the broader institutional context and can help them identify strategies or solutions suited to that context.

Beyond supporting women scholars as individuals, mentoring programs may contribute to change in organizational cultures when they prepare women to enter leadership roles with tools to counter the impact of implicit bias and to promote policies and processes that nurture inclusive, supportive environments. Mentoring and networking activities have symbolic as well as functional value. By investing in women faculty members in ways that help ensure their success as scholars and as institutional citizens and leaders, universities and colleges can highlight their commitment to building a diverse faculty.

Purpose

Mentoring and networking activities may serve several purposes simultaneously:

- *Support for career development.* These programs seek to support women scholars, regardless of their career stage, in developing productive, satisfying, and successful careers. They may provide opportunities for women to sharpen their skills in leadership and career decision-making, envision career options, and interact with more senior women, who can serve as role models.
- *Assistance in problem-solving.* Mentoring and networking opportunities are sometimes organized to help women find support in identifying appropriate steps or options to solve challenges.
- *Collegial connections and communities of support.* Typically, mentoring and networking activities provide occasions for women to develop relationships with people who can offer collegial encouragement and guidance. Such support can help reduce anxiety, especially for early-career faculty unsure how to interpret or handle various situations they may face.
- *Visibility and professional sponsorship.* Program models that include connecting early-career faculty with distinguished external scholars can offer additional benefits, such as sponsorship in the discipline, which makes the early-career scholar more visible in her field. Senior scholars may serve as exemplars of accomplishment and possibility for early-career faculty. Especially for those with few women colleagues in their field or at their campus, interactions with visiting scholars can offer a form of mentoring that is not otherwise available.

Audience

Mentoring and networking activities in ADVANCE institutions have addressed several audiences. Efforts focused on early- or mid-career women faculty seek to enhance their career-related skills and deepen their knowledge of the institution and its culture. Other programs have focused on providing mid-career and senior women with the skills and knowledge needed to compete for and be effective in leadership roles inside or outside their institution. Still other programs have sought to foster skills among faculty of any gender who hold institutional leadership roles, perhaps as deans and department chairs.

A few early ADVANCE institutions aimed to prepare graduate students and postdoctoral scholars for academic positions by providing mentoring and networking opportunities for those considering academic careers. Such initiatives were permitted only under the early program solicitations (Laursen & De Welde, 2019) and are not discussed here.

Models

A fairly wide literature addresses mentorship of various kinds; of note, however, is the general lack of clear definitions and systematic frameworks for analyzing or planning mentoring activities. Mentoring and networking took quite diverse forms across the ADVANCE institutions we studied and even varied over time in particular institutions. Many institutions took a somewhat experimental approach, trying out particular forms of mentoring and then adjusting, discontinuing, or replacing them or inventing new forms, depending on faculty responses and the assessment of campus needs.

We include coaching as part of the broad range of options that we label "mentoring." Coaching sometimes denotes a relationship that has a targeted goal, such as helping women develop senior-level leadership skills. It can also imply relationships in which the coach is scaffolding the woman's own decision-making (with less emphasis on the coach's views), which is different than relationships in which senior colleagues share their expertise, experiences, advice, and perspectives with less experienced colleagues.

An article by Dawson (2014), based on an extensive literature review, outlined 16 design elements that characterize the variety of mentoring options. Some of the choices to be considered in designing mentoring plans include:

- *Objectives of mentoring.* What purposes is it intended to address? Some ADVANCE mentoring and networking activities focused on helping new faculty members to understand expectations, policies, and the institutional culture and to develop their career goals. Some programs focused on introducing mid-career women to possibilities in leadership. Other objectives included responding to emerging problems or challenges; ensuring that new faculty establish themselves as productive scholars; and easing the transition of new department chairs by helping them gain the institutional knowledge and professional skills needed for leading a unit.

- *Roles.* What roles and functions will be played by the mentor and by the mentee? Some ADVANCE projects expected mentors to provide specific knowledge (e.g., information about institutional policies or guidance about negotiation strategies). Others urged a more fluid, organic approach in which mentors and mentees together determined their respective roles.
- *Cardinality.* How many people will be involved in each role? One-to-one mentoring, with either matched mentor-mentee pairs or self-selected teams, was tried at several ADVANCE institutions. However, often this approach was replaced over time with one-to-many or many-to-many networking models that brought together groups of peers or mixed groups of pre-tenure and senior faculty.
- *Seniority.* What is the expertise, experience, and status level of each person in the relationship? Some ADVANCE institutions offered activities to connect early-career and senior faculty, in which senior colleagues shared perspectives based on their greater experience. Others crafted peer mentoring opportunities, in which colleagues at similar career stages served as peer or near-peer mentors.
- *Time.* What are the expectations for the amount of time each person devotes to the relationship, the extent and regularity of interactions, and the duration of the relationship? In some cases, ADVANCE mentoring programs extended across a semester or a year (or more), such as the University of Texas at El Paso's regular meetings for pre-tenure faculty and their mentors, or Hunter College's sponsorship program for women scientists, which could extend to three years. At the other end of the continuum, Case Western Reserve's hotline coaching offered immediate mentoring over the phone or in a few sessions to help women with specific and immediate concerns. Between these two ends of the spectrum were examples such as occasional networking luncheons to enable mentoring conversations between pre-tenure faculty and experienced

senior colleagues around specific topics, such as tenure and promotion, work/life issues, or grant writing.

- *Location of the mentoring program.* One issue not included in Dawson's (2014) list is where to situate a mentoring program within the organization's structure. Some institutions organized mentoring and networking activities at the institutional level, perhaps located in the teaching and learning center or in the office of faculty development or faculty affairs. Other projects helped colleges or departments to develop their own mentoring and networking plans responsive to local needs.

Dawson (2014) mentioned other issues, including how mentors and mentees are selected and connected, how participants are trained or guided for the mentoring process, and the resources, such as space and technology, available to support mentoring relationships. Corneille and coauthors (2019) identified mentoring as a salient issue for faculty women of color and suggested that traditional mentoring models may be less effective for women of color.

Examples

Most institutions that incorporated mentoring or networking activities as interventions in their change portfolios used several different forms, and often these forms changed over time. The ADVANCE project at Case Western Reserve University (Cohort 2) developed a comprehensive approach to mentoring, with long- and short-term options, opportunities for faculty and administrative leaders, and institution-situated as well as college-located mentoring options. The specifics included:

- *Mentoring committees and mentoring lunches.* ADVANCE leaders initially planned to establish mentoring committees for faculty women of all races and ethnicities and faculty men of color, which consisted of three experienced colleagues: one in the department, one outside it, and one outside the university. However, response to this model was not strong, and some resistance was expressed to its formality. The committees were replaced with less formal junior faculty mentoring lunches, which emphasized building relationships among early-career faculty, senior faculty, and administrators by opening conversations about a wide variety of topics.
- *Executive coaching for deans, chairs, and individual faculty women.* Coaching focused on helping people achieve personal and professional goals

through targeted guidance from experienced leaders and on supporting them to lead change in the institution.

- *Hotline mentoring.* This innovative approach to mentoring enabled women scholars and leaders to request a telephone conversation with an experienced colleague to brainstorm approaches to serious, often time-sensitive challenges that women encountered in salary negotiations, work/life navigation, promotion and tenure processes, or interpersonal dynamics.
- *Speed mentoring.* Speed mentoring events of 90 minutes each were open to all faculty members, postdoctoral fellows, and graduate students. These short, focused interactions with mentors focused on such issues as CV design and career-building strategies.

The University of Texas at El Paso (Cohort 2) offered an institution-wide, formal one-to-one mentoring approach combined with networking opportunities. The faculty mentoring program for women targeted all pre-tenure women faculty to help them become acculturated to the university and "increase their effectiveness and visibility" by having access to information and resources. All new women faculty members were matched with mentors for guidance on handling teaching, research, and service responsibilities; managing family issues; and setting priorities.

Early-career faculty participated in informal monthly luncheons to discuss such topics as promotion and tenure processes and departmental and university-level service. They also attended a mid-year workshop organized to help mentor-mentee pairs assess and adjust their relationships. Formative evaluation across several years showed that the faculty participants assessed the mentoring relationships to be very useful.

The sponsorship program at Hunter College (Cohort 1) was carefully designed to address the specific challenges early-career women may face as researchers and to foster increased research success.

Eight to twelve associates at any rank were selected each year to receive funding for up to three years, not necessarily contiguous. Each associate was matched with a successful senior scholar (of any gender) in the same field, but not the same department, for communication every two weeks to support research accomplishments. Associates each received up to $10,000 per year for research-related support, while sponsors received up to $2,500 per semester to acknowledge the time they spent supporting the associate.

Monthly workshops focused on career development, writing and publishing, mentoring processes, and work/life balance. These were infused with information about gender schemas and the role of accumulated disadvantage in women's careers.

Quantitative assessments showed that participants increased their research productivity, while interview data provided descriptions of the positive impact on participants' knowledge, confidence, and contributions to their departments.

Responding to campus interest, the LEAP project at the University of Colorado Boulder (Cohort 1) shifted from one mentoring model to another during its grant period. Initially, LEAP offered a coaching model that matched early-career faculty with senior faculty trained as coaches. While evaluation data showed benefits to both coaches and their pre-tenure partners, after two years the project leaders decided to move toward activities that emphasized networking. Among their reasons was the modest level of interest in coaching from early-career faculty, possibly because of perceptions that expressing interest in coaching might imply that the faculty member was struggling.

This shift toward networking was viewed as successful at Colorado. Networking activities included lunches, book groups, and workshops; they targeted early-career faculty, associate professors, senior faculty, and department chairs. Informed by the philosophy that a rising tide raises all ships, the networking events were open to all women faculty, STEM and non-STEM.

The approach of the University of Washington (Cohort 1) illustrated the ways in which faculty development or leadership development topics can be used to attract academics to events that foster networking. Mentoring-for-leadership lunches were designed to encourage women in STEM fields to consider career paths involving leadership roles. The lunches featured discussion after a 20-minute presentation by a woman in a formal (positional) or informal (nonpositional) leadership role who outlined her personal history, challenges, and success strategies. Quarterly formative evaluations and a summative evaluation indicated that participants felt less isolated and expressed more likelihood to pursue leadership opportunities.

Quarterly professional development workshops for all pre-tenure faculty in the University of Washington's ADVANCE departments addressed career-related topics (e.g., time management, negotiating the tenure process, advising graduate students, and balancing multiple roles). Evaluation results showed that applicants gained a greater sense of being part of a community; they also learned enhanced strategies for balancing teaching, research, and service.

The University of Rhode Island's (Cohort 2) approach to mentoring illustrated ways to situate mentoring in the contexts of individual colleges. ADVANCE leaders met with college deans to review overall institutional mentoring goals and supported each college in developing a mentoring policy tailored for its faculty. They also developed resources to assist colleges, such as a web tutorial, a handbook, and a training workshop on mentoring.

The mentoring program at Lehigh University (Cohort 5) targeted STEM women who had been recently tenured and promoted to associate professor and supported them to pursue promotion to full professor by developing a career success plan and interacting with an external senior mentor. The program's framing as leadership development was adjusted in response to data that showed that Lehigh faculty women did not equate "leadership" to holding specific positions as university administrators, but rather held broad and diverse definitions of leadership that encompassed taking intellectual leadership in their scholarly fields and other interests. While the number of people eligible for the program was not large each year, a high fraction participated, and evaluation data indicated they valued the program. The program was extended to a wider range of regional institutions through an ADVANCE partnership project, entitled MAPWISEly, with the intent to use this broader sample in a research study to improve understanding of how best to mentor women faculty at mid-career (see Laursen & Austin, 2014c).

At Texas A&M University (TAMU, Cohort 5), two models illustrated the ways formal and informal mentoring can meet the needs of different constituencies. Success circles were peer mentoring groups formed around specific interests. Robust groups developed around topics related to challenges faced by women at different career stages: academic writing circles fostered peer mentoring and accountability around writing; the "moms group" offered support around work/life challenges for faculty parents; and women department heads organized to share information, offer support to each other, and troubleshoot among their small number, who were widely dispersed across a large and decentralized institution. While initially the circles received scheduling support from the TAMU ADVANCE Center, several of them continued as self-organized circles after the grant ended.

The ADVANCE Scholars Program was developed to support early-career women of color. It is notable as an example of an intersectional approach crafted to respond to the specific challenges women of color experience in their faculty roles, such as high but informal service demands and everyday incivilities from faculty colleagues, staff, and students (Turner, 2002; Stanley, 2006a, 2006b). The two-year program connected women of color who were assistant professors with an internal advocate from TAMU and provided travel support for each scholar to interact with an external eminent scholar in her discipline, who was invited to serve as a mentor. Group activities and retreats fostered connections among the scholars and developed the internal advocates' understanding and support for early-career scholars of color. The developers were able to institutionalize the program in the university's Office of Diversity, with the intent that this office would support the group-level activities while colleges would support the individual scholars from their colleges. This design enables all colleges, not just STEM units, to support scholars from groups historically underrepresented at TAMU and makes it possible to include other faculty from underrepresented groups, especially men of color.

Finally, many institutions incorporated informal networking into their other program activities, such as celebrations for women who received promotion, tenure, or faculty awards; events to recognize small grant recipients; or receptions for visiting scholars. At the University of Texas at Rio Grande Valley (Cohort 6), the ADVANCE project invited all women faculty to a *merienda* (high tea), where they discovered shared interests and concerns. This group developed into the lively Women's Faculty Network, which became a voice for women faculty with the university administration (Laursen & Austin, 2014f).

In another example of informal networking, the TAMU ADVANCE Center used a distributed leadership structure that engaged more than 100 faculty from across campus in designing and leading 12 distinct program activities. While this structure added organizational complexity, it had positive side effects because working together on a shared project served to connect faculty across colleges and departments and to strengthen networks among senior women and senior male allies (Laursen, 2017). TAMU's climate surveys showed that engaging with this work had positive ripple effects for senior women and their departments (Taylor et al., 2017).

Evaluation

Mentoring and networking activities were assessed in a variety of ways. Extent of participation was an easy measure that could be tracked over time. Often, general observations of enrollment and interest were used to determine whether activities were meeting perceived needs and responding to the interests of women faculty. Some programs used interviews or written surveys of both mentees and mentors to gather formative evaluation data on satisfaction, areas of interest of participants, and preferred topics for mentoring workshops, and summative data about program outcomes.

In general, approaches to evaluation work best when they are appropriately scaled to match the depth and expected impact of the intervention. The analysis by Carter-Sowell and coauthors (2019) is an example of an in-depth evaluation of a substantial mentoring program, the ADVANCE Scholars Program at TAMU. Laursen and colleagues (2005) used a combination of surveys, interviews, and focus groups to provide formative and outcome evaluations for a coaching program at the University of Colorado Boulder. Buch and coauthors (2011) described the use of faculty surveys at the University of North Carolina at Charlotte (Cohort 3) to first assess the needs of mid-career faculty, and then to monitor participation and outcomes for those who participated in the program they designed.

Affordances and Limitations

Overall, mentoring and networking activities provide opportunities for individuals to enhance their professional skills and knowledge, gain deeper understanding of institutional resources and culture, and cultivate professional connections that can support, inform, and assist them in handling professional and personal responsibilities and challenges. The greatest obstacle is the time required for people to participate. Often, tangible costs are modest: for food and services for mentoring gatherings. Stipends may be budgeted to support time and travel for more intensive forms of mentoring, and more formal programs should likewise support training for mentors and coaches. Specific forms of mentoring and networking activities vary significantly in their particular benefits and limitations.

INDIVIDUAL ONE-TO-ONE MENTORING

There is one major affordance for this type of mentoring:

- Individual mentees can develop personal relationships over time with a more senior person, who focuses on the specific situation, interests and needs of the mentee.

The limitations include:

- Early-career faculty members may be concerned that expressions of interest in being mentored could be perceived as signals of weakness, uncertainty, or problems in performance. One way to address this issue is by requiring all new faculty to have a mentor. The challenge thus becomes making good matches that are meaningful and not pro forma.
- Early-career faculty also may be concerned about revealing questions, challenges, or issues to a colleague within the same department, for fear

that the senior colleague may be in an evaluative role at a later time and the shared information could compromise the assessment of the early-career colleague's strengths. One solution is to match people with a mentor from outside the department, although there is some risk that the mentor may not fully understand the specific issues confronting the early-career faculty member.

- Some senior colleagues who volunteer as mentors may not have the personal qualities needed to be effective. Programs should offer training for mentors and coaches; they may need to refrain from matching some mentors and follow up on pairings with discreet check-ins. Because there is an uneven power dynamic between pre-tenure and senior faculty, mentoring programs should be prepared to protect pre-tenure faculty and offer a graceful mechanism by which a mentee can extract herself from a pairing that is not a good fit.

MENTORING COMMITTEES WITH COLLEAGUES FROM WITHIN AND OUTSIDE THE MENTEE'S DEPARTMENT

There is one significant affordance for this committee approach:

- In addition to the affordances of one-to-one mentoring, mentees receive the guidance and perspectives of multiple advisors.

The limitations of this approach include:

- Arranging meeting times can be challenging when more people are involved.
- Unless mentoring is required for all, faculty may worry that requesting a mentoring committee could undermine how they are viewed by others.

PROGRAMS THAT CONNECT EARLY-CAREER FACULTY WITH EXTERNAL EMINENT SCHOLARS

Affordances for this type of mentoring include:

- Receiving advice, mentoring, and the opportunity to interact with a disciplinary role model who can describe their experiences and offer guidance about professional and work/life issues.
- These interactions may lead in particular to research career benefits, such as reviews of manuscripts; advice about research; reciprocal invitations to visit and speak at the mentor's institution; collaborations on research

grants or projects; and introductions and networking opportunities in the broader disciplinary community.

- An external scholar who becomes knowledgeable about the early-career scholar's work may be called upon as an external reviewer.
- The external scholar in turn has an opportunity to be generative while also being honored, and they may benefit from enriched knowledge of other institutions' programs and expanded collegial networks of their own.

There is one major limitation of this approach:

- If a visiting scholar program is targeted to early-career women faculty, other colleagues may feel left out or resentful. Careful explanation of the purpose of the program can preclude or diminish this problem.

NETWORKING ACTIVITIES WITH PEERS OR WITH MIXED GROUPS

Affordances of these approaches include:

- Compared to individual mentoring, networking activities provide a more informal environment in which a range of perspectives and experiences can be shared.
- Mentees may learn about a variety of strategies or approaches to consider, without the pressure of feeling that they should follow the advice of a specific person, and they may make multiple connections simultaneously.
- Peer mentoring enables people to exchange ideas with others having similar experiences, thus avoiding the risk of sharing uncertainties with more senior colleagues who may later be in an evaluative role.
- All forms of networking create connections across a campus that enhance the overall capacity and knowledge of faculty and administrators, which can in turn positively influence the campus culture.

There is one significant limitation:

- Networking activities may not focus on the specific needs of an individual faculty member. Individuals may need to identify those in their mentoring network who can be most helpful in regard to specific questions or issues.

Summary

Connections made through mentoring and networking programs can offer insider knowledge, new perspectives, and personalized support for women at a variety of career stages. Mentors can help to normalize common challenges, solve problems, and identify situations where other help is needed. However, several ADVANCE institutions found that the design of mentoring programs was sensitive to local cultures and norms around mentoring, which influenced how the program was communicated and perceived. Thus, clarity about the program's purpose, methods for preparing mentors, and good formative evaluation are essential to developing a program that is responsive to participants' needs and interests.

Networking efforts can be designed to be synergistic with other programs, such as faculty development activities and leadership development programs and celebrations. Working together on institutional equity can also be a way to strengthen faculty networks.

FURTHER READING

Kram, K. E. (1983). Phases of the mentor relationship. *Academy of Management Journal*, 26(4), 608–625.

Rabinowitz, V. C., & Valian, V. (2007). Beyond mentoring: A sponsorship program to improve women's success. In A. J. Stewart, J. E. Malley, & D. LaVaque-Manty (Eds.), *Transforming science and engineering: Advancing academic women* (pp. 96–115). Ann Arbor: University of Michigan Press.

Yen, J. W., et al. (2007). The ADVANCE mentoring-for-leadership lunch series for women faculty in STEM at the University of Washington. *Journal of Women and Minorities in Science and Engineering*, 13(3), 191–206.

Zellers, D. F., Howard, V. M., & Barcic, M. A. (2008). Faculty mentoring programs: Reenvisioning rather than reinventing the wheel. *Review of Educational Research*, 78(3), 552–588.

Chapter Seven

New Frontiers of Research and Practice

Some new systemic change strategies have emerged from the ideas and work of ADVANCE IT grantees who received awards later in the program's lifetime, often a result of applying different theoretical frameworks and disciplinary lenses to the goal of developing a more equitable institution. These new ideas enrich our notions of how institutions can lead efforts for social justice and identify areas where more work is needed.

WE HAVE PRESENTED a historical perspective based on studying institutions that received ADVANCE Institutional Transformation awards early in the history of the program. We chose to investigate those institutions so that we could learn something about whether and how their strategies had worked and were lasting. We have continued to observe, talk with, and learn from the leaders of newer ADVANCE projects, who have drawn on the research and development work done by earlier grantees and developed increasingly sophisticated theoretical models, contextual variations, and plans for implementation, in part due to the NSF's expectations and encouragement. The ADVANCE program's increasing emphasis on and opportunity for research has further strengthened community knowledge; indeed, in updating materials in our StratEGIC Toolkit for this volume, we found many new and exciting results relevant to equity in higher education, and no doubt missed many more. Thus, the set of strategies that we have presented is not complete.

We highlight in this chapter some exciting new types of strategies, distinct from those already presented in chapters 3–6, to advance gender equity in institutions of higher education. We have not analyzed these projects in detail but offer them as examples of other systemic approaches that are under development or ripe for further work.

Addressing Other Arenas of Bias

Many ADVANCE IT projects drew on the literature about implicit bias to de-velop interventions for faculty hiring (Strategy 1) and tenure and promotion (Strategy 2), recognizing these processes as deeply shaping the composition of the faculty at key recruitment and retention stages. They observed that such efforts had ripple effects, as faculty who had undergone training in the context of a search committee used their knowledge in other arenas, such as discussing applications for graduate student admissions, writing recommendation letters, or selecting winners of faculty awards. These situations all involve faculty members as the biased evaluators of other faculty or of students. But biased judgments of faculty by students and staff also influence faculty success, such as when students evaluate teaching through end-of-course questionnaires, or when staff do not complete work requested by early-career women but do complete work for senior men in the department.

Based on evidence from surveys and focus groups with women faculty about disrespectful gendered treatment by students and staff, the ADVANCE Center at Texas A&M University (Cohort 5) began to work on these issues. The center worked with the student affairs office to develop a training module for new student orientation about the "Aggie values" of respect and equality. It also supported departmental teams of faculty and staff in joint work to learn about bias, understand how it manifests for both faculty and staff members, and develop projects to improve department climate (http://advance.tamu.edu).

Approaching Equity through Analysis of Power and Privilege

While ADVANCE IT projects have been focused on the persistent underrepresentation of women in STEM disciplines, such underrepresentation is a result of broader, systemic patterns of sexism that are linked to racism, classism, ableism, heterosexism, ageism, and other forms of marginalization, all reflecting the unequal distribution of privilege and power. Oregon State University's (Cohort 7) ADVANCE project recognizes that "efforts to drive systemic change [for STEM women] can fall short if they do not also attend to all aspects of socially just change and engage in activities necessary to achieve the central aim of equity" (John et al., 2016, n.p.). Using a distinctive, seminar-based approach, Oregon State's team has applied a social justice lens to influence recruitment and promotion policies and practices, elevate values of justice and equity in institutional cultures, and raise faculty members' and leaders' awareness of difference, power, and discrimination in the academy so that they are better prepared to take action to support equity, inclusion, and justice (https://advance.oregonstate.edu).

Equalizing Workloads and Their Impact on Advancement

Research shows that academic women perform more service work than men, and it is more likely to be work that is important but less visible and valued, such as mentoring, writing recommendations, and informal advising, rather than task-based service that is more public and more readily quantified, such as chairing a committee (Babcock et al., 2017; Hanasono et al., 2019; Misra et al., 2011). Similar patterns are found for faculty of color (both men and women) and for trans and nonbinary faculty members. A key question is then, how is such gendered "secret service" valued (or not) in institutional advancement processes? (Hanasono et al., 2019). Efforts to study, clarify, make public, and address these differential workloads have been pioneered by the ADVANCE team at the University of Maryland, College Park, and the team's subsequent Faculty Workloads and Rewards Project (O'Meara, Kuvaeva, & Nyunt, 2017; O'Meara et al., 2017; O'Meara et al., 2018; O'Meara et al., 2019; see also https://www.advance.umd.edu/gender-on-campus -service; https://facultyworkloadandrewardsproject.umd.edu).

Reflecting similar goals but a different approach, SU ADVANCE, an IT project at Seattle University (Cohort 8), a private institution in the Jesuit tradition, is studying and revising promotion guidelines to reflect the institution's comprehensive educational goals and give appropriate value in promotion decisions to teaching, community engagement, and service leadership (https://www.seattleu .edu/advance). The project is exploring how the university is supporting (or not) multiple paths to promotion and reducing inequities between tenure-stream and contract faculty. This team has found that the concept of service stands in as a default category for many varied activities in which faculty participate, but they don't know how to include on their CVs (O'Brien et al., 2019, p. 5). Yet analysis reveals several categories of such work that are important to the institution and aligned with its purpose as a mission-driven, comprehensive liberal arts university: academic program development, student mentoring, institutional governance, community engagement, and more. The team's participatory action research is now feeding university-level efforts to revise promotion guidelines and to develop a mentoring program that will both mentor faculty for careers that are well aligned to the institutional mission, and mentor-the-mentors by guiding chairs and deans on the connections between diversity, inclusion, and the wide range of faculty activities that have value in this institution.

Combating Sexual and Gender-Based Harassment

Awareness of harassment in academia and its entanglement with gender and race has been elevated in recent years. A consensus study from the National Academies of Science, Engineering, and Medicine (Johnson, Widnall, & Benya, 2018) showed that harassment is very prevalent in STEM fields as a consequence of masculinized cultures—and exacerbated by organizational tolerance and inaction, power dynamics inherent in STEM educational structures and in research labs, and by the isolating environments where scientists work, such as labs and field sites where research is conducted. The report's emphasis on organizational cultures and structures points to the opportunity for institution-based work to combat harassment, but analyses have suggested that colleges and universities lag rather than lead in this work (Cantalupo & Kidder, 2018, 2019; Libarkin et al., 2019).

Leadership on this topic so far has come from a few professional societies and funding agencies, such as policies to retract proven harassers' funding and recognition by the National Science Foundation and the National Academy of Sciences, respectively, and discipline-based efforts to reduce sexual harassment at conferences and to change disciplinary cultures, such as the work being done by ADVANCEGeo (https://serc.carleton.edu/advancegeo).

Some ADVANCE awardees, including the University of New Hampshire (Cohort 6), the University of Massachusetts Lowell (Cohort 8), and Florida International University (Cohort 8), have worked on projects to reduce faculty bullying and microaggressions and to strengthen bystander intervention.

Honoring Intersectional Identities

In the early years of ADVANCE, the experiences of white, cisgender, heterosexual women tended to shape the thinking and design of IT projects (Laursen & De Welde, 2019). This framing masks and homogenizes the perspectives and experiences of US women of color, Native American women, and those born in other countries; women with disabilities; transgender women; women who identify as lesbian, bisexual, or queer; and nonbinary people. Important work by institutional ADVANCE projects at historically Black and Hispanic-serving institutions, such as the University of Texas at El Paso (Cohort 2), the University of Texas at Rio Grande Valley (Cohort 6), Jackson State University (Cohort 5), Howard University (Cohort 6), and North Carolina A&T (Cohort 7), highlights how gender equity may be framed differently at institutions where racial equality is already built into the mission.

Research by Armstrong and Jovanovic (2015, 2017) highlighted the challenges of conceiving and designing intersectional approaches to change, especially at majority white institutions. As they noted, "Without an intersectional perspective, the systemic issues particular to [underrepresented minority] women can remain hidden in a structural 'blind spot,' unseen and unaddressed by the institutions that wish to support them" (Armstrong & Jovanovic, 2017, p. 226). By extending a gender-based framing to include other forms of intersectional identity, the entire community benefits from new thinking and strategies that further inclusion.

Including Contingent Faculty

A major issue for higher education is its increasing reliance on non-tenure-track faculty, which includes a range of people with long-term, short-term, and course-to-course appointments. Rachel Levy (2019) coined the term VITAL faculty, which refers to the visitors, instructors, teaching assistants, adjuncts, and lecturers in this category. In mathematics and other fields, they teach large numbers of students and are thus particularly important as role models, advisors, and mentors for undergraduates. By the NSF's definition, the ADVANCE program does not extend to non-tenure-track faculty, focusing instead on women who are seen as permanent members of the faculty and can rise into institutional leadership roles. However, it is important for institutions to find avenues and resources for addressing the needs of this essential group of colleagues—many of whom make long-term commitments to institutions too, as teaching- and research-focused specialists. Institutions that fail to do so are undervaluing the important contributions of VITAL faculty and risk making them a permanently marginalized class. Gappa, Austin, and Trice (2007) suggested ways to ensure respect and support for those in roles not protected by the tenure system, and further work in this area is needed.

Summary

These newer areas of equity work reflect a growing awareness in universities and colleges of the range of ways in which people can be marginalized. While much work has been done to make the academy more inclusive and equitable, the emergence of these additional interventions and strategies highlights the continuing challenges in higher education. They also provide more avenues for effecting change, which leaders and designers of institutional equity projects may consider as they build a change portfolio.

PART III Building and Enacting a
          Change Portfolio

Chapter Eight

Put It All Together

Three case studies illustrate how institutions can build a portfolio of change strategies well suited to their particular contexts. Developing synergy among multiple strategies creates a greater impact, and there are some common pitfalls to avoid in comprehensive change projects.

WE HAVE DISCUSSED 12 strategies that institutions of higher education have developed to foster more equitable working environments for women STEM faculty members. These interventions are intended

- to address bias in evaluating people during decision-making for hiring, advancement, and rewards
- to enhance the everyday experiences and visibility of women in STEM workplaces
- to help people navigate life challenges without derailing their careers
- to support women's growth in the knowledge, skills, and connections needed to operate at the highest levels of their profession

It is clear, however, that no single intervention from any of these categories can single-handedly achieve the broad transformational goals of ADVANCE. Indeed, if the problems of institutionalized sexism in academia were that simple to ameliorate, they would be solved already! To accomplish real and lasting change requires multiple approaches that operate on different levels and sectors of the institution. Thus, under ADVANCE, institutions have developed plans that combine interventions of multiple types and that act on multiple parts of the institutional system.

Here, we present three brief case studies of ADVANCE IT projects as they were planned and implemented at specific campuses. These are examples of how dif-

ferent institutions combined multiple interventions into an overall change portfolio. The case studies show how the institutional context influenced each project,
how each team identified core problems for STEM women faculty on their own
campus, what interventions they chose to pursue, how they designed and implemented those interventions, and how the chosen interventions succeeded in their
context, singly and combined. If the strategies detailed in chapters 3–6 are the
menu of offerings, then these case studies represent each diner's order.

The cases presented here are taken from a larger set of 15 case studies, all based
on data collected in 2009–2010 as the Institutional Transformation projects supported in the first two rounds of ADVANCE funding were ending and we could
begin to see what they had accomplished and learned. As described in appendix
B, we gathered documents and conducted interviews with project leaders. During
five site visits conducted in 2011–2012, we interviewed many faculty members,
administrators, and staff connected to the local ADVANCE work. Direct quotations in the case studies are taken from these documents and interview transcripts. This source material was organized, analyzed, and synthesized by our research team, and each case study was then reviewed and approved by its institutional
team, whose members corrected some errors of fact and offered helpful clarifica-
tions. Teams were also invited to provide an update on their work through late 2014,
and many elected to do so. Their comments emphasize the long time frame that is
needed to achieve some types of change. We also discuss the variety of models for
sustaining and institutionalizing ADVANCE programming after grant funding
ends—which may suggest ways to incorporate this programming into the regular operations of the institution from the start.

These case studies summarize major features of each project but do not provide
a detailed history. Often, more extensive information is available on the institution's ADVANCE project website or is documented in the project's publications.
Each case study is organized with a common structure:

- *Identifying details* note the institution's name, location, ADVANCE IT
  award dates, and leadership team.
- *Key elements of the overall change strategy* outline the goals and design of
  the ADVANCE project and indicate its theory of change, whether
  explicitly stated or as extracted by the research team.
- *Relevant elements in the institutional context* are the particular features that
  influenced the project team's identification of the problems on which to
  focus, the choice of interventions to address those problems, and the

success of these interventions. We also include some general institutional features based on the Carnegie Classification of Institutions of Higher Education (n.d.; see also Indiana University Center for Postsecondary Research, 2018).

- *Scope* identifies the disciplines, departments, and faculty audiences addressed by the project. Because ADVANCE is a program offered by the National Science Foundation, the scope of projects was limited to disciplines supported by the NSF for the duration of the award and implemented in varied ways that reflected each campus's context.
- *Program elements* are the major components and activities of the ADVANCE Institutional Transformation project.
- *Outcomes* include the key results of the project, especially changes in women's representation and advancement, campus climate, and institutionalization of ADVANCE programs. These are drawn from institutional data, evaluation reports, and interviews, and may include both positive outcomes and areas where progress was less readily achieved or measured.
- *Research team observations* are analytical insights from our research team. They highlight strengths or challenges of the project and areas of focus or difference from other projects in the ADVANCE community.
- *Project team observations* include comments from the institution's ADVANCE team, if they chose to offer any, on the status, outcomes, and institutionalization of their work as of 2014 and updated by some in 2019.
- *Further reading* provides references to websites, published papers, and other resources for learning more about the ADVANCE work at a specific institution.

To highlight a range of approaches, models, and outcomes for institutional change efforts, we chose Case Western Reserve University in Cleveland, Ohio; the University of Texas at El Paso; and the University of Wisconsin–Madison. Like any small set of examples, these three cases do not show every variation, but they do represent different types of institutions in the US higher education landscape: private, public regional, and public flagship universities, and larger and smaller universities. Due to their different histories and missions, gender inequities manifest somewhat differently in each organization's context. The cases thus illustrate different emphases—on policy, practice, or leadership development; on recruiting or retaining women—and different approaches to institutionalizing their ADVANCE efforts. Together, they highlight a range of possible approaches and raise questions for readers to consider in their own contexts.

Our conclusions about the affordances and limitations of these models are derived from our close, comparative study of many institutions. Readers may review other examples at the StratEGIC Toolkit website: 12 additional written case studies from Cohorts 1–2 of ADVANCE IT awards have a similar format (they can be found under "Institutional Portfolios"), and 11 video vignettes introduce a set of institutions from Cohorts 3–6, initially awarded in 2006–2012 (see appendix A for a full list of awardees). These additional examples further illustrate the range of ways that institutional teams have perceived the challenges of gender equity at their own institution and designed approaches to addressing them.

Case Study 1

Case Western Reserve University
ADVANCE IT project: Academic Careers in Engineering
and Science (ACES)
Cleveland, Ohio

Dates of grant: September 2003–August 2008 (Cohort 2)
PI: Lynn Singer
Co-PIs: John Angus, Mary Barkley, Diana Bilimoria, Donald Feke,
Hunter Peckham
Project coordinator: Amanda Shaffer

Key Elements of the Overall Change Strategy

ACES was a multifaceted initiative to accomplish "institutional transformation that would lead to increased transparency and accountability as well as more equitable practices, policies, procedures, and structures and increased participation of women science and engineering (S&E) faculty at all levels and in leadership." The change theory was not explicit, but we infer some core ideas:

- Change is accomplished through a mix of grassroots and top-down initiatives that make policies and practices more equitable, create opportunities for women to succeed, and educate everyone to improve the climate.
- Departments are key workplace units that shape faculty work lives, and thus they are the best places to reach faculty.

- Leaders of departments and schools are key people in setting a tone, controlling and distributing resources, developing and executing plans, and maintaining accountability. For this reason, the knowledge, attitudes, and empowerment of these leaders are key targets of the change initiative.

Relevant Elements in the Institutional Context

- Prior work included an institutional self-study of resource allocation as well as focus groups of women. These data revealed low morale among women faculty and identified some serious issues around equity and climate. Before the award, Case Western had recently established the President's Advisory Council on Women and the Flora Stone Mather Center for Women as "a central hub of communication, education, research, and programming."
- Case Western Reserve was the first private university to receive an ADVANCE IT award. This was important, interviewees suggested, because at a private institution, there is less access to data and less required transparency than in public institutions.
- Case Western Reserve is situated on an urban campus in the US Midwest. Follow-up work under the NSF ADVANCE PAID (Partnerships for Adaptation, Implementation and Dissemination) and PLAN (Partnerships for Learning and Adaptation Networks) awards has extended to other research universities in northeastern Ohio and Pennsylvania.
- The project experienced extensive turnover of members of the upper administration during the grant period; there was also a financial crisis and votes of no confidence in the president and provost. The ADVANCE team reported greater success in colleges where leadership was stable and less success in those where it was not.
- Carnegie classification: private, nonprofit doctoral university with very high research activity. Comprehensive programs with medical/veterinary school. Enrollment in 2017 was ~12,000 students, majority graduate.

Scope of ACES

Departmental. The ADVANCE award supported 31 departments in NSF-funded fields from four colleges. Faculty access to ACES programs was provided to a few departments at a time, as each department was phased in over a four-year period.

Demographic. In addition to its focus on women, the project sought to increase the recruitment of minority faculty and students. Some resources were developed to support faculty from groups marginalized in other ways, such as LGBT, Jewish, Black, and Latinx faculty. Men could participate in some program offerings.

Program Elements

The main efforts of ACES focused on faculty development, faculty recruitment, and improvement of transparency, communication, and leadership in institutional processes and policies. Data-gathering efforts were used to engage key players as well as to gather information.

FACULTY DEVELOPMENT

- Executive coaching for individual women faculty was intended to help people to "achieve professional and organizational goals, and to undertake positive change" in their units. Hotline coaching for women enabled them to address emergent (or urgent) issues or opportunities.
- A formal mentoring program was established, but it met with resistance and was underused. It was replaced by informal and peer mentoring opportunities, organized by college.
- Opportunity grants to women faculty aimed to improve their chances of career success, seed new or hard-to-fund projects, and address timeout and work/life issues in women's careers.
- New awards were established for women leaders, and they were recognized at an annual celebration of women's accomplishments. A distinguished lecturer series brought to campus women leaders in STEM, who presented scientific work and also offered personal narratives of their career trajectories.
- Leadership development included the annual Provost's Leadership Retreat, which is ongoing, and individualized executive coaching of chairs and deans. Chairs attended departmental leadership workshops held at the University of Washington (see Strategy 4).
- Department grants funded climate-related initiatives of the awarded department's choosing.

FACULTY RECRUITMENT AND HIRING

- Efforts to improve the search process included direct work with search committees to strengthen the recruiting of women and diversify the pool; increased accountability for deans in signing off on the candidate pool; training for chairs on reducing bias in searches; improved data gathering on pool diversity; and cultural competency training for all faculty. Much of the training and support was done by the new faculty diversity specialist, a role that was later elevated and made permanent.

- Work to attract diverse faculty included a local partner-hiring network, family leave policies, and welcome packets about local resources and opportunities for specific faculty groups. The faculty diversity officer met with candidates, and searches included informal meetings with women faculty who were not on the search committee.
- Efforts to encourage diverse scholars to enter academic careers included a minority faculty exchange program with minority-serving institutions, which provided students with role models who are successful minority faculty and strengthened minority student persistence, and summer research positions for students from marginalized groups. Some career activities were directed to postdocs and graduate students. Efforts such as these to build the so-called pipeline were permitted under early ADVANCE solicitations, but not in later rounds (see Laursen & De Welde, 2019).

EQUITY, TRANSPARENCY, AND ACCOUNTABILITY IN INSTITUTIONAL PROCESSES

- Case Western formalized several previously informal policies on automatic tenure-clock stoppage, family leave, dual-career hires, and domestic partners (despite the fact that the state banned same-sex marriage at the time).
- Consistent, locally customized communication efforts about ADVANCE addressed varied constituencies across campus, including individual departments and chairs.
- Data-gathering efforts were improved in several areas related to faculty diversity, and the team developed ways of feeding data back to those who can act on them, such as presenting reports on faculty diversity at the annual Provost's Leadership Retreat.
- The accountability of chairs and deans was strengthened by setting specific diversity goals for each unit, and then including these goals in the annual review of the chair or dean. Deans were given the authority to approve search pools before candidates could be invited to campus.

Outcomes

- The trends in numbers of women faculty members were positive but college-dependent, showing increases in the numbers of STEM women in the College of Arts and Sciences and the College of Engineering, but decreases in their numbers in the Colleges of Medicine and Management. This result reflects an increase in the proportions of women in hiring pools and among those hired, and also reflects the variability in the opportunity to hire (e.g., there were more hires in engineering than in medicine). The College of Management suffered overall cuts in faculty size during this time, so for this college remaining steady was seen as a win.

- There were more women chairs in arts and sciences and in engineering, and there were some successes in advancing women to higher rank and into endowed chairs.
- Climate measures were mixed; some improved and others declined from 2004 to 2007. Data from the COACHE (Collaborative on Academic Careers in Higher Education) survey indicated that pre-tenure faculty were less satisfied than a similar group at peer institutions. Informal observations suggested that women's morale improved and overall gender equity awareness increased.
- Salary equity improved with help from specific administrative efforts to remedy disparities identified in the institutional self-study.
- Institutionalization was strong in some areas, mixed in others. Policies were formalized, and hiring procedures were strengthened and formalized with support from people in permanent positions in the provost's office and in two schools. Leaders' accountability and institutional data collection became stronger. Several of the faculty-level activities, such as workshops, networking events, and celebrations, were made permanent at the Flora Stone Mather Center for Women.

Research Team Observations

- The team was strong and stable despite institutional changes, including the PI's promotion to interim provost. This stability seems to have been a positive force in communicating with departments and engaging pockets of resistance.
- Colleges at Case Western Reserve are fairly autonomous, which may explain the project's emphasis on formalizing and making transparent the processes and policies that shape faculty life.
- Hiring was a major focus, while tenure and promotion were not formally addressed in the initial phase.

- Formal activities focused on structures and processes rather than on cultural change. Some culturally focused activities did take place, particularly through a male allies group, department grants, and the dean's fellows for collegiality. Several of these were later, spontaneous additions to the project portfolio in response to emerging needs.

Project Team Observations

Many activities developed under ACES were sustained under the banner of ACES+, including faculty opportunity grants, executive coaching, and the Provost's Leadership Retreat. Other processes initiated under ACES continue under the Office of Academic and Faculty Affairs and the Office for Inclusion, Diversity and Equal Opportunity, including bias workshops for search committee members and workshops for administrators who oversee searches. Data collection and communication efforts remain important: for example, a faculty climate survey was initiated with analyses of gender and ethnicity, and it is now institutionalized to occur every three years, with findings shared on the university's website. Annual gender salary analyses and periodic faculty climate surveys have also been institutionalized.

Lessons learned at Case Western have been extended and adapted to other contexts through the IDEAL and IDEAL-N networks. As a result of the award, team members published a book (Bilimoria & Liang, 2012) and several chapters and articles (Bilimoria et al., 2007; Bilimoria, Joy, & Liang, 2008; Bilimoria et al., 2013; Bilimoria & Singer, 2019; Bilimoria & Stewart, 2009; Jordan & Bilimoria, 2007; Liang & Bilimoria, 2007).

FURTHER READING

The ACES+ website describes its current work, including specific programs and activities that have been sustained since NSF funding ended. The "History" section documents some of the project's activities under the original NSF ADVANCE award. http://www.case.edu/admin/aces.

The Collaborative on Academic Careers in Higher Education (COACHE) offers research-based surveys of faculty job satisfaction, which are intended to help academic leaders in diagnosing issues that reduce the job satisfaction and retention of an excellent and diverse faculty. https://coache.gse.harvard.edu.

Singer, L., et al. (2019). IDEAL: Institutions Developing Excellence in Academic Leadership: Equity in STEM: Disciplinary differences and contexts. Retrieved from https://ssrn.com/abstract=3344656.

Case Study 2

University of Texas at El Paso
ADVANCE IT project: UTEP ADVANCE
El Paso, Texas

Dates of grant: September 2003–February 2010 (Cohort 2)
PI: Evelyn Posey
Co-PIs: Elizabeth Anthony, Ann Gates, Christine Reimers, Patricia
Witherspoon

Key Elements of the Overall Change Strategy

This project identified two main barriers to women's representation: institutional impediments, especially shortfalls in guidance, role models, and support, and issues in balancing family needs with the demands of an academic career. These obstacles are well documented in the literature, and they were locally identified issues of prominence. The team at UTEP tackled these barriers through three strands of activity:

- recruitment and policy initiatives to develop a diverse faculty and ensure that all are fairly treated
- faculty development to inform faculty, help them acculturate to the university, and guide them in developing and carrying out a holistic career plan
- collaborative leadership to improve climate, develop faculty leaders, and share best practices by engaging faculty members and departments

The strands were coordinated but separately led. While the set of activities undertaken was not necessarily novel, the three-strand design assigned a rationale and leadership responsibility for each. There was little focus on implicit bias; rather, the focus was on setting a positive atmosphere where all can succeed.

Relevant Elements in the Institutional Context

- Historically a mining and metallurgy school, UTEP remains strong in STEM fields. The campus emphasis on engineering was one factor accounting for low proportions of women at the onset of the project.
- The campus is a regionally focused research university with a strong sense of mission to its local community and its Hispanic students, who

are 75% Mexican American. It is the only US research university with a majority Hispanic population and one of six NSF-designated Model Institutions for Excellence because of its success in graduating STEM students from underrepresented groups.

- An evaluator described the campus as "lean": salaries are low and teaching loads high. Pressure to demonstrate research productivity and bring in grant funding has risen in recent years as UTEP seeks to become a tier 1 institution in the University of Texas system.
- UTEP's president during the ADVANCE period, Diana Natalicio, had served more than 25 years. Natalicio was known for her high interest in the regional mission of the campus and nationally recognized for her leadership on diversity and inclusion.
- Carnegie classification: public, nonprofit doctoral university with high research activity; the rating has increased to "very high" since the time of the grant. Comprehensive doctoral programs with no medical/veterinary school. Enrollment in 2017 was ~25,000 students, majority undergraduate.

Scope of UTEP ADVANCE

Departmental. The project addressed 18 STEM departments in four colleges, including social science and business fields supported by the NSF.

Demographic. Many activities targeted women; some included men. UTEP ADVANCE made a special effort to involve Hispanic faculty and to include international faculty in its gender diversity efforts, noting the importance of these groups in faculty composition and as role models for the university's students.

Program Elements

Activities were organized under three strands. One centered on institutional policy, which is subdivided here into efforts on recruitment and on retention. Two other strands focused on building faculty capacities.

POLICY AND PRACTICE AROUND FACULTY RECRUITMENT

A variety of activities addressed transparency and equity in institutional recruitment processes. Four faculty fellows (one in each college) worked on recruitment and retention issues. These positions were formalized as associate deans for faculty affairs, with a counterpart position in the provost's office. A dual-career hiring policy was formulated and assistance given to individual couples; this task became the purview of the human resources office. Some grant funds were used to facilitate dual-career hires. The HR office also distributed the search committee manual and maintained oversight of search processes and pool diversity. Departments could request extra funds to interview a well-ranked woman candidate. ADVANCE contributions to faculty start-up packages led to a broader examination of these packages for inequity, and more transparent practices were put in place to ensure equity in start-up when hires are made.

POLICY AND PRACTICE AROUND FACULTY RETENTION

Third-year reviews of pre-tenure faculty were instituted in all four colleges, and a tenure-clock extension policy was approved. A brochure was developed to publicize and explain the family leave policy.

FACULTY DEVELOPMENT

These activities included a mix of efforts to develop future institutional leaders and to support individual women's career advancement. An intensive, cohort-based career development program enrolled more than 50 faculty to design integrated career plans and develop leadership skills. Formal coaching reached most pre-tenure women faculty; it was later opened to all pre-tenure faculty. A grants program directed resources to individual faculty for scholarly development and assisted with start-up funding for newly hired women. One-off talks and lunches were used to share information and promote networking.

COLLABORATIVE LEADERSHIP

These activities focused on giving faculty members ways to have impact on their own workplaces, directing conversations toward solutions rather than problems, and drawing on people's ideas and expertise. Chair development sessions were offered, and chairs' input was sought. Focus groups and faculty forums provided input and fostered connections. This program continued through the university's Sam Donaldson Center for Communication Studies.

Collectively, these activities engaged what appears to be a high fraction of the faculty. Project leaders made extensive efforts to communicate with stakeholders, especially internal stakeholders: faculty members, chairs, deans, departments, and offices with relevant specialties. Substantial data-gathering efforts were carried out, and several of these processes were institutionalized as long-term campuswide monitoring.

Outcomes

- During the award period, 38% of tenure-track faculty hires in STEM were women. UTEP ADVANCE found that women candidates were very competitive if they were invited to interview: if 33% of a UTEP on-campus interview pool were women, there was a 57% probability that the first job offer would go to a woman.
- A dozen dual-career hires were made.
- The overall proportion of women in STEM fields rose by half compared to pre-ADVANCE years, when these proportions were quite steady. There were increases in the number of women at all ranks in departments served by ADVANCE. Among the women hired, 31% were Hispanic.
- Climate survey results indicated positive changes in women's perception of the general institutional climate and in men's awareness of diversity issues; gender-based gaps in perceptions decreased (see Ryabov & Wang, 2011). The survey also indicated positive changes in faculty satisfaction with hiring and with tenure and promotion processes. Some comments suggested the campus was developing a culture of mentoring, where mentoring is seen as being of value to all and not remedial (see also Strategy 12).
- Some sustained practices emerged from policy, recruitment, and data collection work. At the end of the grant period, all policies were formalized and in use, except for the dual-career policy, which was not formally applied because of a lack of funding to support it.

Research Team Observations

- The project was thoughtfully constructed and carried out. The team chose key strategies that reached high numbers of faculty members, providing sufficient intensity without targeting extensive resources toward a few people.
- Several aspects of the project were attentive to the local culture and demographics, including a qualitative research study of Latina STEM faculty (Ryabov & Witherspoon, 2008) and very successful efforts to hire Latina faculty members. Efforts to institute partner hiring and to communicate work/life policies addressed potential hires' concerns about moving to El Paso and sought to establish and communicate a welcoming atmosphere.
- Faculty at UTEP had a high consciousness of the institutional mission and a seriousness about diversity. ADVANCE was described as adding gender

to the preexisting diversity conversation on campus—a next step, rather than a first step, in campus discussions of equity.

- The UTEP team reached out to ADVANCE projects at several other institutions to draw on existing resources or collaboratively develop some activities.
- Institutionalization has distributed program elements and responsibilities to various campus entities rather than keeping them united under the ADVANCE banner. The project team noted that this decentralization made it more difficult to track the ongoing evolution and impact of the program.

FURTHER READING

The UTEP ADVANCE website documents the project's activities under the NSF ADVANCE award. https://www.utep.edu/nsfadvance.

Posey, E., et al. (2019). NSF ADVANCE Institutional Transformation for faculty diversity: Equity in STEM: Measurements, methodologies, and metrics for research and evaluation. Retrieved from https://ssrn.com/abstract=3344655.

Ryabov, I., & Wang, G.-Z. (2011). Assessing academic climate change in gender diversity in the areas of science and engineering. *Journal of Women & Minorities in Science & Engineering*, 17(4), 371–388.

Ryabov, I., & Witherspoon, P. D. (2008). Diverse pathways to the PhD: A study of women faculty in the sciences and engineering at a Hispanic-serving institution. *Journal of Women & Minorities in Science & Engineering*, 14(3), 225–243.

Case Study 3

University of Wisconsin–Madison
ADVANCE IT project: Women in Science & Engineering
   Leadership Institute (WISELI)
Madison, Wisconsin

   Dates of grant: January 2002–June 2007 (Cohort 1)
   PI: Molly Carnes
   Co-PI: Jo Handelsman
   Executive and research director: Jennifer Sheridan

Key Elements of the Overall Change Strategy

The Women in Science & Engineering Leadership Institute was established as a centralized, visible administrative structure with a mission to address impediments to women's academic advancement and to make the concerns of women engineers and scientists more visible within the university. WISELI sought "to answer two questions: What are the barriers impeding the participation and advancement of women in science and engineering? How can we eliminate or overcome these barriers?"

The original proposal did not espouse an explicit theory of change, but there was some thought about what levers would or would not result in desired change. Over time, the project incorporated a "stages of change" model that recognized the psychological adjustments involved in making a major change and that compared the transformation of institutions to individual transformations, such as stopping smoking (Carnes, Handelsman, & Sheridan, 2005). Areas such as individual leadership development and mentoring were thought to be well addressed on campus already and thus were not targeted. The project developed a focus on unconscious bias, since evaluation data from its workshops persuaded the team that providing new knowledge about unconscious bias made a difference in participants' attitudes and thus potentially could influence their behavior. A sizable research and evaluation effort treated the university as a living laboratory for studying gender equity, implementing solutions to problems, and assessing their impact.

Relevant Elements in the Institutional Context

- The large size of the institution led the leaders to decide to work with 70 science and engineering departments in the biological and physical sciences rather than take a narrower approach.
- The history of decentralization at UW was felt to be an advantage, since the project leaders did not need permission or sign-offs from senior administrators to take steps toward action or experiment with new ideas. On the other hand, the decentralized environment made measuring the effects of different interventions more challenging.
- Several work/life policies and programs for women already existed on campus, including mentoring and childcare programs, policies such as tenure-clock extension for family leave, and a process for salary equity review. Thus, the project could experiment with and shape new initiatives beyond basic policies.
- A campus culture of strong faculty governance and leadership played a role in how the team structured WISELI programs. For example, workshops were organized around faculty-to-faculty peer teaching, guided by the assumption that academics value interacting with other faculty members.

- The support of the provost's office was important, but overall WISELI was seen as a faculty-driven initiative, which is consistent with the culture and history of the university.
- Carnegie classification: public, nonprofit research university with very high research activity. Comprehensive doctoral programs with a medical/veterinary school. Enrollment in 2017 was ~43,000 students, majority undergraduate.

Scope of the ADVANCE Initiative

The WISELI project focused on biological and physical sciences (including engineering) faculty and staff in the six schools with the largest faculties in these areas: the Colleges of Engineering, Letters and Science, and Agricultural and Life Sciences, and the Schools of Veterinary Medicine, Pharmacy, and Medicine and Public Health. Overall, the project targeted approximately 70 units and 1,200 faculty.

Program Elements

Significant components of WISELI's work included:

- *Hiring workshops.* Originally developed for the chairs of faculty search committees, a workshop series called Searching for Excellence and Diversity was successful in guiding faculty searches, and it was then extended to all members of search committees. WISELI now offers train-the-trainer workshops to help other institutions develop their own workshops on this topic, which brings in revenue to support ongoing WISELI programs.
- *Departmental climate workshops.* These workshops brought together groups of chairs to survey their departments and use the survey results to identify issues and develop plans to enhance their department's working environment. Almost all physical sciences departments participated as did about one-third of departments in the biological sciences. Chairs reported these workshops to be very useful, and departments that resurveyed showed improvements. However, campus-wide climate survey data did not always show immediate positive impacts in individual units.
- *Life cycle professorships.* This program provided funding to support faculty women and men at critical points when life events were negatively affecting their scholarly careers. These very popular grants were ultimately

funded with private donations (although the university stepped in one year when the endowment was hit hard by the economy). The Vilas Life Cycle Professorship Program has been honored by the ACE/Sloan Award for Faculty Career Flexibility, and versions of this program have been adopted at other institutions.

- *Increasing women's visibility.* Grants for "celebrating women in science and engineering" enabled groups, including graduate students, to bring women speakers to campus for departmental brown-bag events or lecture series, thus increasing women's visibility. This program brought 66 women to campus between 2002 and 2006, and it continues with support from various colleges and schools. For many years, WISELI hosted an annual distinguished lecture, investing its effort in a single, high-profile event instead of many smaller events, based on the team's observation that attendance at their campus-wide events lessened over time.

- *Evaluation and research.* The program gathered data on gender equity indicators and campus climate; evaluated campus programs for their effectiveness in enhancing gender equity; and studied topics such as departmental climate, why women leave the faculty, and the efficacy of appointment changes from academic staff to faculty.

Outcomes

- As of the end of the grant period, the proportion of women faculty had increased in biological and physical sciences departments (15.3% in 2000 to 20% in 2006). Women's presence as chairs in these fields rose from 4.5% in 2000 to 14.7% in 2006. Men's and women's salaries were approximately the same after controlling for rank and division. However, women were still leaving the university at higher rates than men, and there was no change in the number of women directing centers or institutes.

- Workshops for members of faculty hiring committees led to increases in offers to and hiring of women candidates. There was also evidence of increased satisfaction among the new hires and of increased awareness of climate issues more generally.

- In the short term, evidence about the impact of WISELI activities on attitudes was mixed. Overall data from campus-wide climate surveys showed that faculty perceptions of the climate were more positive, but women as a group, and separately faculty of color as a group, reported experiences of a more negative climate. Participation in WISELI events was associated with more negative views of institutional climate, which the team viewed as signaling greater recognition and awareness of the issues faced by underrepresented faculty. Similarly, positive perceptions of departmental climate declined among chairs who took part in the climate workshops, as they became more aware of climate-related issues.

- The program is well institutionalized, as WISELI became very visible on campus and nationally. It is housed in the College of Engineering, and its space and staff are funded by various UW colleges and through other grants. Project leaders tracked which colleges used what percentage of WISELI resources, which helped them to secure funding from those colleges to sustain WISELI. Some activities are revenue-generating since the institute provides other campuses with consulting, workshops, publications, and resources on issues for women in science and engineering.

Research Team Observations

- The project demonstrated how a clear and selective focus on addressing knowledge and beliefs about hiring can serve as a means to influence institutional culture more broadly. Blunt measures, such as climate surveys, did not always show these changes in the short term, but the team's research over the long term has offered evidence that change has taken root in both attitudes and behaviors.

- Creating WISELI outside the central administration enabled the project leaders to have considerable autonomy in how they organized their work. They sought to craft a faculty-led project where, they explained, faculty members could talk with other faculty members. The role of the provost's office was to provide support but not to intrude or to manage the project. The project did not identify as needs, nor seek to address, formal issues of institutional policy or procedures, which would have required more involvement of administrators holding specific institutional roles.

- The team's final report offered thoughtful analysis of some things that did not work well: initially expecting faculty to attend many meetings, focusing some initial workshops on single departments, and trying to encourage changes for women from non-tenure-track appointments to tenure-stream appointments. These comments demonstrate the importance of an experimental approach to change projects that makes use of formative evaluation and responsive decision-making in identifying and acting on the successes and failures of project initiatives.

Project Team Observations

Since the end of Wisconsin's ADVANCE IT award in 2007, WISELI has continued to implement all of the major initiatives begun with the initial award and to
innovate in research and programming to promote the advancement of women in
academic science and engineering at the University of Wisconsin–Madison and
nationally. WISELI has disseminated the team's copyrighted "Searching for Excellence and Diversity" hiring workshop to more than 30 colleges and universities
via on-site train-the-trainer workshops. WISELI also worked with nine universities to disseminate a workshop called Enhancing Department Climate.

In 2009, WISELI was awarded a grant from the National Institutes of Health
(NIH) to create a new offering entitled Breaking the Bias Habit. Presented at the
department level, this two-and-a-half-hour workshop was shown in an experimental study to positively affect awareness of bias, motivation to act without bias,
and actions to reduce bias (Carnes et al., 2015). Some measures of climate at the
department level improved for departments that received the workshop, and both
hiring of women faculty and retention of men faculty in the experimental departments increased (Devine et al., 2017). Detailed workshop materials and video
clips for facilitators are available on the WISELI website, and WISELI is available
to administer the workshop on other campuses, which the team has done for more
than a dozen institutions.

WISELI is continuing to research the effectiveness of the Breaking the Bias
Habit approach with an NIH-funded multisite trial entitled Bias Reduction in Internal Medicine (BRIM). More information on that study is available at https://
brim.medicine.wisc.edu.

FURTHER READING

WISELI's website provides details on its programs, resources, and reports, and it includes
an extensive publication list. https://wiseli.wisc.edu.

Lessons from the Case Studies

The institutional features highlighted in these three cases show that an institution's context—its history, mission, location, and culture—shape what is important for a change project to address and which approaches are more likely to
succeed. Many more examples can be found in the institutional portfolios available in the online StratEGIC Toolkit. For example, Wisconsin's identity as a ma-

jor research university led to a plan that was strongly grounded in applying and producing research. UTEP's approach arose out of its mission to serve the US-Mexico border region of West Texas. To benefit UTEP's predominantly Latinx student body, it was important to recruit and retain Latina faculty as role models and leaders. UTEP had a strong preexisting institutional narrative about the value of ethnic diversity, but the team identified work to be done around gender diversity. Traditions of strong, centralized leadership at UTEP enabled a centralized project design, while Wisconsin, a large and decentralized campus, chose to work with departments. At Case Western Reserve, a private institution, a lack of transparency was identified as obscuring inequities in status and salary for women, so the ADVANCE project emphasized gathering, sharing, and using data, and making processes and leadership decisions more transparent and open.

Two other features are evident in these cases: contextual differences shaped not only general approaches but specific programs in these ADVANCE projects, and multiple programs were combined to work on multiple fronts. UTEP, like other more rural institutions we studied, made particular effort to lower the barriers for dual-career academic couples to accept jobs at the university. At the same time, the ADVANCE team worked to reduce implicit bias in hiring and offered incentives to departments to encourage them to invite well-qualified women for campus interviews. Other ADVANCE efforts supported women after they were hired—through the mentoring of individuals and through policy changes to formalize early, pre-tenure feedback—so that the faculty members they had worked hard to recruit could succeed and thrive. And collaborative leadership programming sought to engage more senior faculty in supporting early-career faculty and improving work environments.

With traditions of strong faculty governance, Wisconsin emphasized faculty-to-faculty communication about the research base behind implicit bias as a means to shift attitudes, which would then influence hiring and evaluation behaviors and improve climate in departments. Members of hiring committees and department heads were the initial targets as key influencers with the potential to bring others along. At the same time as it targeted cultural practices, WISELI offered other programs to support individual women. At this campus, the identified needs were not met by faculty development, but by providing a means to obtain bridging support to maintain or restart scholarship in the face of life events.

At Case Western Reserve, data showed persistent low morale and equity concerns among women, but departments were strong and independent, and college deans had high autonomy: a singular, top-down approach would not be welcomed.

The ACES team was strategic in selecting multilayered approaches, including leadership development to strengthen the knowledge and skills of department chairs and deans. Accountability strategies were set in place by the provost to value this development, empower the deans and in turn the chairs, and hold units accountable for progress on equity and inclusion. At the same time, opportunity grants and hotline coaching supported the professional growth and formal advancement of individual women, and celebrations of women's accomplishments raised their visibility campus-wide. In all three of these institutions, strong communication and broad engagement of faculty members were essential to securing successes.

As these cases show, the scope of ADVANCE Institutional Transformation projects was initially defined by the NSF's ADVANCE program solicitation, which included disciplines from science, technology, engineering, and mathematics and the social and behavioral sciences (SBS), which are supported by the NSF more generally. In these fields, the issues of women's representation and experience are particularly salient and visible, so STEM and SBS departments served well as laboratories for developing and refining interventions. However, recognizing that these issues were by no means limited to particular departments, many institutions broadened the reach of ADVANCE-derived programming when they institutionalized their efforts after NSF funding ended. For example, Case Western Reserve continued some of its ADVANCE programs from the deputy provost's office to serve faculty from all units. Similarly, the University of Michigan (Cohort 1) formalized its ADVANCE program as a stand-alone center and opened programs to all colleges and departments, with institutional support. In many institutions, leaders whose skills and vision developed under ADVANCE have continued to lead equity work, an example of how capacity building has been another lasting impact of the grant-funded project. Because of the pioneering work of ADVANCE institutions, the research-based guidance we offer about these strategies can be deployed across disciplines—guided by local data and shaped by local resources.

These examples also reflect a variety of approaches to sustaining programs and measuring their impact. For example, WISELI continued at the University of Wisconsin as a self-supporting research unit, while UTEP folded insights from ADVANCE programs into the work of other offices. It is clear from our research that there is no single right answer for how to sustain or institutionalize ADVANCE work; it is also clear that planning for sustainability should start early, because the work of transformation is not complete after a five-year grant. New policies and practices take time to prepare and enact; cultures are slow to change; and some measures of impact do not respond quickly. For example, at the University of Michigan, cumulative measures from repeated faculty climate surveys began to show real and positive impact on the experiences of women in STEM departments more than a decade after ADVANCE began (Flaherty, 2014; UM ADVANCE, 2013). Moreover, work to educate faculty about the issues for women may first yield a drop in faculty perceptions of the climate as men become educated about the problem and realize that the situation is less rosy than they thought (Laursen, 2009; Nielsen et al., 2005). This is also the case for white faculty members' perception of the climate for colleagues of other races. At Texas A&M (Cohort 5), Taylor and colleagues (2017) developed an analytical approach to connect change in climate measures at the department level to the department's participation in ADVANCE, taking advantage of the large samples available at their institution and a change model that engaged STEM faculty in ADVANCE leadership across multiple initiatives. Their findings are useful in demonstrating a cumulative impact of TAMU's multifaceted program, but also in revealing the broader implication that progress is uneven in systemic change initiatives.

Another element of the projects' scope is evident in these three cases. In the early years, most institutions did not take an intersectional approach to ADVANCE, nor did the program solicitation invite this orientation: women were treated as a monolithic group, with other identities treated as add-ons (Armstrong & Jovanovic, 2015; Hunt et al., 2012; Laursen & De Welde, 2019). As Jovanovic and Armstrong (2014) described, programs targeted to women have not typically accounted for differences in women's experiences that arise because they also belong to a particular race, ethnicity, sexual orientation, or culture. Thus, programs that do not account for multiple, intersecting identities not only may miss the mark for diverse women but may erase intersectional identities and increase individuals' risk and stress (Armstrong & Jovanovic, 2015; Corneille et al., 2019). UTEP's ADVANCE project was an early exception to this pattern because of its intentional and successful efforts to study the experiences of Latinas in STEM and to recruit them to the UTEP faculty. In their edited volume, De Welde and Stepnick (2015b) offered more examples of the intersectional inequalities faced by women who are Black, parents, lesbians, caring for elders, and more. Women's experiences of campus climate likewise vary among departments and colleges, and this is another reason that it is important to recognize differences in local climate and offer solutions that can adapt to different settings.

Some later ADVANCE institutions initiated exciting approaches that were more explicitly intersectional. For example, at Florida International University (Cohort 8), a high proportion of STEM faculty are international men, and its project aimed at addressing the cultural, racial, and gender biases of this group. ADVANCE work at Jackson State University (Cohort 5), a historically Black institution, sought to foster women's success, especially at mid-career, in a setting where there is a high consciousness of racial diversity and pride but where women's advancement, promotion, and leadership have lagged. At Oregon State University (Cohort 7), intensive training for institutional leaders connected sexism to a more general framework about power dynamics and the systemic oppression of marginalized people. Research by Armstrong and Jovanovic (2015, 2017), also based on ADVANCE IT projects, identified enabling institutional factors for change efforts that fully include women of multiple marginalized identities, especially women of color, and offered guidance on designing change strategies that are intersectional in multipronged and synergistic ways.

Three detailed case studies do not reveal the full range of institutional approaches, programs, and outcomes. Our online StratEGIC Toolkit (www.strategictoolkit.org) offers additional examples of how institutions combined multiple interventions strategically in ways that responded to specific issues for women on their campus and were explicitly designed with the institutional context in mind. The toolkit includes institutional portfolios, similar to these case studies, for several other institutions that received ADVANCE IT awards in Cohorts 1–2 (initially funded in 2001–2004), and video vignettes of several more institutions supported by ADVANCE in Cohorts 3–6 (funded in 2006–2012).

Chapter Nine

Design a Change Portfolio to Advance Equity

INSTITUTIONAL TRANSFORMATION IS challenging and time-consuming and requires a systemic approach to both the change process and the change goals. In this book, we have explained why institutional change to create more inclusive academic workplaces is critically important—for the quality of the lives of the people who work in the academy, for the ability of higher education institutions to fulfill their missions, and for the betterment of society. The talents, insights, and perspectives of people from a wide array of backgrounds and identities are needed to address the daunting problems facing our communities, the nation, and the globe. In support of institutions seeking to build diverse, inclusive, and welcoming academic workplaces, we have offered a set of strategies and interventions drawn from the experiences of institutions that received National Science Foundation ADVANCE Institutional Transformation awards, which have been adapted with success in institutional contexts. Case examples have shown how universities take strategic approaches in their efforts to foster more inclusive workplaces, but each reflects distinctive institutional contexts and characteristics and showcases different ways to construct comprehensive change portfolios.

Having served as consultants and evaluators for several institutions as they prepared and implemented ADVANCE projects, including at our own universities, we are often asked for advice about strategies to include in institutions' proposals for ADVANCE funding or in their plans to move the needle toward goals of inclusivity and diversity. What interventions have other institutions used with good results? In this final chapter, we offer our response and some advice to those who are designing their own change portfolios.

A theme throughout this book is that higher education institutions are complex and multifaceted; thus, plans to effect significant organizational change must account for that complexity. Prior research on change processes and our own study and experiences all indicate that successful transformation processes require a comprehensive, strategic approach that goes beyond replicating the work of other institutions.

In this chapter, we provide suggestions and guidelines for leaders who are committed to the overall goal of institutional transformation in service to inclusive academic workplaces. First, we define what we mean by "taking a strategic approach" to the problem and the context in which this problem and possible interventions are situated. Then we focus on deciding what to do, including the notion of theories of change and the process of selecting strategies and interventions. We discuss implementing the chosen interventions, including the key roles of change leaders, persistence over time, strategic communication, and evaluation. We conclude by discussing the challenge of sustainability.

Taking a Systemic and Strategic Approach to Transformation

We start by identifying the problem; framing what is to be accomplished, solved, or improved; and selecting a set of levers that can be used to address the problem and move the institution toward its goals. This systemic and strategic approach involves recognizing that higher education institutions are complex and multifaceted organizations. Any successful change requires analyzing how the problem affects individual faculty members, students, and staff; determining what elements of the problem are evident at the departmental, college, and institutional levels; and then carefully developing a change strategy that is appropriate for the problem, the institution, and its unique context. It also involves choosing multiple levers for change that work together to affect different levels of the institution in different ways.

Identifying and Framing the Problem

Key to taking a systemic and strategic approach is determining what problem the change process will address. The overall problem considered in this book is the inadequate representation of women and individuals of color in the academy, particularly in STEM fields; the related goal is to increase the recruitment, retention, and success of women faculty in STEM fields. To achieve this goal, we must recognize that women, especially in STEM fields, face a range of challenges, including implicit bias that stymies their advancement, inadequate structures and policies to support them in managing professional and personal responsibilities, infrequent opportunities for visibility and upward mobility, and limited support for growth and development. Identifying which specific challenges are the targets for change in a given situation is an essential step in planning an institutional change endeavor, because choosing the set of specific interventions depends on what problems the institution has decided to address.

A few examples illustrate our point. In deciding how to focus their ADVANCE project, leaders at Jackson State University (Cohort 5) recognized that women faculty of color were isolated and underrepresented as full professors; they did not have the same levels of external funding and research collaborations as their male colleagues did. As a historically Black institution, Jackson State was founded to educate those who had been denied access to higher education, and this heritage remains important to the institution's mission. In recent years, the university has sought to deepen and expand its research mission. To increase women's representation as full professors—and to show students examples of women of color who are successful scholars—women associate professors needed support for research-oriented writing. After clearly articulating this problem, Jackson State leaders took steps to design a program to support STEM women in achieving their professional writing goals and to foster community among women scholars even as these faculty also fulfilled responsibilities as dedicated teachers and mentors.

At Lehigh University (Cohort 5), senior institutional leaders recognized the need to recruit and hire more women faculty. Yet hiring clusters of women or clusters of scholars of color to provide a critical mass in specific departments would be difficult to accomplish in this smaller university, where departments often do not have the number of openings needed to make cluster hires. Guided by research suggesting that women are drawn toward interdisciplinary work (Rhoten & Pfirman, 2007; Van Rijnsoever & Hessels, 2011), the Lehigh team hypothesized that breaking down disciplinary silos and fostering connections across departments might make the university very attractive to women scholars. In Lehigh's institutional culture, departmental boundaries are relatively easy to cross, so the Lehigh team focused on leveraging, highlighting, and supporting the interdisciplinary work already in place in order to attract more women. They recognized another problem too: while early-career faculty were carefully mentored, those at mid-career received little mentoring, even as they were being asked to accept new responsibilities. Identifying this problem led Lehigh leaders to develop strategies for supporting mid-career faculty to gain leadership skills useful both inside the institution and beyond it.

The examples of Jackson State and Lehigh illustrate how institutions can identify specific problems to address within the wider challenge of creating more inclusive and equitable environments.

Analyzing the Context

Context shapes the decision about the problem to be addressed and the choice of strategies and interventions. A comprehensive, thoughtful, and strategic approach to change requires consideration of the particular culture and climate of an institution: its history, including earlier efforts to advance diversity and inclusion; public or private status; rural or urban location; demographics of the faculty; faculty governance structures, including participation in collective bargaining; and the stability, characteristics, and style of senior institutional leadership over recent years. Those planning institutional change projects may ask, for example, how do faculty and administrators interact, and to what extent does a sense of trust and collegiality pervade the campus? How hierarchical is the decision-making process, and who is involved in what kinds of decisions? Where data show different levels of participation by different members of the community, a change project may focus on increasing leadership skills and broadening engagement.

How does geography influence the experiences of women faculty and their partners? Faculty in urban institutions may find that their partners relatively easily secure appropriate employment, while jobs for partners in rural towns may be harder to find. For an institutional transformation project, such geographical aspects of context may shape the choice to include, or not, a focus on dual-career policies.

What values and traditions are important to the institution due to its history, affiliations, or location? How does the institution's size affect the ways community members interact? What are key demographics among the faculty? An institution with many faculty who remain at associate professor rank for long periods may decide to create and implement strategies to guide these advanced mid-career faculty to successful promotion.

In designing their ADVANCE proposal, leaders at the University of Texas at El Paso (Cohort 2) recognized that many women faculty had significant family responsibilities, consistent with cultural traditions in its Mexican American border community. Responding to this important part of the cultural landscape, the ADVANCE leaders worked to ensure that institutional policies, such as leave policies, were family-friendly.

Leaders at Montana State (Cohort 6) also considered key contextual factors in designing their ADVANCE grant, identifying values prevalent in its Rocky Mountain location, such as independence, decentralization, deregulation, and respect for bootstrapping to accomplish their goals. The change leaders then created a university transformation project that respected these elements of local culture. In particular, drawing on theories of relational autonomy and self-determination theory, they identified relatedness, competence, and autonomy as basic human needs that the academic workplace should meet for its faculty. With the backdrop of this contextual analysis, the institutional change leaders designed and evaluated each part of their project in terms of faculty responses to these important human needs (Smith et al., 2017).

What are ways to explore and understand the institutional context? Institutional data on faculty composition, hiring, and promotion can begin to outline some features of context, particularly in comparison with peer institutions. Focus groups, interviews, and climate surveys have been useful tactics as initial work to identify the focus and strategies for a proposed ADVANCE project. Such studies may be designed to determine problems, areas of tension, or concerns in an institution: whether and where faculty with various identities feel included or excluded, comfortable or devalued; what characteristics define the institution at large and shape specific units; what institutional values may undermine commitment to equity, diversity, and social justice; and what issues most concern faculty. Many institutions have made good use of the surveys offered by COACHE (Collaborative on Academic Careers in Higher Education). Repeating these studies regularly provides a means of seeing change over time and measuring progress.

Another way to identify the organizational context and the problems to be addressed is through systematic organizational analysis. One useful approach is to examine the institution through the four frames explained by Bolman and Deal (2017): structural, human resource, political, and symbolic. Each of these frames or lenses guides observers to notice important features of the organization. For example, using a structural lens highlights institutional policies and processes and how they work in the organization: how recruitment occurs, how processes for tenure and promotion operate, and how space is allocated. Analyzing the institution through a human resource lens may highlight the demographics of those who are hired and promoted and their needs for professional development. The political lens draws attention to how power and influence are allocated and used in the academy, such as who serves in leadership roles and receives awards and who may be routinely excluded from such opportunities. The cultural or symbolic lens focuses awareness on the values of the institution and the messages that convey those values. Looking through the cultural lens draws attention to messages about the relative importance of gender equity, the abilities of women as researchers and leaders, and the extent to which their contributions are valued.

Analyzing a university through Bolman and Deal's (2017) frames shows how the institution works and where problems or challenges lie. For example, leaders concerned about low numbers of women scientists and engineers may be guided by the structural lens to ask how many women STEM faculty apply for open positions, how many new scientists graduate each year in the relevant fields, how many are invited to interview, and whether they accept a job offer. If such analysis finds that the issue is not in recruiting scientists to join the institution but in retaining them, solving this problem will require an approach other than a hiring-focused effort. Such analysis, situated in a structural perspective, could help leaders see problematic elements of institutional processes.

Considering the symbolic frame may highlight the messages conveyed within the institution. Do news articles more often elevate the work of male colleagues, or do campus celebrations highlight some community members more than others? Explicit attention to the institution's culture and symbolic messages can deepen understanding of exactly what the problem is that the institution wants to address.

In sum, determining the specific institutional problems to be addressed is an essential step in designing a productive and impactful change process. Identifying key aspects of the institutional culture that may influence the success of a change initiative is an important prerequisite to selecting specific change interventions. Climate studies and institutional analysis using the four lenses suggested by Bolman and Deal (2017) are examples of ways to identify organizational problems that an institution wants to tackle and to understand organizational cultures that will shape the choice and design of strategies to advance gender equity.

Choosing the Strategies and Interventions

With a particular local problem in mind, change leaders sometimes want to decide quickly on specific strategies and interventions to address that problem, perhaps emulating those used at other institutions. However, choosing effective interventions requires consideration of the specific problem, context, and needs of each institution. What are ways to design plans that are appropriate for a specific institutional context?

One useful step is to consider social science theories that offer explanations for human and organizational behavior relevant to the institution's challenges and circumstances. While some leaders believe they should find one theory of change to guide their work, experienced change leaders tend to draw on more than one theory. Indeed, one study of institutional changes to improve undergraduate STEM education (Kezar, 2018) emphasized that effective change processes are informed by multiple theories of change. Theories of change may come directly from the literature on organizational theory, or they may emerge as working understandings of why the problem exists and what interventions might make a difference. Different theories may address the problem at different levels, such as psychosocial theories to address faculty experiences and organizational theories to address institutional practices.

West Virginia University (Cohort 5) provides a useful example of how drawing on more than one theory can be helpful. Consistent with research and theories about the structure of organizations of higher education and of academic work, change leaders at West Virginia University recognized that faculty members spend a great deal of time working within their departments. Departmental practices and policies greatly influence academic life; theory and research on academic work indicate that participation in faculty governance is a key element of how institutions function. Yet these practices and policies may be gendered in ways that are invisible to department members. So the ADVANCE team chose to work on making these processes more effective, for example ensuring that all faculty members participated actively in department meetings and had a voice in decision-making processes. Several theories about the role of departments in higher education institutions, the gendering of organizations, and the importance of engagement for building commitment and equity informed their thinking and design (Bird & Latimer, 2019; Latimer et al., 2014). Specifically articulating the theories that are influencing leaders' thinking can help make expectations and decisions more explicit, and can point to change interventions that follow logically from the theory.

Creating logic models can also help change leaders to select interventions and strategies most relevant to their situations. Logic models are frameworks that show the overall goal of a project and its desired short- and longer-term outcomes in moving toward and ultimately achieving the broader goal (Knowlton & Phillips, 2012). Articulating a logic model can help project teams reach greater clarity about what strategies they will use, why these are appropriate choices, and how they will know if they are making headway. Several key questions can help change teams develop a logic model to guide their work:

- What are the overall goals that the project seeks to achieve?
- What strategies or interventions do leaders believe will help to achieve that goal? Why do we believe these strategies will work? How do various strategies complement each other?
- How will we know if we have been successful? What short-term and longer-term indicators will show progress toward the goal?

Often, the process of developing a change model will help teams recognize that some chosen strategies may not be directly relevant to their goals, or that they need additional strategies to move the institution in the desired direction (e.g., see Hardcastle et al., 2019).

In the end, success in advancing toward a major change goal, such as creating more diverse and inclusive academic workplaces, requires the strategic use of multiple levers for change. Since colleges and universities are complex organizations with multiple parts, deploying multiple well-chosen interventions is likely to be more effective than pursuing one intervention alone. For example, the impact of family-friendly policies is enhanced when coupled with efforts to cultivate a culture that encourages faculty members to use such policies without worrying that they will appear uncommitted to their work. The impact of providing leadership development opportunities for women becomes more profound when tenure and promotion processes include provisions to recognize and value participation in such programs.

Just as Bolman and Deal's (2017) four organizational lenses are useful for analyzing the institution, reflecting on these lenses can also provide some help in designing an effective portfolio of change strategies. A strong set of interventions is likely to address structural, human resource, political, and symbolic issues. For example, having identified a problem with women's advancement into senior roles in the organization, change leaders may choose to review and clarify tenure and promotion policies (addressing structural issues), while also providing faculty development and mentoring support to candidates as they approach promotion and tenure (addressing human resource issues) and offering leadership development to department chairs on mentoring early- and mid-career faculty (addressing political issues by preparing leaders with the power to help effect change). At the same time, change leaders might enhance perceptions of women as disciplinary leaders by highlighting the expertise of visiting scholars—an intervention using the power of symbols. Choosing a set of interventions that together address structural, human resource, political, and symbolic aspects of the problem as it is situated in the organization is an example of taking a strategic and systemic approach toward change goals.

At the same time, single strategies can sometimes influence the organization in multiple ways. Kansas State's (Cohort 2) grant program for women faculty members (Strategy 11) provides an example of a dual impact from an intervention. Early-career women could apply for grants to invite senior colleagues to visit the university and discuss their research—a human resource intervention to strengthen the professional connections of untenured faculty. While visiting, the senior scholar would meet with senior institutional leaders to discuss opportunities for women in their field, and give a public talk, thus serving as a highly visible symbol of the contributions of women scholars.

These examples show how effective change initiatives are built from multiple interventions that are mutually reinforcing and complementary. When strategically chosen, the interventions together address particular institutional problems in various ways and at multiple levels of the organization. Some strategies may support individual faculty members, and others may encourage more congenial departmental environments. Some may change institutional policies and processes to ensure greater equity and fairness, and others may help department chairs and deans shape institutional cultures with greater awareness of how systemic privilege undermines inclusiveness.

Anchoring Strategies for Change

Although we offer guidelines, ideas, and examples to help change leaders select interventions that are strategic and contextually responsive for their institution, we often are pushed to declare which interventions are the most important and impactful. We counsel that strategies should be chosen on the basis of how they address and align with the institution's context and specific change goals, and how as a set they can have a strategic impact. But we also acknowledge that certain strategies have become the core of many change portfolios. Based on our research, three anchoring interventions are especially noteworthy in their impact and seem to link in synergistic ways to other strategies to bring about more equitable and inclusive academic work environments.

The first of these powerful strategies is institutional attention to implicit bias in processes of evaluating faculty. Efforts to expand awareness and understanding of how implicit bias functions to undermine diversity and inclusion, and to embed this awareness in institutional practices, such as hiring and promotion, have been a key element of cultural change at many of the institutions that received ADVANCE grants. So far, the best documented interventions have addressed bias in hiring processes (Strategy 1), but because implicit bias can play a role in many institutional evaluation processes across the span of a career, the ideas are also appropriate in evaluating faculty for tenure, promotion, and institutional awards (Strategy 2), where useful interventions can also be designed. It is crucial not only to educate people who hold evaluation roles, but to give them practical strategies to catch and counter bias and to hold people accountable. However, as chapter 1 details, biased evaluation processes are just one of the barriers to women in the institution, so attention to bias alone is not sufficient to change institutional culture, and this approach must be combined with other strategies suited to the nature and urgency of each institution's issues.

Strengthening institutional leadership at the middle and higher levels of the institution is another intervention that we see as particularly effective in the long run (Strategy 4). For example, creating a group of institutional leaders who understand the issues and are empowered to create more inclusive academic environments can have a strong impact on their units and across campus by integrating change efforts throughout the institution. This strategy may also involve strengthening the leadership skills of women and others from groups that are underrepresented in leadership positions: preparing them to advance in their careers and assume leadership roles if they so choose. The scope of leadership development need not be limited to those interested in formal leadership positions. Such programs also may be used to cultivate people who can lead change efforts; become champions of diversity, equity, and inclusion in their departments; and serve as organizational catalysts for change. It also need not be limited to formal training for leadership; indeed, on-the-job collaborative work as a workshop facilitator, coach, mentor, or co-convener of a working group or policy task force can also serve to develop leadership skills when the faculty member is appropriately supported. This strategy has the potential to make substantial impact across an institution. At the same time, it is often not very visible and its impact may not be obvious, so this approach may work best when combined with other interventions that are seen to have more direct and immediate impacts on faculty lives.

Related to leadership, direct approaches to improving department climate (Strategy 5) did not appear in our data as frequently as some of the other interventions. However, more recent ADVANCE work has further developed this strategy, and we see its considerable potential as a third anchoring strategy. A focus on improving the climate of the department has an impact on all faculty, not only women. Thus, this strategy may have particular appeal in institutions where change leaders perceive that change efforts will be most readily appreciated if they lead to benefits for all.

In addition to these three anchoring strategies, we also observe the strategic benefits of an overarching approach to communication. Developing and sustaining a proactive and comprehensive multichannel communications plan has served ADVANCE IT projects very well. This includes informing faculty, staff, and administrators across the campus and inviting them to participate, engaging with institutional bodies and stakeholder groups that have the potential to assist (or interfere) with the project's work, elevating the visibility and progress of the project as it proceeds, claiming and sharing credit where it is due, and celebrating successes. This is hard and not generally glorious work that requires a good deal of personal time and attention, but it is possible to be strategic in choosing and preparing project ambassadors to interact with different groups, preparing text and online materials that serve multiple purposes, and using events and meetings as opportunities to inform constituencies and make the case for the project and its importance. Approaching communication opportunities as invitations to participate, some projects found help in unexpected quarters. One of our favorite examples is the popular women's basketball coach who helped to raise money for childcare facilities at Utah State (Cohort 2). Strategy 6 offers more ideas about communication.

Our overall message is that selecting the interventions to include in a change plan involves carefully analyzing the context, clarifying the goals to be achieved, and committing to a systemic approach. We have shared our perceptions of some strategies that make productive anchors for institutional change plans. While highlighting these core strategies, however, we emphasize the strategic effects of leveraging a purposefully chosen set of complementary interventions to create a powerful change portfolio. Because the net impact of such a change effort depends on not only the design of initiatives but how they are understood and embraced, effective leaders also recognize the power of an effective communication strategy to build commitment across the institution to the goals and processes of change.

Implementing the Strategic Change Plan

Our research also has yielded insights on how institutions have implemented their plans successfully. Several themes stand out across institutions.

Ensuring the Involvement of Committed, Articulate Leaders

Undertaking an institutional change process requires several kinds of leadership to frame the issues and navigate the process. Successful institutional ADVANCE programs have been led by teams composed of diverse individuals who each bring distinctive talents. Leadership teams often include the project's principal investigator (PI) or director, a project manager, and an executive leadership group or advisory board. Often, the PI is a senior institutional leader, such as a provost, whose presence provides credibility and visibility to the work. The co-PIs may include one or more faculty members or administrators with sufficient time and commitment to navigate the project's daily work and to make connections across campus.

Initiators of ADVANCE projects are often very strategic in how they construct their leadership teams, ensuring that the range of knowledge and skills needed for effecting change is explicitly and purposefully represented on the team. Team members may offer many assets: institutional knowledge, vision, creativity, communication and collaboration skills, ability to connect people across disciplines and fields, experience in institutional administration, connection to institutional governance bodies, scholarly or practical knowledge of how higher education institutions work, energy, persistence, or collegiality. No single leader will have all these qualities, but a leadership team can together have these skills.

Examples of how the composition of leadership teams directly and strategically relates to success in change projects abound across ADVANCE projects. At Case Western Reserve University, the active involvement of a senior woman administrator in the leadership team over multiple years helped to ensure ongoing momentum for the ADVANCE project, even during times of significant institutional administrative change. At other universities, the ADVANCE effort benefited from the connections of some leadership team members to campus governance bodies, where they could encourage decision-making favorable to work/life policies. Faculty members with expertise on theories and practices of organizational change or on how higher education institutions function have been important participants in some projects, as have staff members who know the university well and can coordinate the logistics of running a project. At some universities, including Lehigh,

Virginia Tech, and the University of California, Irvine, men have served as senior members of the ADVANCE project team. Their presence and explicit commitment to the principle and goal of gender equity in itself advances the work.

As team members or not, the explicit support of senior institutional leaders, such as the provost, is critically important to the success of a change effort. They can frame the overall institutional commitment to diversity, equity, and inclusion; call out organizational structures and processes that have fostered inequities; and articulate why equity and inclusion are essential to institutional quality. ADVANCE teams were most successful in enlisting this support when they could articulate how the goals of ADVANCE aligned with other goals important to senior leaders, such as those prioritized in an institution's overall strategic plan.

Getting Started and Maintaining Persistence

The leaders we interviewed encouraged careful analysis and selection of strategies, but they also counseled others not to be afraid to initiate a change process. Some advised starting small, with the support of those interested and willing to do the work. Spending time trying to convince those who are uninterested is not a worthwhile expenditure of energy. But identifying and including supporters can help initiate good ideas, leverage them over time, and encourage others to see the possibilities for positive impacts on the institution.

Persistence is equally important. Change leaders need to recognize and remind others that substantive change takes time. Early leaders and supporters are needed; wider involvement requires patience and continuing effort. Those encountering obstacles must find creative ways to advance. At one university, departures of the president and provost who had supported the ADVANCE project led to challenges because the new senior leaders had their own ideas to cultivate and did not provide the same enthusiasm or support. Recognizing that their efforts could become stalled, the team worked on getting ADVANCE-friendly colleagues elected to the faculty senate, where they could work on changing campus policies in order to strengthen gender equity. Instead of being halted by the change in the institutional leaders' approach, they found other ways to advance the project's goals.

Establishing Buy-In, Identifying Allies, and Communicating Effectively

Our data reflect the importance of including as many people as possible in the promise and excitement of institutional transformation. Identifying allies is an essential part of establishing organizational commitment to the goal and raising the cross-institutional support needed to create change. Allies are individuals or groups across campus with shared interests in fostering a more inclusive orga-nizational environment. Allies may have expertise on the needs of another un-derrepresented group or on the types of programs that are planned; they may align philosophically with those working for gender equity.

To find allies, develop a sense of inclusion, and gain support, project leaders need to find opportunities to talk with a wide range of stakeholders and ask them to identify issues of concern. Leaders should invite and listen to the perspectives of a variety of people and encourage their involvement in the work. At Iowa State University (Cohort 3), working at multiple levels of the institution meant talking with faculty members as well as administrators. Finding opportunities to talk with faculty within their departmental contexts can be especially productive since the department is where faculty time and efforts are primarily directed. ADVANCE leaders at North Dakota State University (Cohort 4) were proactive in seeking male allies and advocates and providing avenues for them to share insights and input. At the University of Houston (Cohort 7), faculty members responded enthusiasti-cally to invitations to come together to discuss common interests. In each of these examples, change leaders were purposeful in inviting colleagues into the conver-sation and the process.

While wide engagement is important, change leaders offered a few caveats about involving faculty in a change effort. Faculty members need time to do the work they are asked to carry out; this is important, skilled work that should be compensated and not treated as a service responsibility or an overload. Providing a course release or summer salary can be attractive options for recognizing this kind of work. If faculty members are asked to lead teams or facilitate workshops and meetings, they must be appropriately trained. When leaders encounter resis-tance or reluctance to get involved, they may wish to ask their colleagues to help them figure out what would strengthen the quality of the environment.

In addition to explicit efforts to engage faculty and win their buy-in, support, and ideas, symbolic messages play an important role in change initiatives. In the early years of the ADVANCE IT project at the University of Nebraska–Lincoln (Co-hort 4), the provost included a printed note on the university's holiday greeting card that celebrated the institution's commitment to diversity and inclusion and the ADVANCE project. At Utah State University (Cohort 2), the tower on campus was illuminated with a large A when the institution received its ADVANCE grant, celebrating the award while also encouraging campus-wide conversation about the meaning of greater diversity and inclusion.

Tracking, Monitoring, and Evaluating the Change Outcomes and Processes

Gathering data, monitoring key indicators relevant to the change process, and taking time to evaluate progress and challenges are ways to move a change process forward. If the goals of the transformation project are clearly articulated, team leaders can identify progress by monitoring the same indicators used to identify the problem. At the University of Nebraska–Lincoln, for example, the ADVANCE team shared data with department chairs about applicant pools and hires at several points during the project. Over a shared meal, department chairs received data about their own department's applicant pools and hiring results as well as comparative data about doctoral graduates in the field nationally, in peer institutions, and in their own colleges. Conversations around these data enabled everyone to reflect on their progress toward the goal of more inclusive searches and hiring practices, to explore the evidence for change and areas where more attention was needed, and to brainstorm further strategies to be enlisted.

To meet NSF expectations for project evaluation, ADVANCE Institutional Transformation projects have included internal and external evaluators. Internal evaluators are responsible for monitoring progress on the activities in the change portfolio and for providing formative data to help project leaders make mid-course adjustments where needed. Usually based inside the institution so they can work closely with the project, they may be faculty members or researchers in higher education, sociology, organizational psychology, or other fields that offer theories and perspectives useful for understanding organizational dynamics, academic work, and change processes. Institutional research or evaluation units may have staff with expertise in program evaluation and organizational analysis.

Internal evaluators may design data collection processes about specific program elements, such as mentoring experiences or workshops. They may design, implement, and analyze institutional climate studies to identify problems and prioritize needs. As the project progresses, climate studies can be repeated to illuminate areas of progress or continuing concern. Because they are on-site, these evaluators can collect data on a regular basis; knowing the institution well can help them interpret the data.

External evaluators are often able to see the big picture in terms of organizational climate, and they can situate the specific problems in the university within the broader national context. They may be faculty members, researchers, or full-time evaluators located at other organizations, often with expertise on gender-related issues or on organizational change processes. They may ask insightful questions and provide guidance as project teams firm up plans. Coming from outside the institution enables external evaluators to see elements of the institution or the change process that are less evident to those inside the organization. They can offer a more distanced perspective and share observations and ideas from other institutions. External evaluators also often enjoy a level of respect simply because they are from outside the institution.

Ideally, project teams consider evaluation right from the start of project planning, since evaluation is most useful when incorporated at all stages. The insights and input of internal and external evaluators, who often work collaboratively or at least in coordination with each other, provide the project team with feedback and ideas that are essential to designing and implementing change projects for optimal impact.

Sustaining Change over Time

A major challenge to any kind of organizational change effort, regardless of its purpose, is to ensure lasting results. Leaders of ADVANCE Institutional Transformation projects need to consider what will be the long-term legacy of their work and how gains in diversity and inclusiveness can be maintained for the long term. They should consider sustainability from the start. What approaches help to ensure that the advances made are sustained over time?

One idea is to attract and engage in the work a substantial number of people from across the institutional community. If inclusion and equity are to be advanced, many members of the community must commit to these values and incorporate them into their daily work. Strategies to find allies and enlist the interest and ongoing involvement of senior institutional leaders also cultivate a wide base of support. Indeed, change in faculty members' everyday behaviors and practices may be a signal of deep and lasting cultural change. At the same time, cultural change must be backed by equitable structures, such as formal policies and practices, in order to prevent backsliding and reversion to old patterns (Hardcastle et al., 2019).

Another strategy is to find ways to embed into regular institutional budgetary processes the financial resources to support the work. For example, if a faculty mentoring program is a valued and successful part of the change portfolio, then change leaders should explore—well in advance of the end of grant funding—how to embed program costs into the regular institutional budget process. This may require some modifications of the program over time.

Anticipating the end of grant funding for their transformation projects, some teams focused their efforts on institutional policies, such as promotion and tenure policies or family leave policies, reasoning that policies, once approved by normal governance processes, become well established and difficult to remove. Some teams moved ADVANCE programs into existing offices, where funding and leadership could become embedded. At Michigan State University (Cohort 4), for example, the Faculty Excellence Advocate Program, started under the university's ADVANCE IT project, was embedded in the work of each college and coordinated by the Office of the Associate Provost for Academic Human Resources.

At some institutions, maintaining the actual name ADVANCE Institutional Transformation has been important; elsewhere, sustainability has been best supported through integrating the program into permanent institutional structures, even though the program's original name is gone. In the ADVANCE community, there are examples of several forms of sustainability; for change leaders, the key point is to begin to consider avenues for sustainability from the onset of the project.

Reflections and Next Steps

As we complete the writing of this book, we are reflecting on the contributions that we hope it makes as well as on the work still needed to create more equitable academic environments. We have explained various practical strategies and interventions that are being used across institutions of higher education to enhance gender equity among STEM faculties. We have focused on each strategy on its own, examining its purposes and the variations we have seen in its use, some models used in actual institutional contexts, and the strategy's affordances and limitations as an approach to change. This inventory and analysis of well-used strategies is intended to aid institutions as they sort through the problems they wish to address and the options available to them.

We also urge higher education leaders to take a systemic approach to organizational change—to go beyond simply selecting a few strategies and, instead, to take a comprehensive, integrated, and strategic approach. In this book, being strategic means analyzing the context and identifying particular issues confronting the institution; carefully and purposefully selecting strategies in alignment with the particular problems that have been identified; and implementing an integrated change portfolio that aligns with both the institutional context and the nature of the issues to be addressed. Such a portfolio should connect a set of change strategies in ways that leverage their unique contributions toward impactful and sustainable change. Systemic efforts also involve selecting strategies to address the structural, political, human resource, and cultural aspects of the organization. Institutional leaders must understand that such efforts require the involvement of many people across campus working together. Our research provides evidence that such a systemic organizational approach is necessary if effective and lasting change is to take shape.

We also see where further study would be useful. While the work presented here emphasizes practical strategies to create more inclusive academic institutions, we have learned about additional organizational processes that play a role in institutional change, such as connecting with allies and handling resistance. We plan to share findings about these processes in future writing. Moreover, we recognize that institution-level work, as necessary and important as it is, does not alleviate the need to address the broader societal sexism and racism that enable inequities to persist. With the scholars and activists who are examining and disrupting these embedded societal forces and envisioning alternative futures, we share the goal of supporting movement toward a more just and equitable academy in which the full array of talent is fully welcomed. While different in focus than ours, such work is a powerful force for change because it informs and inspires institution-level change efforts.

Leaders at the National Science Foundation who have envisioned, initiated, and nurtured the ADVANCE program also deserve much appreciation. Their commitment, leadership, persistence, and vision have provided critically important scaffolding, urgency, and legitimacy to the work taken up by institutional teams. Meetings to convene ADVANCE institutional leaders have fostered community, connections, and collaboration among those engaged in the daunting work of institutional transformation to advance gender equity; these convenings too have served as a critically important force for change. Together, the analyses and urgings of program leaders at the NSF, the diligent work and hard-earned insights of institutional leaders of ADVANCE programs, and the efforts of researchers and evaluators have enabled newer projects to build on and extend the successes and lessons forged in the work of the early institutional grantees.

At the same time as we appreciate all that has been achieved, we see the need to find more ways to measure and document progress and success. We are often asked "what works?" and find that the level of evidence we can offer for particular interventions and for entire change portfolios is sometimes disappointing to the questioner. Perhaps the next phase of ADVANCE should be about expanding ways to measure success. One area needing creative and ongoing attention is evaluation of gender equity initiatives and interventions. The federally funded

ADVANCE projects already attend to evaluation, for example, tracking indicators of women's institutional status to look for change over time that may be attributed to the institutional project (Frehill, Jeser-Cannavale, & Malley, 2007). However, everyone involved in this kind of cultural change work realizes how hard it is to move the needle in the short time scale of a five-year grant (De Welde, 2017). Finding ways to evaluate the immediate impact of change efforts, while also recognizing that much of the outcome of change work happens over a longer period, presents a worthy challenge for those interested in evaluation research.

One way to enhance evaluative approaches may emerge from creating regular opportunities for multiple stakeholders in this work to ask and analyze what has been learned across the set of institutions that have purposefully worked on gender equity change. NSF leaders have been reflective about this question over the years as evidenced in the evolving priorities and expectations in the ADVANCE solicitation (Laursen & De Welde, 2019). Efforts to invite nontraditional and creative approaches to evaluation may be useful. For example, the ADVANCE community may want to join together in asking what "success" may mean. What are appropriate and reasonable criteria for short-term success at the institutional level (within five-year time frames, for example), and what are useful indicators of longer-term institutional change? How might community members work together to reflect about what has been learned and how change efforts need to evolve and adapt over time?

Funders can encourage change leaders to consider and explicitly address in their planning the kinds of evaluation work that will accompany their intervention strategies. While already expected in grant proposals, more focused consideration could be directed to such questions so as to deepen and provide more nuance in the evidence base about change strategies. For example, what do change leaders hope will be the impact of specific interventions? Who will be affected and how? And what elements of the intervention are most important and should be evaluated? Not all interventions may need extensive evaluation. For example, convenings of women to discuss issues around which they want to collaborate may require only some records of interest and attendance, while other efforts, such as new mentoring programs, may merit well-designed and thorough evaluation. As proposals are developed and as implementation plans unfold, discerning which efforts and initiatives should receive robust and explicit evaluation—and which do not require this—is important.

In the same vein, formative evaluation should be recognized to be as important as summative evaluation, and synergies should be recognized between evaluation and research. Formative evaluation can foster institutional learning as initiatives are developed and first implemented; planning for how to collect and use ongoing formative feedback is strategically wise to ensure that plans attend to local contextual features and needs. Such work can pave the way so that over time, a change portfolio can be responsive and impactful in meeting specific institutional needs. Often, research initiatives connected to ADVANCE projects develop useful insights that have substantial evaluative value; creative approaches may be required to mine the research data and capture these insights along the way, before they have value only in hindsight.

We also encourage community-wide discussion of evaluation at meetings and in relevant published materials. Grantees have appreciated past convenings of ADVANCE investigators as opportunities for the generous and honest exchange of lessons and ideas. We hope that such gatherings continue to provide opportunities to consider systematically which evaluation approaches are working most productively for different kinds of interventions and for different kinds of goals. Structured conversations, in which key themes and lessons are systematically captured and distilled for broader dissemination, may help to identify circumstances and factors that challenge or undermine change initiatives, such as the departure of supportive senior-level institutional leaders.

A systematic approach to developing case studies of mature change projects would also be useful in cross-institutional discussions and exchanges of experience and knowledge. Case studies might focus on how institutions have grappled with definitions of impact and success, what measurable outcomes they have found to be feasible and useful, and what approaches they have developed and refined for evaluating specific interventions and measuring overall project impact. In taking up these questions of how to define and operationalize success, case studies may also consider issues of sustainability. What forms has sustainability taken across ADVANCE institutions, and how have project leaders addressed sustainability as the projects develop? Because sustainability can take various forms, such as incorporating specific strategies into the portfolios of well-established offices or morphing interventions to adapt to the institution's needs and context, responses to these questions will need to be receptive to a range of ways in which projects may become embedded in institutional work and culture. Sometimes, integration into the local context is so successful that the change is no longer easily attributed to the influence of ADVANCE.

Concluding Thoughts

Much has already been learned from the work supported by ADVANCE to change institutions to effect greater gender equity—and more lessons remain to be identified and shared. Significant institutional change involves action, learning, commitment, and community. It requires systemic and purposeful change approaches with careful evaluation and research to identify and extract key lessons. It improves with honest sharing of what works—and what doesn't—with a generous and supportive community of colleagues who share common goals and a common vision. Everyone—the nation, the scientific enterprise, the institution, and the faculty member—benefits from more inclusive and nurturing academic environments that tap into the talents of all community members.

We urge those working to establish such environments to consider the examples we have provided and the recommendations we have offered for taking a strategic and systemic approach. We also call for continuing commitment to systematically study and learn from the courageous work occurring on many campuses. We honor all those who are working together—each in their unique organizational context—with commitment to a shared vision of equity and excellence. We hope the analyses, examples, and ideas in this book will be a productive addition to this significant work in the higher education landscape. Our collective efforts can and must create the kinds of academic workplaces that will produce the knowledge needed to address daunting societal issues and prepare the next generation of scientists, mathematicians, and engineers, who will represent diverse perspectives, value inclusion, and pursue justice in their own spheres.

Appendix A

ADVANCE Institutional Transformation Awards by Cohort through 2019

Award cohort	Institution	State	Award start date	NSF award number
1	Georgia Institute of Technology (Georgia Tech)	GA	2001	0123690
1	Hunter College, City University of New York	NY	2001	0123609
1	New Mexico State University	NM	2001	0123636
1	University of California, Irvine	CA	2001	0123654
1	University of Colorado Boulder	CO	2002	0123532
1	University of Michigan	MI	2001	0123682
1	University of Puerto Rico at Humacao	PR	2001	0123571
1	University of Washington (UW)	WA	2001	0123552
1	University of Wisconsin–Madison	WI	2002	0123666
2	Case Western Reserve University	OH	2003	0245054
2	Earth Institute at Columbia University	NY	2004	0244984
2	Kansas State University	KS	2003	0245039
2	University of Alabama at Birmingham (UAB)	AL	2003	0244880
2	University of Maryland, Baltimore County (UMBC)	MD	2003	0244922
2	University of Montana	MT	2003	0245014
2	University of Rhode Island	RI	2003	0245090
2	University of Texas at El Paso (UTEP)	TX	2003	0245094
2	Utah State University	UT	2003	0245071
2	Virginia Polytechnic Institute (Virginia Tech)	VA	2003	0244916
3	Brown University	RI	2006	0548311
3	California State Polytechnic University, Pomona (Cal Poly Pomona)	CA	2006	0548426
3	Cornell University	NY	2006	0547373
3	Iowa State University	IA	2006	0548113
3	Marshall University Research Corporation	WV	2006	0547427
3	New Jersey Institute of Technology	NJ	2006	0600399
3	Rensselaer Polytechnic Institute	NY	2006	0548354
3	William March Rice University (Rice)	TX	2005	0548130
3	University of Arizona	AZ	2006	0546843
3	University of Illinois, Chicago	IL	2006	0548401
3	University of North Carolina at Charlotte	NC	2006	0542562

Award cohort	Institution	State	Award start date	NSF award number
4	Michigan State University	MI	2008	0811205
4	North Dakota State University	ND	2008	0811239
4	Northeastern University	MA	2008	0811170
4	Ohio State University	OH	2008	0811123
4	Purdue University	IN	2008	0811194
4	Rutgers University	NJ	2008	0810978
4	University of Nebraska–Lincoln	NE	2008	0811250
4	Washington State University	WA	2008	0810927
4	Wright State University	OH	2008	0810989
5	Jackson State University	MS	2010	1008708
5	Lehigh University	PA	2010	1008375
5	Syracuse University	NY	2010	1008643
5	Texas A&M University (TAMU)	TX	2010	1008385
5	University of Maine	ME	2010	1008498
5	University of Maryland, College Park	MD	2010	1008117
5	West Virginia University	WV	2010	1007978
6	Howard University	DC	2012	1208880
6	Montana State University	MT	2012	1208831
6	Rochester Institute of Technology	NY	2012	1209115
6	University of California, Davis	CA	2012	1209235
6	University of Cincinnati	OH	2012	1209169
6	University of New Hampshire	NH	2012	1209189
6	University of Texas at Rio Grande Valley (formerly UT Pan American)	TX	2012	1209210
6	University of Virginia	VA	2012	1209197
7	North Carolina Agricultural and Technical State University (NCA&T)	NC	2014	1409799
7	Oregon State University	OR	2014	1409171
7	University of Delaware	DE	2014	1409472
7	University of Houston	TX	2014	1409928
8	Clemson University	SC	2016	1629934
8	Florida International University	FL	2016	1629889
8	Seattle University	WA	2016	1629875
8	University of Massachusetts Lowell	MA	2016	1629761
8	University of New Mexico	NM	2016	1628471
9	Arizona State University	AZ	2018	1824260
9	Florida A&M University	FL	2018	1824267
9	University of Massachusetts Amherst	MA	2018	1824090
9	Villanova University	PA	2018	1824237
9	Virginia Commonwealth University	VA	2018	1824015

Appendix B

Research Methods

Our study used a mixed-methods approach guided by conceptual frameworks on organizational change and faculty work. The work was funded by an ADVANCE PAID (Partnerships for Adaptation, Implementation and Dissemination) award from the National Science Foundation (HRD-0930097, 2010–2015) and a workshop grant (HRD-1830185, 2018–2019). All research procedures were approved by the Institutional Review Board of Michigan State University under an interinstitutional agreement with the University of Colorado Boulder, and all interviewees provided their informed consent. Authors Laursen and Austin worked on this study since its inception; others who worked on the research team at different times include Melissa Soto, Dalinda Martinez, and Anne-Barrie Hunter. Kris De Welde joined our team in 2018.

We examined in detail the 19 institutions awarded ADVANCE Institutional Transformation grants in 2001–2004 in Cohorts 1–2 (see appendix A). When we began the work in 2010, these institutional teams had completed their projects (or nearly so): they had designed, implemented, refined, and evaluated programs; reviewed, adjusted, or developed policies; and had observed and documented the outcomes of these actions. They had faced challenges and considered how to sustain their activities and accomplishments. Thus, this group was best positioned to reflect on the outcomes and procesess of their work. They included large public research institutions, private institutions, and smaller institutions; some focused on research while others emphasized undergraduate education. They were distributed geographically and were diverse in institutional mission and culture.

The data we gathered about these institutions included:

- Nearly 150 documents, including proposals, annual and final reports, brochures, presentations, publications, and evaluation reports totaling 160 MB of text data and covering the span of each institution's activities (typically 5–7 years). These documents were gathered from project websites and from project leaders. While what we could gather varied in the depth of information, with few exceptions we were able to assemble a fairly complete set of documents, giving special importance to the original proposal, the annual report prepared for the third-year site visit conducted by the ADVANCE program, and the final report to the NSF.
- Transcripts of 19 interviews with ADVANCE leaders from these schools. The interviews were conducted by telephone and typically lasted 50–70 minutes. We spoke with leaders from 18 institutions (two leaders were from one institution) but were unable to secure an interview with a leader from the nineteenth institution.
- Transcripts of 115 interviews with 171 individuals, including ADVANCE project leaders, staff, faculty, and administrators from five institutions selected for site visits.

The locations for site visits were carefully chosen. First, we prepared structured analytical summaries of our findings about each institution based on analysis of the documents and interviews, and reviewed these with our advisory board, discussing features of interest to explore in depth and parameters to define the scope and variation of the cases. With their advice, we chose three institutions, completed these site visits, and then reflected on what we had learned before choosing the final two cases, seeking to balance the range of institutions and strategies represented in the data. All institutions that we invited to participate in the case studies agreed to do so, and we conducted all five two-and-a-half-day site visits in 2011–2012. A typical site visit included about 25 interviews and focus groups with 30–45 individuals, which were conducted separately by two researchers. Interviewees included project leaders, evaluators, and many deans, department chairs, and faculty who had participated in the local ADVANCE program. We debriefed with the ADVANCE leadership team at the end of each visit to share some of our observations and seek their reactions. The five cases represent public and private institutions in different geographic regions that took diverse approaches to institutional change in support of women STEM scholars: Case Western Reserve University, Kansas State University, University of Texas at El Paso, University of California, Irvine, and Utah State University.

We carried out detailed analyses of these data, including:

- Coding the document set for each institution using a rubric based on the literature, which focused on the project's theory of change (explicit or implicit), the types of institutional change strategies chosen, and the rationale for them. We drew on prior studies that identified the types of actions taken by ADVANCE institutions (Bilimoria, Joy, & Liang, 2008; Fox, 2008) to construct our rubric, which had 14 main categories and 75 subcategories that we used to classify project activities, verify whether activities described in the proposal were enacted or not, and ascertain the longevity of activities (e.g., if activities continued throughout the project or were tried but then dropped).
- Preparing a narrative summary for each institution drawing on the coded reports and the interviews. Each summary explained the goals and key elements of an institution's overall change strategy, relevant contextual elements, program elements, outcomes, and other noteworthy features observed by the research team. These 19 summaries were used in discussion with our advisory board to select the five institutions for in-depth case study.
- Coding in detail, using NVivo software from QSR (Brisbane, Australia), the original 19 interviews and the 115 interviews from the five case study sites. Our coding scheme was developed both from theory and empirically from the data. The codebook was developed using an iterative and collaborative process: researchers read several interviews, identified themes, and discussed them to arrive at main coding categories and agree on their definitions (Hsieh & Shannon, 2005). This refinement process continued as more interviews were coded, and new codes were added to capture emergent themes. In the end, nearly 6,000 passages were coded using 41 codes that labeled distinct concepts spanning interventions, processes, theories of change, evaluation, and leadership activities. The software made it

straightforward to find illustrative quotes, further divide analytical subcategories, and count the relative weight of opinion in different categories.

Nearly all the coded passages can be grouped under five major topics:

- interventions used by institutions (~30% of passages)
- processes that were important in running the project (~30%)
- information about the institution's needs, context, and choice of strategies (~18%)
- observations about departments, disciplines, and faculty life (~11%)
- information about individuals' histories, motivations to participate, and career impacts of taking part in ADVANCE (~8%)

From the data, we identified and analyzed 13 common interventions used by these institutions to advance women in STEM, and we reported these in the strategic intervention briefs shared on our online StratEGIC Toolkit: Strategies for Effecting Gender Equity and Institutional Change (Laursen & Austin, 2014a). The strategies presented in this book are adapted from the toolkit with some refinements. For example, we broke one intervention described there into two parts that aligned with different strategies presented in this book, and we have grouped the strategies in order to better highlight their purposes and the problems each was intended to address. In this book, we have included additional examples of the strategies derived from the working meetings

The narrative summaries initially prepared for selecting cases for site visits were further refined and elaborated, reviewed by institutional teams, and shared, with each team's permission, as the institutional portraits on the StratEGIC Toolkit website. We selected the case studies here to highlight institutions that developed combinations of strategies well suited to their institutional context and that offered some evidence about the combined impacts of their work. The toolkit includes additional examples of how institutions design comprehensive change plans composed of multiple strategies.

We used working meetings in 2015 and 2018 to gather additional data about specific interventions, innovative or distinctive approaches, context-sensitive choices and adaptation, and organizational change processes. We have drawn on these data to provide additional examples of strategies (chapters 3–6), to identify new arenas of institutional transformation work (chapter 7), and to describe how institutions build change plans (chapters 8–9). Details about how we conducted and carried out these meetings, which we call "focus group workshops," can be found in our reports (Austin & Laursen, 2015; Laursen, De Welde, & Austin, 2019). Briefly, we conducted structured conversations with 16–18 people about issues that were of interest to us as researchers and about which we anticipated the participants would have insights from their work as leaders, evaluators, researchers, or observers of institutional change projects. An analysis of the program solicitations (calls for proposals) from NSF ADVANCE also informed this book, and the methods for that study are described in a separate publication (Laursen & De Welde, 2019).

References

ADVANCE Project TRACS. (2017). *Strategies to enhance work-life integration.* Retrieved from http://www.montana.edu/nsfadvance/worklife/howto.html.

Ahlqvist, V., et al. (2013). *Observations on gender equality in a selection of the Swedish Research Council's evaluation panels.* Stockholm, Sweden: Vetenskapsrådet.

Allen, J., Smith, J. L., & Ransdell, L. B. (2019). Missing or seizing the opportunity? The effect of an opportunity hire on job offers to science faculty candidates. *Equality, Diversity and Inclusion: An International Journal, 38*(2), 160–177.

American Mathematical Society [AMS]. (2019). *Annual survey of the mathematical sciences: Demographics in the mathematical sciences.* Retrieved from http://www.ams.org/profession/data/annual-survey/demographics.

Anderson-Knott, M., Wonch Hill, T., & Watanabe, M. (2013). *ADVANCE Nebraska: Internal evaluation summative report.* Lincoln: Survey, Statistics, and Psychometrics Core Facility, University of Nebraska. Retrieved from http://advance.unl.edu/files/ADVANCE-NebraskaInternalEvaluationSummativeReport.pdf.

Anicha, C. L., Burnett, A., & Bilen-Green, C. (2015). Men faculty gender-equity advocates: A qualitative analysis of theory and praxis. *Journal of Men's Studies, 23*(1), 21–43.

Antecol, H., Bedard, K., & Stearns, J. (2018). Equal but inequitable: Who benefits from gender-neutral tenure clock stopping policies? *American Economic Review, 108*(9), 2420–2441.

Antonio, A. L., Astin, H. S., & Cress, C. M. (2000). Community service in higher education: A look at the nation's faculty. *Review of Higher Education, 23*(4), 373–397.

Archie, T., Kogan, M., & Laursen, S. L. (2015). Do labmates matter? The relative importance of workplace climate and work-life satisfaction in women scientists' job satisfaction. *International Journal of Gender, Science and Technology, 7*(3), 343–368.

Armstrong, M. A., & Jovanovic, J. (2015). Starting at the crossroads: Intersectional approaches to institutionally supporting underrepresented minority women STEM faculty. *Journal of Women and Minorities in Science and Engineering, 21*(2), 141–157.

Armstrong, M. A., & Jovanovic, J. (2017). The intersectional matrix: Rethinking institutional change for URM women in STEM. *Journal of Diversity in Higher Education, 10*(3), 216–231.

Ashcraft, C., & Breitzman, A. (2012). *Who invents IT? Women's participation in information technology patenting, 2012 update.* Boulder, CO: National Center for Women and Information Technology. Retrieved from https://www.ncwit.org/sites/default/files/resources/2012whoinventsit_web_1.pdf.

Astin, H. S., & Milem, J. F. (1997). The status of academic couples in US institutions. In M. A. Ferber & J. W. Loeb (Eds.), *Academic couples: Problems and promises* (pp. 128–155). Urbana: University of Illinois Press.

Atherton, T. J., et al. (2016). LGBT+ climate in physics: Building an inclusive community. College Park, MD: American Physical Society. Retrieved from http://www.aps.org/programs/lgbt/.

Austin, A. E. (1992). Supporting junior faculty through a teaching fellows program. In M. D. Sorcinelli, & A. E. Austin (Eds.), *Developing new and junior faculty* (pp. 73–86). San Francisco, CA: Jossey-Bass.

Austin, A. E. (2003). Creating a bridge to the future: Preparing new faculty to face changing expectations in a shifting context. *Review of Higher Education, 26*(2), 119–144.

Austin, A. E. (2006a). Foreword. In S. J. Bracken, J. K. Allen, & D. R. Dean (Eds.), *The balancing act: Gendered perspectives in faculty roles and work lives* (pp. ix–xiv). Sterling, VA: Stylus.

Austin, A. E. (2006b). Conclusion. In S. J. Bracken, J. K. Allen, & D. R. Dean (Eds.), *The balancing act: Gendered perspectives in faculty roles and work lives* (pp. 147–157). Sterling, VA: Stylus.

Austin, A. E. (2010a). Expectations and experiences of aspiring and early career academics. In L. McAlpine & G. S. Akerlind (Eds.), *Becoming an academic: International perspectives* (pp. 18–44). New York: Palgrave Macmillan.

Austin, A. E. (2010b). Supporting faculty members across their careers. In K. Gillespie, D. L. Robertson, and Associates (Eds.), *A guide to faculty development* (2nd ed., pp. 363–378). San Francisco, CA: Jossey-Bass.

Austin, A. E. (2011). The socialization of future faculty in a changing context: Traditions, challenges, and possibilities. In J. C. Hermanowicz (Ed.), *The American profession: Transformation in contemporary higher education* (pp. 145–167). Baltimore, MD: Johns Hopkins University Press.

Austin, A. E., & Laursen, S. L. (2015). *Organizational change strategies in ADVANCE Institutional Transformation projects: Synthesis of a working meeting.* Boulder, CO, and East Lansing, MI. Retrieved from https://www.colorado.edu/eer/content/workshop-report-public113015.

Austin, A. E., & McDaniels, M. (2006). Preparing the professoriate of the future: Graduate student socialization for faculty roles. In J. C. Smart (Ed.), *Higher education: Handbook of theory and research* (vol. 21, pp. 397–456). Dordrecht, Netherlands: Springer.

Austin, A. E., & Rice, R. E. (1998). Making tenure viable: Listening to early career faculty. *American Behavioral Scientist, 41*(5), 736–754.

Austin, A. E., Sorcinelli, M. D., & McDaniels, M. (2007). Understanding new faculty: Background, aspirations, challenges, and growth. In P. Perry & J. Smart (Eds.), *The scholarship of teaching and learning in higher education: An evidence-based perspective* (pp. 39–89). Dordrecht, Netherlands: Springer.

Avallone, L., et al. (2013). Supporting the retention and advancement of women in the atmospheric sciences: What women are saying. *Bulletin of the American Meteorological Society, 94*(9), 1313–1316.

Aycock, L. M., et al. (2019). Sexual harassment reported by undergraduate female physicists. *Physical Review Physics Education Research, 15*(1). Retrieved from https://journals.aps.org/prper/abstract/10.1103/PhysRevPhysEducRes.15.010121.

Babcock, L., et al. (2017). Gender differences in accepting and receiving requests for tasks with low promotability. *American Economic Review, 107,* 714–747.

Baker, V. L., et al. (Eds.). (2018). *Success after tenure: Supporting mid-career faculty.* Sterling, VA: Stylus.

Bakian, A. V., & Sullivan, K. A. (2010). The effectiveness of institutional intervention on minimizing demographic inertia and improving the representation of women faculty in higher education. *International Journal of Gender, Science and Technology, 2*(2), 207–234.

Baldwin, R., et al. (2008). Mapping the terrain of mid-career faculty at a research university: Implications for faculty and academic leaders. *Change: The Magazine of Higher Learning, 40*(5), 46–55.

Beach, A. L., et al. (2016). *Faculty development in the age of evidence: Current practices, future imperatives.* Stylus, VA: Stylus.

Beddoes, K., & Pawley, A. L. (2014). "Different people have different priorities": Work-family balance, gender, and the discourse of choice. *Studies in Higher Education, 39*(9), 1573–1585.

Bedi, G., Van Dam, N. T., & Munafo, M. (2012). Gender inequality in awarded research grants. *Lancet, 380*(9840), 474.

Beemyn, G. (Ed.). (2019). *Trans people in higher education.* Albany: State University of New York Press.

Bellas, M. L., & Toutkoushian, R. K. (1999). Faculty time allocations and research productivity: Gender, race and family effects. *Review of Higher Education, 22*(4), 367–390.

Bertrand, M. (2018). Coase Lecture: The glass ceiling. *Economica, 85*(338), 205–231.

Bilen-Green, C., et al. (2015). Implementation of advocates and allies programs to support and promote gender equity in academia. Paper presented at 122nd ASEE Annual Conference & Exposition, Seattle, WA, June.

Bilimoria, D., et al. (2007). Executive coaching: An effective strategy for faculty development. In A. J. Stewart, J. Malley, & D. LaVaque-Manty (Eds.), *Transforming science and engineering: Advancing academic women* (pp. 187–203). Ann Arbor: University of Michigan Press.

Bilimoria, D., Joy, S., & Liang, X. (2008). Breaking barriers and creating inclusiveness: Lessons of organizational transformation to advance women faculty in academic science and engineering. *Human Resources Management, 47*(3), 423–441.

Bilimoria, D., & Liang, X. (2012). *Gender equity in science and engineering: Advancing change in higher education.* New York: Routledge.

Bilimoria, D., et al. (2013). Faculty at early, middle, and late career stages: Gender effects. In S. Vinnicombe et al. (Eds.), *Handbook of research on promoting women's careers* (pp. 304–325). Northampton, MA: Edward Elgar.

Bilimoria, D., et al. (2006). How do female and male faculty members construct job satisfaction? The roles of perceived institutional leadership and mentoring and their mediating processes. *Journal of Technology Transfer, 31*(3), 355–365.

Bilimoria, D., & Singer, L. T. (2019). Institutions Developing Excellence in Academic Leadership (IDEAL): A partnership to advance gender equity, diversity, and inclusion in academic STEM. *Equality, Diversity and Inclusion: An International Journal, 38*(3), 362–381.

Bilimoria, D., & Stewart, A. J. (2009). "Don't ask, don't tell": The academic climate for lesbian, gay, bisexual and transgender faculty in science and engineering. *NWSA Journal, 21*(2), 85–103.

Bird, S. R. (2011). Unsettling universities' incongruous, gendered bureaucratic structures: A case-study approach. *Gender, Work, & Organization, 18*(2), 202–230.

Bird, S., & Latimer, M. (2019). Examining models of departmental engagement for greater equity: A case study of two applications of the dual agenda approach. *Equality, Diversity and Inclusion: An International Journal, 38*(2), 211–225.

Blackburn, H. (2017). The status of women in STEM in higher education: A review of the literature, 2007–2017. *Science & Technology Libraries, 36*(3), 235–273.

Boice, R. (1992). *The new faculty member: Supporting and fostering professional development.* San Francisco, CA: Jossey-Bass.

Bolman, L. G., & Deal, T. E. (2017). *Reframing organizations: Artistry, choice, and leadership* (6th ed.). San Francisco, CA: Jossey-Bass.

Borello, L. J., et al. (2015). International status of women in the chemical sciences. In W. Pearson, L. M. Frehill, & C. L. McNeely (Eds.), *Advancing women in science* (pp. 131–171). Cham, Switzerland: Springer.

Bowman, N. A. (2010). College diversity experiences and cognitive development: A meta-analysis. *Review of Educational Research, 80*(1), 4–33.

Bowman, N. A. (2011). Promoting participation in a diverse democracy: A meta-analysis of college diversity experiences and civic engagement. *Review of Educational Research, 81*(1), 29–68.

Bracken, S. J., Allen, J. K., & Dean, D. R. (Eds.). (2006). *The balancing act: Gendered perspectives in faculty roles and work lives.* Sterling, VA: Stylus.

Britton, D. M. (2017). Beyond the chilly climate: The salience of gender in women's academic careers. *Gender & Society, 31*(1), 5–27.

Britton, D. M., et al. A. (2012). Surveying the campus climate for faculty: A comparison of the assessments of STEM and non-STEM faculty. *International Journal of Gender, Science and Technology, 4*(1), 102–122.

Buch, K., et al. (2011). Removing the barriers to full professor: A mentoring program for associate professors. *Change: The Magazine of Higher Learning, 43*(6), 38–45.

Bug, A. (2010). Swimming against the unseen tide. *Physics World* (August), 16–17.

Building Engineering & Science Talent [BEST]. (2004). *A bridge for all: Higher education design principles to broaden participation in science, technology, engineering and mathematics.* San Diego, CA: BEST. Retrieved from http://www.bestworkforce.org/sites/default/files/research/downloads/Bridge%20for%20All%20Higher%20Ed%20report.pdf.

Burack, C., & Franks, S. E. (2006). Evaluating STEM department websites for diversity. *WEPAN 2006 Conference Proceedings.* Retrieved from https://journals.psu.edu/wepan/article/viewFile/58443/58131.

Burgess, D. J., et al. (2012). Does stereotype threat affect women in academic medicine? *Academic Medicine, 87*(4), 506–512.

Bystydzienski, J. M., & Bird, S. R. (Eds.). (2006). *Removing barriers: Women in academic science, technology, engineering, and mathematics*. Bloomington: Indiana University Press.

Caleo, S., & Heilman, M. E. (2019). What could go wrong? Some unintended consequences of gender bias interventions. *Archives of Scientific Psychology, 7*, 71–80.

Callister, R. R. (2006). The impact of gender and department climate on job satisfaction and intentions to quit for faculty in science and engineering fields. *Journal of Technology Transfer, 31*(3), 367–375.

Campbell, C. M., & O'Meara, K. (2014). Faculty agency: Departmental contexts that matter in faculty careers. *Research in Higher Education, 55*(1), 49–74.

Cantalupo, N. C., & Kidder, W. (2018). A systematic look at a serial problem: Sexual harassment of students by university faculty. *Utah Law Review, 2018*, 671–786.

Cantalupo, N. C., & Kidder, W. (2019). Systematic prevention of a serial problem: Sexual harassment and bridging core concepts of Bakke in the #MeToo era. *UC Davis Law Review, 52*, 2349–2405.

Carnegie Classification of Institutions of Higher Education. (n.d.). About the Carnegie Classification. Retrieved from http://carnegieclassifications.iu.edu.

Carnes, M., et al. (2012). Promoting institutional change through bias literacy. *Journal of Diversity in Higher Education, 5*(2), 63–77.

Carnes, M., et al. (2015). Effect of an intervention to break the gender bias habit for faculty at one institution: A cluster randomized, controlled trial. *Academic Medicine: Journal of the Association of American Medical Colleges, 90*(2), 221–230.

Carnes, M., et al. (2005). NIH director's Pioneer Awards: Could the selection process be biased against women? *Journal of Women's Health, 14*(8), 684–691.

Carnes, M., Handelsman, J., & Sheridan, J. (2005). Diversity in academic medicine: The stages of change model. *Journal of Women's Health, 14*(6), 471–475.

Carter-Sowell, A. R., et al. (2019). ADVANCE Scholar Program: Enhancing minoritized scholars' professional visibility. *Equality, Diversity and Inclusion: An International Journal, 38*(3), 305–327.

Casadevall, A., & Handelsman, J. (2014). The presence of female conveners correlates with a higher proportion of female speakers at scientific symposia. *MBio, 5*(1), e00846-13.

Cech, E. A., & Blair-Loy, M. (2014). Consequences of flexibility stigma among academic scientists and engineers. *Work and Occupations, 41*(1), 86–110.

Cech, E. A., & Blair-Loy, M. (2019). The changing career trajectories of new parents in STEM. *Proceedings of the National Academy of Sciences, 116*(10), 4182–4187.

Cho, S., Crenshaw, K. W., & McCall, L. (2013). Toward a field of intersectionality studies: Theory, applications and praxis. *Signs, 38*(4), 785–810.

Clair, M., & Denis, J. S. (2015). Sociology of racism. In James Wright (Ed.), *International Encyclopedia of the Social and Behavioral Sciences* (2nd ed., vol. 19, pp. 857–863). Amsterdam, Netherlands: Elsevier.

Clancy, K. B., et al. (2017). Double jeopardy in astronomy and planetary science: Women of color face greater risks of gendered and racial harassment. *Journal of Geophysical Research: Planets, 122*(7), 1610–1623.

Clancy, K. B., et al. (2014). Survey of academic field experiences (SAFE): Trainees report harassment and assault. *PLOS One, 9*(7), e102172.

Colbeck, C. L., & Drago, R. (2005). Accept, avoid, resist: How faculty members respond to bias against caregiving . . . and how departments can help. *Change: The Magazine of Higher Learning, 37*(6), 10–17.

Corneille, M., et al. (2019). Barriers to the advancement of women of color faculty in STEM: The need for promoting equity using an intersectional framework. *Equality, Diversity and Inclusion: An International Journal, 38*(2), 328–348.

Correll, S. (2001). Gender and the career choice process: The role of biased self-assessments. *American Journal of Sociology, 106,* 1691–1730.

Correll, S., Benard, S., & Paik, I. (2007). Getting a job: Is there a motherhood penalty? *American Journal of Sociology, 112,* 1297–1338.

Crane, R. L., et al. (2006). Schema disjunction among undergraduate women in computer science. In E. M. Trauth (Ed.), *Encyclopedia of gender and information technology* (pp. 1087–1091). Hershey, PA: Idea Group Reference.

Crenshaw, K. (1991). Mapping the margins: Intersectionality, identity politics, and violence against women of color. *Stanford Law Review, 43*(6), 1241–1299.

Cullen, Z. B., & Perez-Truglia, R. (2019). The old boys' club: Schmoozing and the gender gap. Cambridge, MA: National Bureau of Economic Research. Retrieved from http://www.nber.org/papers/w26530.

Dawson, P. (2014). Beyond a definition: Toward a framework for designing and specifying mentoring models. *Educational Researcher, 43,* 137–145.

Dean, D. J., & Koster, J. B. (2013). *Equitable solutions for retaining a robust STEM workforce: Beyond best practices.* London: Academic.

DeAro, J., Bird, S., & Ryan, S. M. (2019). NSF ADVANCE and gender equity: Past, present and future of systemic institutional transformation strategies. *Equality, Diversity and Inclusion: An International Journal, 38*(2), 131–139.

Demb, A., & Wade, A. (2012). Reality check: Faculty involvement in outreach and engagement. *Journal of Higher Education, 83*(3), 337–366.

Devine, P. G., et al. (2017). A gender bias habit-breaking intervention led to increased hiring of female faculty in STEMM departments. *Journal of Experimental Social Psychology, 73,* 211–215.

De Welde, K. (2017). Moving the needle on equity and inclusion. *Humboldt Journal of Social Relations, 39,* 192–211.

De Welde, K., & Laursen, S. L. (2008). The "ideal type" advisor: How advisors help STEM graduate students find their "scientific feet." *Open Education Journal, 1*(1), 49–61.

De Welde, K., & Laursen, S. L. (2011). The glass obstacle course: Informal and formal barriers for women PhD students in STEM fields. *International Journal of Gender, Science and Technology, 3*(3), 571–595.

De Welde, K., & Stepnick, A. (2015a). From people to policies: Enduring inequalities and inequities from women academics. In K. De Welde & A. Stepnick (Eds.), *Disrupting the culture of silence: Confronting gender inequality and making change in higher education* (pp. 1–28). Sterling, VA: Stylus.

De Welde, K., & Stepnick, A. (Eds.). (2015b). *Disrupting the culture of silence: Confronting gender inequality and making change in higher education.* Sterling, VA: Stylus.

DiAngelo, R. (2012). *What does it mean to be white? Developing white racial literacy.* New York: Peter Lang.

Diehl, A. B., & Dzubinski, L. M. (2016). Making the invisible visible: A cross-sector analysis of gender-based leadership barriers. *Human Resource Development Quarterly, 27*(2), 181–206.

Dobbin, F., & Kalev, A. (2018). Why doesn't diversity training work? The challenge for industry and academia. *Anthropology Now, 10*(2), 48–55.

Drago, R., et al. (2005). Bias against caregiving. *Academe, 91*(5), 22–25.

Drago, R., et al. (2006). The avoidance of bias against caregiving: The case of academic faculty. *American Behavioral Scientist, 49*(9), 1222–1247.

Drago, R., & Williams, J. (2000). A half-time tenure track proposal. *Change: The Magazine of Higher Learning, 32*(6), 46–51.

Duch, J., et al. (2012). The possible role of resource requirements and academic career-choice risk on gender differences in publication rate and impact. *PLOS One, 7*(12), e51332.

Dutt, K., et al. (2016). Gender differences in recommendation letters for postdoctoral fellowships in geoscience. *Nature Geoscience, 9*(11), 805.

Dyer, R. A., & Montelone, B. A. (2007). An institutional approach to establishing professional connections. In A. Stewart, J. Malley, and D. LaVaque-Manty (Eds.), *Transforming science and engineering: Advancing academic women* (pp. 48–61). Ann Arbor: University of Michigan Press.

Eagly, A. H., & Carli, L. L. (2003). The female leadership advantage: An evaluation of the evidence. *Leadership Quarterly, 14*(6), 807–834.

Eaton, A. A., et al. (2020). How gender and race stereotypes impact the advancement of scholars in STEM: Professors' biased evaluations of physics and biology post-doctoral candidates. *Sex Roles, 82*(3–4), 127–141.

Ebert-May, D., et al. (2015). Breaking the cycle: Future faculty begin teaching with learner-centered strategies after professional development. *CBE: Life Sciences Education, 14*(2), ar22.

Edelman, M. W. (2015). It's hard to be what you can't see. *Child Watch Column*. Washington, DC: Children's Defense Fund. Retrieved from https://www.childrensdefense.org/child-watch-columns/health/2015/its-hard-to-be-what-you-cant-see.

Ehrenberg, R. G., et al. (2012). Diversifying the faculty across gender lines: Do trustees and administrators matter? *Economics of Education Review, 31*(1), 9–18.

Espinosa, L. (2011). Pipelines and pathways: Women of color in undergraduate STEM majors and the college experiences that contribute to persistence. *Harvard Educational Review, 81*(2), 209–241.

Espinosa, L. L., McGuire, K., & Jackson, L. M. (2019). *Minority serving institutions: America's underutilized resource for strengthening the STEM workforce*. Washington, DC: National Academies Press.

Estrada, M., et al. (2016). Improving underrepresented minority student persistence in STEM. *CBE: Life Sciences Education, 15*(3), es5.

Estrada, M., Hernandez, P. R., & Schultz, P. W. (2018). A longitudinal study of how quality mentorship and research experience integrate underrepresented minorities into STEM careers. *CBE: Life Sciences Education, 17*(1), ar9.

Etzkowitz, H., et al. (1994). The paradox of critical mass for women in science. *Science, 266*, 51–54.

Fan, Y., et al. (2019). Gender and cultural bias in student evaluations: Why representation matters. *PLOS One, 14*(2), e0209749.

Fassiotto, M., et al. (2016). Women in academic medicine: Measuring stereotype threat among junior faculty. *Journal of Women's Health, 25*(3), 292–298.

Filardo, G., et al. (2016). Trends and comparison of female first authorship in high impact medical journals: Observational study (1994–2014). *BMJ, 352,* i847.

Fine, E., & Handelsman, J. (2012a). *Searching for excellence and diversity: A guide for search committees.* Madison: Women in Science & Engineering Leadership Institute, University of Wisconsin. Retrieved from https://wiseli.wisc.edu/resources/guidebooks-brochures.

Fine, E., & Handelsman, J. (2012b). *Reviewing applicants: Research on bias and assumptions* (2nd ed.). Madison: Women in Science & Engineering Leadership Institute, University of Wisconsin. Retrieved from https://wiseli.wisc.edu/resources/guidebooks-brochures.

Flaherty, C. (2014). U. Michigan climate survey shows gains in morale. *Inside Higher Ed.* Retrieved from https://www.insidehighered.com/quicktakes/2014/07/01/u-michigan-climate-survey-shows-gains-morale.

Flaherty, C. (2016). Forgotten chairs. *Inside Higher Ed.* Retrieved from https://www.insidehighered.com/news/2016/12/01/new-study-suggests-training-department-chairs-woefully-inadequate-most-institutions.

Ford, H. L., et al. (2019). Women from some under-represented minorities are given too few talks at world's largest earth-science conference. *Nature, 576,* 32–35.

Fox, M. F. (1991). Gender, environmental milieu, and productivity in science. In H. Zuckerman, J. Cole, and J. Bruer (Eds.), *The outer circle: Women in the scientific community* (pp. 188–204). New York: Norton.

Fox, M. F. (2001). Women, science, and academia: Graduate education and careers. *Gender and Society, 15,* 654–666.

Fox, M. F. (2008). Institutional transformation and the advancement of women faculty: The case of academic science and engineering. In J. C. Smart (Ed.), *Higher education: Handbook of theory and research* (vol. 23, pp. 73–103). New York: Springer.

Fox, M. F., & Colatrella, C. (2006). Participation, performance, and advancement of women in academic science and engineering: What is at issue and why. *Journal of Technology Transfer, 31*(3), 377–386.

Fox, M. F., & Mohapatra, S. (2007). Social-organizational characteristics of work and publication productivity among academic scientists in doctoral-granting departments. *Journal of Higher Education, 78,* 542–571.

Freeman, R. B., & Huang, W. (2015). Collaborating with people like me: Ethnic coauthorship within the United States. *Journal of Labor Economics, 33*(S1), S289–S318.

Frehill, L. M., Abreu, A., & Zippel, K. (2015). Gender, science, and occupational sex segregation. In W. Pearson, L. M. Frehill, & C. L. McNeely (Eds.), *Advancing women in science* (pp. 51–92). Cham, Switzerland: Springer.

Frehill, L. M., Jeser-Cannavale, C., & Malley, J. E. (2007). Measuring outcomes: Intermediate indicators of institutional transformation. In A. J. Stewart, J. E. Malley, & D. LaVaque-Manty (Eds.), *Transforming science and engineering: Advancing academic women* (pp. 298–323). Ann Arbor: University of Michigan Press.

Furst-Holloway, S., & Miner, K. (2019). ADVANCEing women faculty in STEM: Empirical findings and practical recommendations from National Science Foundation ADVANCE institutions. *Equality, Diversity and Inclusion: An International Journal, 38*(2), 122–130.

Gappa, J. M., Austin, A. E., & Trice, A. G. (2007). *Rethinking faculty work: Higher education's strategic imperative.* San Francisco, CA: Jossey-Bass.

Gardner, S. K., & Blackstone, A. (2013). "Putting in your time": Faculty experiences in the process of promotion to professor. *Innovative Higher Education, 38*(5), 411–425.

Ginther, D. K., Kahn, S., & Schaffer, W. T. (2016). Gender, race/ethnicity, and National Institutes of Health R01 research awards: Is there evidence of a double bind for women of color? *Academic Medicine: Journal of the Association of American Medical Colleges, 91*(8), 1098–1107.

Golde, C. M., & Dore, T. M. (2001). *At cross purposes: What the experiences of today's doctoral students reveal about doctoral education.* Philadelphia, PA: Pew Charitable Trusts.

Goldin, C., & Rouse, C. (2000). Orchestrating impartiality: The impact of "blind" auditions on female musicians. *American Economic Review, 90*(4), 715–741.

González, J. C. (2007). Surviving the doctorate and thriving as faculty: Latina junior faculty reflecting on their doctoral studies experiences. *Equity & Excellence in Education, 40*(4), 291–300.

Greenwald, A. G., & Krieger, L. H. (2006). Implicit bias: Scientific foundations. *California Law Review, 94*(4), 945–967.

Griffin, K. A. (2020). Institutional barriers, strategies, and benefits to increasing the representation of women and men of color in the professoriate. In L. Perna (Ed.), *Higher education: Handbook of theory and research* (vol. 35, pp. 1–73). Cham, Switzerland: Springer. Retrieved from https://doi.org/10.1007/978-3-030-11743-6_4-1.

Griffin, K. A., et al. (2010). Investing in the future: The importance of faculty mentoring in the development of students of color in STEM. *New Directions for Institutional Research, 2010*(148), 95–103.

Gunter, R. (2009). The emergence of gendered participation styles in science-related discussions: Implications for women's place in science. *Journal of Women and Minorities in Science and Engineering, 15*(1), 53–75.

Gunter, R., & Stambach, A. (2003). As balancing act and as game: How women and men science faculty experience the promotion process. *Gender Issues, 21*(1), 24–42.

Gurin, P., et al. (2002). Diversity and higher education: Theory and impact on educational outcomes. *Harvard Educational Review, 72*(3), 330–367.

Guskey, T. R. (2000). *Evaluating professional development.* Thousand Oaks, CA: Corwin.

Hall, R. M., & Sandler, B. R. (1982). The classroom climate: A chilly one for women? Washington, DC: Association of American Colleges and Universities.

Hanasono, L. K., et al. (2019). Secret service: Revealing gender biases in the visibility and value of faculty service. *Journal of Diversity in Higher Education, 12*(1), 85–98.

Handley, I. M., et al. (2015). Quality of evidence revealing subtle gender biases in science is in the eye of the beholder. *Proceedings of the National Academy of Sciences, 112*(43), 13201–13206.

Hardcastle, V. G., et al. (2019). It's complicated: A multi-method approach to broadening participation in STEM. *Equality, Diversity and Inclusion: An International Journal, 38*(3), 349–361.

Harris, J. C., & Nicolazzo, Z. (2017). Navigating the academic borderlands as multiracial and trans* faculty members. *Critical Studies in Education*. Retrieved from https://doi.org /10.1080/17508487.2017.1356340.

Hayward, C. N., Kogan, M., & Laursen, S. L. (2016). Facilitating instructor adoption of inquiry-based learning in college mathematics. *International Journal of Research in Undergraduate Mathematics Education, 2*(1), 59–82.

Hechtman, L. A., et al. (2018). NIH funding longevity by gender. *Proceedings of the National Academy of Sciences, 115*(31), 7943–7948.

Hengel, E. (2017). Publishing while female: Are women held to higher standards? Evidence from peer review. Cambridge Working Paper in Economics 1753. Retrieved from https://www.repository.cam.ac.uk/handle/1810/270621.

Herbers, J. M. (2014). Special issue: Part-time on the tenure track. *ASHE Higher Education Report, 40*(5), 1–161.

Herring, C. (2009). Does diversity pay? Race, gender, and the business case for diversity. *American Sociological Review, 74*(2), 208–224.

Hochschild, A. R. (1989). *The second shift: Working parents and the revolution at home.* New York: Avon.

Holman, L., Stuart-Fox, D., & Hauser, C. E. (2018). The gender gap in science: How long until women are equally represented? *PLOS Biology, 16*(4), e2004956.

Holmes, M. A., O'Connell, S., & Dutt, K. (Eds.). (2015). *Women in the geosciences: Practical, positive practices toward parity.* Washington, DC, and Hoboken, NJ: American Geophysical Union, and Wiley.

Hong, L., & Page, S. E. (2004). Groups of diverse problem solvers can outperform groups of high-ability problem solvers. *Proceedings of the National Academy of Sciences, 101*(46), 16385–16389.

Hoppe, T. A., et al. (2019). Topic choice contributes to the lower rate of NIH awards to African-American/Black scientists. *Science Advances, 5*(10), eaaw7238.

Hsieh, H. F., & Shannon, S. E. (2005). Three approaches to qualitative content analysis. *Qualitative Health Research, 15*(9), 1277–1288.

Hughes, B. E. (2018). Coming out in STEM: Factors affecting retention of sexual minority STEM students. *Science Advances, 4*(3), eaao6373.

Hunt, V., Layton, D., & Prince, S. (2015). Diversity matters. *McKinsey & Company*. Retrieved from https://www.mckinsey.com/~/media/mckinsey/business%20functions/organiza tion/our%20insights/why%20diversity%20matters/diversity%20matters.ashx.

Hunt, V. H., et al. (2012). Intersectionality and dismantling institutional privilege: The case of the NSF ADVANCE program. *Race, Gender & Class, 19*(1–2), 266–290.

Hurtado, S. (2007). Linking diversity with the educational and civic missions of higher education. *Review of Higher Education, 30*(2), 185–196.

Indiana University Center for Postsecondary Research. (2018). *The Carnegie Classification of Institutions of Higher Education.* Bloomington: Indiana University Center for Postsecondary Research.

Isbell, L. A., Young, T. P., & Harcourt, A. H. (2012). Stag parties linger: Continued gender bias in a female-rich scientific discipline. *PLOS One, 7*(11), e49682.

John, D., et al. (2016). Catalyzing equity and inclusion: Provoking institutional transformation through the application of a social justice lens. Poster presented at the ADVANCE/GSE Program Workshop, Baltimore, MD, May 22–24.

Johnson, K. R. (2010). The importance of student and faculty diversity in law schools: One dean's perspective. *Iowa Law Review, 96*, 1549–1577.

Johnson, P. A., Widnall, S. E., & Benya, F. F. (Eds.). (2018). *Sexual harassment of women: Climate, culture, and consequences in academic sciences, engineering, and medicine.* Washington, DC: Committee on the Impacts of Sexual Harassment in Academia; Committee on Women in Science, Engineering, and Medicine; Policy and Global Affairs; National Academies of Sciences, Engineering, and Medicine.

Johnson, S. K., Sitzmann, T., & Nguyen, A. T. (2014). Don't hate me because I'm beautiful: Acknowledging appearance mitigates the "beauty is beastly" effect. *Organizational Behavior and Human Decision Processes, 125*(2), 184–192.

Jordan, C. G., & Bilimoria, D. (2007). Creating a productive and inclusive academic work environment. In A. J. Stewart, J. Malley, and D. LaVaque-Manty (Eds.), *Transforming science and engineering: Advancing academic women* (pp. 225–242). Ann Arbor: University of Michigan Press.

Jovanovic, J., & Armstrong, M. A. (2014). Mission possible: Empowering institutions with strategies for change. *Peer Review, 16*(2), 21–24.

Juraqulova, Z. H., McCluskey, J. J., & Mittelhammer, R. C. (2019). Work-life policies and female faculty representation in US doctoral-granting economics departments. *Industrial Relations Journal, 50*(2), 168–196.

Kaatz, A., et al. (2016). Analysis of National Institutes of Health R01 application critiques, impact, and criteria scores: Does the sex of the principal investigator make a difference? *Academic Medicine: Journal of the Association of American Medical Colleges, 91*(8), 1080–1088.

Kaunas, C. L., Tomaszewski, L., & Yennello, S. L. (2018). Transitioning from "two-body problem" to "dual career opportunity": A long and arduous journey. In M. R. McMahon, M. T. Mora, & A. R. Qubbaj (Eds.), *Advancing women in academic STEM fields through dual career policies and practices* (pp. 53–66). Charlotte, NC: Information Age.

Kessel, C. (2015). Women in mathematics: Change, inertia, stratification, segregation. In W. Pearson, L. M. Frehill, & C. L. McNeely (Eds.), *Advancing women in science* (pp. 173–201). Cham, Switzerland: Springer.

Kezar, A. (2014). *How colleges change: Understanding, leading, and enacting change.* New York: Routledge.

Kezar, A. (2018). *Scaling improvement in STEM learning environments: The strategic role of a national organization.* Washington, DC: Association of American Universities.

Knobloch-Westerwick, S., Glynn, C. J., & Huge, M. (2013). The Matilda effect in science communication: An experiment on gender bias in publication quality perceptions and collaboration interest. *Science Communication, 35*(5), 603–625.

Knowlton, L. W., & Phillips, C. C. (2012). *The logic model guidebook: Better strategies for great results.* Thousand Oaks, CA: Sage.

Kramer, L. (n.d.). Advice for departments that give P&T clock extensions. *Hey Jane!*, *31*. Retrieved from https://socwomen.org/wp-content/uploads/2018/02/HeyJane-Volume-31.pdf.

Kumagai, A. K., et al. (2007). Use of interactive theater for faculty development in multicultural medical education. *Medical Teacher, 29*(4), 335–340.

Kyvik, S., & Teigen, M. (1996). Child care, research collaboration, and gender differences in scientific productivity. *Science, Technology, & Human Values, 21*(1), 54–71.

Laird, J. D., et al. (2007). The science of diversity. *Eos: Transactions of the American Geophysical Union, 88*(20), 220.

Larivière, V., et al. (2013). Bibliometrics: Global gender disparities in science. *Nature News, 504*(7479), 211–213.

Latimer, M., et al. (2014). Organizational change and gender equity in academia: Using dialogical change to promote positive departmental climates. In V. Demos, C. W. Berheide, & M. T. Segal (Eds.), *Advances in gender research: Gender transformation in the academy* (vol. 19, pp. 333–353). Stamford, CT: JAI Press.

Laursen, S. (2008). *Outcomes of LEAP individual growth and department enhancement grants, FY 2007.* Boulder: University of Colorado, Ethnography & Evaluation Research. Retrieved from https://www.colorado.edu/eer/content/leap-mini-grant-report2008.

Laursen, S. (2009). *Summative report on internal evaluation for LEAP, Leadership Education for Advancement and Promotion.* Boulder: University of Colorado, Ethnography & Evaluation Research. Retrieved from https://www.colorado.edu/eer/content/leap-internal-summative-report-2009.

Laursen, S. (2017). *Summative report: External evaluation for Texas A&M ADVANCE, year 7, May 2017.* Boulder: University of Colorado, Ethnography & Evaluation Research. Retrieved from https://www.colorado.edu/eer/node/365/attachment.

Laursen, S. L., & Austin, A. E. (2014a). *The StratEGIC Toolkit: Strategies for effecting gender equity and institutional change.* Boulder, CO, and East Lansing, MI. Retrieved from www.strategictoolkit.org.

Laursen, S. L., & Austin, A. E. (2014b). *StratEGIC Toolkit program perspectives: Interview with Canan Bilen-Green, North Dakota State University.* Retrieved from https://www.youtube.com/watch?v=K43MTkh5HaA.

Laursen, S. L., & Austin, A. E. (2014c). *StratEGIC Toolkit program perspectives: Interview with Patrick Farrell, Lehigh University.* Retrieved from https://www.youtube.com/watch?v=Rx2GA4s5SnE.

Laursen, S. L., & Austin, A. E. (2014d). *StratEGIC Toolkit program perspectives: Interview with Melissa Latimer, West Virginia University.* Retrieved from https://www.youtube.com/watch?v=ZQwphLSadvY.

Laursen, S., & Austin, A. (2014e). *StratEGIC Toolkit program perspectives: Interview with Loretta Moore, Jackson State University.* Retrieved from https://www.youtube.com/watch?v=QoSuDcWxQhg.

Laursen, S. L., & Austin, A. E. (2014f). *StratEGIC Toolkit program perspectives: Interview with Marie Mora, University of Texas at Rio Grande Valley.* Retrieved from https://www.youtube.com/watch?v=Typud62WXsE.

Laursen, S. L., & Austin, A. E. (2018). Faculty development for mid-career women in STEM: Cementing career success, building future leaders. In V. L. Baker et al. (Eds.), *Success after tenure: Supporting mid-career faculty* (pp. 221–242). Sterling, VA: Stylus.

Laursen, S. L., et al. (2015). ADVANCing the agenda for gender equity: Tools for strategic institutional change. *Change: The Magazine of Higher Learning, 47*(4), 16–24.

Laursen, S. L., & De Welde, K. (2019). The changer and the changed: Evolving theories and practices of change in ADVANCE calls for institutional transformation. *Equality, Diversity and Inclusion: An International Journal, 38*(2), 140–159.

Laursen, S. L., De Welde, K., & Austin, A. E. (2019). *Workshop report: ADVANCE and beyond: Thinking strategically about faculty-based institutional change.* Boulder, CO, Charleston, SC, and East Lansing, MI. Retrieved from https://www.colorado.edu/eer /content/advance-beyond-workshop-report-2019.

Laursen, S., et al. (2010). *Undergraduate research in the sciences: Engaging students in real science.* San Francisco, CA: Jossey-Bass.

Laursen, S., et al. (2007). What good is a scientist in the classroom? Participant outcomes and program design features for a short-duration science outreach intervention in K–12 classrooms. *CBE: Life Sciences Education, 6*(1), 49–64.

Laursen, S. L., & Rocque, B. (2009). Faculty development for institutional change: Lessons from an ADVANCE project. *Change: The Magazine of Higher Learning, 41*(2), 18–26.

Laursen, S., et al. (2005). *Outcomes of faculty development initiatives of LEAP, Leadership Education for Advancement and Promotion, an NSF ADVANCE project at the University of Colorado at Boulder: Mid-course evaluation report.* Boulder: University of Colorado, Ethnography & Evaluation Research. Retrieved from https://www.colorado.edu/eer/content/leap -workshop-report-2005.

Laursen, S. L., & Weston, T. J. (2014). Trends in PhD productivity and diversity in top-50 US chemistry departments: An institutional analysis. *Journal of Chemical Education, 91*(11), 1762–1776.

LaVaque-Manty, D., Steiger, J., & Stewart, A. J. (2007). Interactive theatre: Raising issues about the climate with science faculty. In A. Stewart, J. Malley, & D. LaVaque-Manty (Eds.), *Transforming science and engineering: Advancing academic women* (pp. 204–223). Ann Arbor: University of Michigan Press.

Lennartz, C., & O'Meara, K. (2018). Faculty development for mid-career women in STEM: Cementing career success, building future leaders. In V. L. Baker et al. (Eds.), *Success after tenure: Supporting mid-career faculty* (pp. 285–310). Sterling, VA: Stylus.

Lennon, T., Spotts, D., & Mitchell, M. (2013). *Benchmarking women's leadership in the United States.* Denver: Colorado Women's College at the University of Denver. Retrieved from https://www.issuelab.org/resource/benchmarking-women-s-leadership-in-the-united -states.html.

Lerback, J., & Hanson, B. (2017). Journals invite too few women to referee. *Nature, 541,* 455–457.

Lerchenmueller, M. J., Sorenson, O., & Jena, A. B. (2019). Gender differences in how scientists present the importance of their research: Observational study. *BMJ, 367,* l6573.

Levy, R. (2019). VITAL faculty: A growing workforce in colleges and universities. Mathematical Association of America. Retrieved from https://www.mathvalues.org/master blog/vital-faculty.

Leyva, L. A. (2017). Unpacking the male superiority myth and masculinization of mathematics at the intersections: A review of research on gender in mathematics education. *Journal for Research in Mathematics Education, 48*(4), 397–433.

Liang, X., & Bilimoria, D. (2007). The representation and experience of women faculty in STEM fields. In R. Burke & M. Mattis (Eds.), *Women and minorities in science, technology, engineering and mathematics: Upping the numbers* (pp. 317–333). Northampton, MA: Edward Elgar.

Libarkin, J. C., et al. (2019). The inadequacy of academic sexual misconduct policies. Unpublished manuscript in author's possession.

Lincoln, A. E., et al. (2012). The Matilda effect in science: Awards and prizes in the US, 1990s and 2000s. *Social Studies of Science, 42*(2), 307–320.

Long, J. S., & Fox, M. F. (1995). Scientific careers: Universalism and particularism. *Annual Review of Sociology, 21*, 45–71.

Loshbaugh, H. L., Laursen, S. L., & Thiry, H. (2011). Reaction to changing times: Trends and tensions in U.S. chemistry graduate education. *Journal of Chemical Education, 88*, 708–715.

Mack, K. M., Winter, K., & Soto, M. (Eds.). (2019). *Culturally responsive strategies for reforming STEM higher education: Turning the TIDES on inequity.* Bingley, England: Emerald.

MacNell, L., Driscoll, A., & Hunt, A. N. (2015). What's in a name: Exposing gender bias in student ratings of teaching. *Innovative Higher Education, 40*(4), 291–303.

Madera, J. M., Hebl, M. R., & Martin, R. C. (2009). Gender and letters of recommendation for academia: Agentic and communal differences. *Journal of Applied Psychology, 94*(6), 1591–1599.

Malcom, S. M. (1996). Science and diversity: A compelling national interest. *Science, 271*(5257), 1817–1819.

Marschke, R., et al. (2007). Demographic inertia revisited: An immodest proposal to achieve equitable gender representation among faculty in higher education. *Journal of Higher Education, 78*(1), 1–26.

Martell, R. F., Lane, D. M., & Emrich, C. (1996). Male-female differences: A computer simulation. *American Psychologist, 51*, 157–158.

Mason, M. A., & Goulden, M. (2002). Do babies matter? The effect of family formation on the lifelong careers of academic men and women. *Academe, 88*(6), 21–27.

Mason, M. A., & Goulden, M. (2004). Do babies matter? Part II: Closing the baby gap. *Academe, 90*(6), 10–15.

Mason, M. A., Goulden, M., & Frasch, K. (2009). Why graduate students reject the fast track. *Academe, 95*(1), 11–16.

Mason, M. A., Wolfinger, N. H., & Goulden, M. (2013). *Do babies matter? Gender and family in the ivory tower.* New Brunswick, NJ: Rutgers University Press.

McClelland, S. I., & Holland, K. J. (2015). You, me, or her: Leaders' perceptions of responsibility for increasing gender diversity in STEM departments. *Psychology of Women Quarterly, 39*(2), 210–225.

McCoy, S. K., Newell, E. E., & Gardner, S. K. (2013). Seeking balance: The importance of environmental conditions in men and women faculty's well-being. *Innovative Higher Education, 38*(4), 309–322.

Misra, J., et al. (2011). The ivory ceiling of service work. *Academe, 97*(1), 22–26.

Misra, J., Lundquist, J. H., & Templer, A. (2012). Gender, work time, and care responsibilities among faculty. *Sociological Forum, 27*(2), 300–323.

Mitchneck, B., Smith, J. L., & Latimer, M. (2016). A recipe for change: Creating a more inclusive academy. *Science, 352*(6282), 148–149.

Monroe, K. R., et al. (2014). Gender equality in the ivory tower, and how best to achieve it. *PS: Political Science & Politics, 47*(2), 418–426.

Moody, J. (2010). *Rising above cognitive errors: Guidelines for search, tenure review, and other evaluation committees* (rev. ed.). Kindle Direct Publishing.

Moore, L. A., et al. (2016). Building support for faculty women of color in STEM. *Diverse: Issues in Higher Education*. Retrieved from https://dc.law.mc.edu/faculty-journals/139/.

Morgan, A. C., et al. (n.d.). Paid parental leave at US and Canadian universities: A dataset of parental leave policies. Retrieved from https://aaronclauset.github.io/parental-leave.

Morimoto, S. A., et al. (2013). Beyond binders full of women: NSF ADVANCE and initiatives for institutional transformation. *Sociological Spectrum, 33*(5), 397–415.

Morton, S. (2018). Understanding gendered negotiations in the academic dual-career hiring process. *Sociological Perspectives, 61*(5), 748–765.

Morton, S., & Kmec, J. A. (2018). Risk-taking in the academic dual-hiring process: How risk shapes later work experiences. *Journal of Risk Research, 21*(12), 1517–1532.

Moss-Racusin, C. A., et al. (2012). Science faculty's subtle gender biases favor male students. *Proceedings of the National Academy of Sciences, 109*(41), 16474–16479.

Moss-Racusin, C. A., Molenda, A. K., & Cramer, C. R. (2015). Can evidence impact attitudes? Public reactions to evidence of gender bias in STEM fields. *Psychology of Women Quarterly, 39*(2), 194–209.

Munoz, S. M., et al. (2017). (Counter)narratives and complexities: Critical perspectives from a university cluster hire focused on diversity, equity, and inclusion. *Journal of Critical Thought and Practice, 6*(2), article 1.

National Academies of Sciences, Engineering, and Medicine. (2019). *The science of effective mentorship in STEMM*. Washington, DC: National Academies Press.

National Research Council. (2007). *Beyond bias and barriers: Fulfilling the potential of women in academic science and engineering*. Washington, DC: National Academies Press.

National Research Council. (2015). *Reaching students: What research says about effective instruction in undergraduate science and engineering*. Washington, DC: National Academies Press. Retrieved from https//:doi.org/10.17226/18687.

National Research Council, Committee on Underrepresented Groups and the Expansion of the Science and Engineering Workforce Pipeline. (2011). *Expanding underrepresented minority participation: America's science and technology talent at the crossroads*. Washington, DC: National Academies Press.

National Science Foundation [NSF], National Center for Science and Engineering Statistics [NCSES]. (2018). *Doctorate recipients from U.S. universities: 2017*. Alexandria, VA: National Science Foundation. Retrieved from https://ncses.nsf.gov/pubs/nsf19301.

National Science Foundation [NSF], National Center for Science and Engineering Statistics [NCSES]. (2019). *Women, minorities, and persons with disabilities in science and engineering*. Alexandria, VA: National Science Foundation. Retrieved from https://www.nsf.gov/statistics/wmpd.

Nielsen, J. M., et al. (2005). Vital variables and gender equity in academe: Confessions from a feminist empiricist project. *Signs: Journal of Women in Culture and Society, 31*(1), 1–28.

Nielsen, M. W., et al. (2017). Opinion: Gender diversity leads to better science. *Proceedings of the National Academy of Sciences, 114*(8), 1740–1742.

Nielsen, M. W., Bloch, C. W., & Schiebinger, L. (2018). Making gender diversity work for scientific discovery and innovation. *Nature Human Behaviour, 2,* 726–734.

O'Brien, J., et al. (2019). *What counts as success? Recognizing and rewarding women faculty's differential contributions in a comprehensive liberal arts university: NSF ADVANCE: Institutional Transformation, Seattle University, interim report, year 3, September 2018–March 2019.* Seattle, WA: Seattle University ADVANCE.

Oh, D., Buck, E. A., & Todorov, A. (2019). Revealing hidden gender biases in competence impressions of faces. *Psychological Science, 30*(1), 65–79.

O'Meara, K. (2002). Uncovering the values in faculty evaluation of service as scholarship. *Review of Higher Education,* Summer, 57–80.

O'Meara, K., Eatman, T., & Petersen, S. (2015). Advancing engaged scholarship in promotion and tenure: A roadmap and call for reform. *Liberal Education, 101*(3). Retrieved from https://www.aacu.org/liberaleducation/2015/summer/0%27meara.

O'Meara, K., et al. (2018). Undoing disparities in faculty workloads: A randomized trial experiment. *PLOS One 13*(12). Retrieved from https://doi.org/10.1371/journal.pone.0207316.

O'Meara, K., Kuvaeva, A., & Nyunt, G. (2017). Constrained choices: A view of campus service inequality from annual faculty reports. *Journal of Higher Education, 88*(5), 672–700.

O'Meara, K., et al. (2017). Asked more often: Gender differences in faculty workload in research universities and the work interactions that shape them. *American Educational Research Journal, 54*(6), 1154–1186.

O'Meara, K., et al. (2019). Department conditions and practices associated with faculty workload satisfaction and perceptions of equity. *Journal of Higher Education, 90*(5), 744–772.

O'Meara, K., Lounder, A., & Campbell, C. M. (2014). To heaven or hell: Sensemaking about why faculty leave. *Journal of Higher Education, 85*(5), 603–632.

O'Meara, K., & Rice, R. E. (Eds.). (2005). *Faculty priorities reconsidered: Encouraging multiple forms of scholarship.* San Francisco, CA: Jossey-Bass.

O'Meara, K., et al. (2011). Studying the professional lives and work of faculty involved in community engagement. *Innovative Higher Education, 36*(2), 83–96.

Ong, M., Smith, J. M., & Ko, L. T. (2018). Counterspaces for women of color in STEM higher education: Marginal and central spaces for persistence and success. *Journal of Research in Science Teaching, 55*(2), 206–245.

Ong, M., et al. (2011). Inside the double bind: A synthesis of empirical research on undergraduate and graduate women of color in science, technology, engineering, and mathematics. *Harvard Educational Review, 81*(2), 172–209.

Open Chemistry Collaborative in Diversity Equity [OXIDE]. (2019). Demographics data. Retrieved from http://oxide.jhu.edu/2/demographics.

Page, S. E. (2007). *The difference: How the power of diversity creates better groups, firms, schools, and societies.* Princeton, NJ: Princeton University Press.

Page, S. E. (2017). *The diversity bonus: How great teams pay off in the knowledge economy* (vol. 2). Princeton, NJ: Princeton University Press.

Peplow, M. (2019). Women's work. *Nature Reviews Chemistry, 3*(5), 283–286.

Phelan, J. E., Moss-Racusin, C. A., & Rudman, L. A. (2008). Competent yet out in the cold: Shifting criteria for hiring reflect backlash toward agentic women. *Psychology of Women Quarterly, 32*(4), 406–413.

Phillips, K. W. (2014). How diversity works. *Scientific American, 311*(4), 42–47.

Pribbenow, C. M., & Benting, D. (2004). *WISELI's life cycle research grant program: Formative and summative evaluation.* Madison, WI. Retrieved from https://wiseli.wisc.edu /reports/wiselis-life-cycle-research-grant-program-formative-and-summative-eval uation.

Quinn, K., Lange, S. E., & Riskin, E. A. (2007). Part-time tenure-track policies: Assessing utilization. Paper presented at the Women in Engineering ProActive Network 2004 Conference, Albuquerque, NM, June 6–9. Retrieved from https://journals.psu.edu /wepan/article/download/58344/58032.

Radde, H. D. (2018). Sexual harassment among California archaeologists: Results of the Gender Equity and Sexual Harassment Survey. *California Archaeology, 10*(2), 231–255.

Ramirez, F. O., & Kwak, N. (2015). Women's enrollments in STEM in higher education: Cross-national trends, 1970–2010. In W. Pearson, L. M. Frehill, & C. L. McNeely (Eds.), *Advancing women in science* (pp. 9–49). Cham, Switzerland: Springer.

Rankin, S., & Reason, R. (2008). Transformational tapestry model: A comprehensive approach to transforming campus climate. *Journal of Diversity in Higher Education, 1*(4), 262–274.

Reuben, E., Sapienza, P., & Zingales, L. (2014). How stereotypes impair women's careers in science. *Proceedings of the National Academy of Sciences, 111*(12), 4403–4408.

Rhoten, D., & Pfirman, S. (2007). Women in interdisciplinary science: Exploring preferences and consequences. *Research Policy, 36*(1), 56–75.

Rice, R. E., Sorcinelli, M. D., & Austin, A. E. (2000). *Heeding new voices: Academic careers for a new generation.* Washington, DC: American Association of Higher Education.

Rice, S., Wolf-Wendel, L. E., & Twombly, S. B. (2007). Helping or hurting women? The case of a dual career couple policy at the University of Kansas. In M. A. D. Sagaria (Ed.), *Women, universities, and change: Gender equality in the European Union and the United States* (pp. 197–214). New York: Palgrave Macmillan.

Richey, C. R., et al. (2019). Gender and sexual minorities in astronomy and planetary science face increased risks of harassment and assault. *Bulletin of the American Astronomical Society.* Retrieved from https://113qx216in8z1kdeyi404hgf-wpengine.netdna-ssl .com/wp-content/uploads/2019/12/Richey-et-al-LGBTQPAN.pdf.

Roberson, L., et al. (2003). Stereotype threat and feedback seeking in the workplace. *Journal of Vocational Behavior, 62*(1), 176–188.

Rosser, S. V. (2004). Using POWRE to ADVANCE: Institutional barriers identified by women scientists and engineers. *NWSA Journal, 16*(1), 50–78.

Rosser, S. V. (2007). Leveling the playing field for women in tenure and promotion. *NWSA Journal, 19*(3), 190–198.

Rosser, S. V. (2010). Building two-way streets to implement—policies that work for gender and science. In B. Riegraf et al. (Eds.), *GenderChange in academia* (pp. 289–303). Wiesbaden, Germany: Verlag für Sozialwissenschaften.

Rosser, S. V. (2017). *Academic women in STEM faculty: Views beyond a decade after POWRE.* Cham, Switzerland: Palgrave Macmillan.

Rosser, V. J. (2003). Faculty and staff members' perceptions of effective leadership: Are there differences between women and men leaders? *Equity & Excellence in Education, 36*(1), 71–81.

Rudman, L. A. (1998). Self promotion as a risk factor for women: The costs and benefits of counterstereotypical impression management. *Journal of Personality and Social Psychology, 74*(3), 629–645.

Ryabov, I., & Wang, G.-Z. (2011). Assessing academic climate change in gender diversity in the areas of science and engineering. *Journal of Women and Minorities in Science and Engineering, 17*(4), 371–388.

Ryabov, I., & Witherspoon, P. D. (2008). Diverse pathways to the PhD: A study of women faculty in the sciences and engineering at a Hispanic-serving institution. *Journal of Women and Minorities in Science and Engineering, 14*(3), 225–243.

Sá, C. M. (2008a). "Interdisciplinary strategies" in US research universities. *Higher Education, 55*(5), 537–552.

Sá, C. M. (2008b). Strategic faculty hiring in two public research universities: Pursuing interdisciplinary connections. *Tertiary Education and Management, 14*(4), 285–301.

Sardelis, S., & Drew, J. A. (2016). Not "pulling up the ladder": Women who organize conference symposia provide greater opportunities for women to speak at conservation conferences. *PLOS One, 11*(7), e0160015.

Sarsons, H. (2017). Recognition for group work: Gender differences in academia. *American Economic Review, 107*(5), 141–145.

Schiebinger, L. (Ed.). (2008). *Gendered innovations in science and engineering.* Stanford, CA: Stanford University Press.

Schiebinger, L., Davies Henderson, A., & Gilmartin, S. K. (2008). *Dual-career academic couples: What universities need to know.* Stanford, CA: Michelle R. Clayman Institute for Gender Research, Stanford University. Retrieved from https://gender.sites.stanford .edu/sites/g/files/sbiybj5961/f/publications/dualcareerfinal_0.pdf.

Schiebinger, L., & Gilmartin, S. K. (2010). Housework is an academic issue. *Academe, 96*(1), 39–44.

Schimpf, C., et al. (2013). STEM faculty and parental leave: Understanding an institution's policy within a national policy context through structuration theory. *International Journal of Gender, Science and Technology, 5*(2), 102–125.

Schimpf, C. T., Santiago, M. M., & Pawley, A. L. (2012). *Access and definition: Exploring how STEM faculty, department heads, and university policy administrators navigate the implementation of a parental leave policy.* West Lafayette, IN: Purdue University, School of Engineering Education. Retrieved from http://docs.lib.purdue.edu/enegs/24.

Schloss, E. P., et al. (2009). Some hidden costs of faculty turnover in clinical departments in one academic medical center. *Academic Medicine, 84*(1), 32–36.

Schroeder, J., et al. (2013). Fewer invited talks by women in evolutionary biology symposia. *Journal of Evolutionary Biology, 26*(9), 2063–2069.

Sege, R., Nykiel-Bub, L., & Selk, S. (2015). Sex differences in institutional support for junior biomedical researchers. *JAMA, 314*(11), 1175–1177.

Sekaquaptewa, D., et al. (2019). An evidence-based faculty recruitment workshop influences departmental hiring practice perceptions among university faculty. *Equality, Diversity and Inclusion: An International Journal, 38*(2), 188–210.

Settles, I. H., Buchanan, N. T., & Dotson, K. (2019). Scrutinized but not recognized: (In)visibility and hypervisibility experiences of faculty of color. *Journal of Vocational Behavior, 113*, 62–74.

Settles, I. H., et al. (2006). The climate for women in academic science: The good, the bad, and the changeable. *Psychology of Women Quarterly, 30*(1), 47–58.

Seymour, E. (1995). The loss of women from science, mathematics, and engineering undergraduate majors: An explanatory account. *Science Education, 79*(4), 437–473.

Seymour, E., & Hewitt, N. M. (1997). *Talking about leaving: Why undergraduates leave the sciences.* Boulder, CO: Westview.

Shaw, A. K., & Stanton, D. E. (2012). Leaks in the pipeline: Separating demographic inertia from ongoing gender differences in academia. *Proceedings of the Royal Society B: Biological Sciences, 279*(1743), 3736–3741.

Shea, C. M., et al. (2019). Interactive theater: An effective tool to reduce gender bias in faculty searches. *Equality, Diversity and Inclusion: An International Journal, 38*(2), 178–187.

Sheltzer, J. M. (2018). Gender disparities among independent fellows in biomedical research. *Nature Biotechnology, 36*(10), 1018–1021.

Sheltzer, J. M., & Smith, J. C. (2014). Elite male faculty in the life sciences employ fewer women. *Proceedings of the National Academy of Sciences, 111*(28), 10107–10112.

Sheridan, J., et al. (2017). Write more articles, get more grants: The impact of department climate on faculty research productivity. *Journal of Women's Health, 26*(5), 587–596.

Smith, D. G., et al. (2004). Interrupting the usual: Successful strategies for hiring diverse faculty. *Journal of Higher Education, 75*(2), 133–160.

Smith, G. C., & Waltman, J. A. (2006). *Designing and implementing family-friendly policies in higher education.* Ann Arbor: Center for the Education of Women, University of Michigan. Retrieved from http://cew.umich.edu/PDFs/designing06.pdf.

Smith, J. L., et al. (2017). Added benefits: How supporting women faculty in STEM improves everyone's job satisfaction. *Journal of Diversity in Higher Education, 11*(4), 502–517.

Smith, J. L., et al. (2015). Now hiring! Empirically testing a three-step intervention to increase faculty gender diversity in STEM. *BioScience, 65*(11), 1084–1087.

Social Sciences Feminist Network Research Interest Group. (2017). The burden of invisible work in academia: Social inequalities and time use in five university departments. *Humboldt Journal of Social Relations, 39*, 228–245.

Sonnert, G., & Holton, G. (1995). *Gender differences in science careers: The Project Access Study.* New Brunswick, NJ: Rutgers University Press.

Sorcinelli, M. D., & Austin, A. E. (Eds.). (1992). *Developing new and junior faculty.* San Francisco, CA: Jossey-Bass.

Sorcinelli, M. D., et al. (2006). *Creating the future of faculty development: Learning from the past, understanding the present.* Bolton, MA: Anker.

Staats, C., et al. (2015). *State of the science: Implicit bias review, 2015.* Columbus: Kirwan Institute, Ohio State University.

Stanley, C. A. (2006a). Coloring the academic landscape: Faculty of color breaking the silence in predominantly white colleges and universities. *American Educational Research Journal, 43*(4), 701–736.

Stanley, C. A. (Ed.). (2006b). *Faculty of color: Teaching in predominantly white colleges and universities*. Bolton, MA: Anker.

Steinpreis, R. E., Anders, K. A., & Ritzke, D. (1999). The impact of gender on the review of the curricula vitae of job applicants and tenure candidates: A national empirical study. *Sex Roles, 41*(7–8), 509–528.

Stepan-Norris, J., & Kerissey, J. (2016). Enhancing gender equity in academia: Lessons from the ADVANCE program. *Sociological Perspectives, 59*(2), 225–245.

Stepan-Norris, J., with Lind, B. (2007). *ADVANCE program: 2006/2007 equity advisor report analysis*. Retrieved from http://archive.advance.uci.edu/Reports-Recent.html.

Stewart, A. J., Malley, J. E., & Herzog, K. A. (2016). Increasing the representation of women faculty in STEM departments: What makes a difference? *Journal of Women and Minorities in Science and Engineering, 22*(1), 23–47.

Stewart, A. J., Malley, J. E., & LaVaque-Manty, D. (Eds.). (2007). *Transforming science and engineering: Advancing academic women*. Ann Arbor: University of Michigan Press.

Stewart, A. J., & Valian, V. (2018). *An inclusive academy: Achieving diversity and excellence*. Cambridge, MA: MIT Press.

Sturm, S. (2006). The architecture of inclusion: Advancing workplace equity in higher education. *Harvard Journal of Law and Gender, 29*, 247–334.

Sturm, S. (2007). Gender equity as institutional transformation: The pivotal role of "organizational catalysts." In A. J. Stewart, J. E. Malley, & D. LaVaque-Manty (Eds.), *Transforming science and engineering: Advancing academic women* (pp. 262–280). Ann Arbor: University of Michigan Press.

Taylor, L. L., et al. (2017). Reducing inequality in higher education: The link between faculty empowerment and climate and retention. *Innovative Higher Education, 42*(5–6), 391–405.

Thiry, H., Laursen, S. L., & Hunter, A. B. (2008). Professional development needs and outcomes for education-engaged scientists: A research-based framework. *Journal of Geoscience Education, 56*(3), 235–246.

Thiry, H., Laursen, S. L., & Liston, C. (2007). Valuing teaching in the academy: Why are underrepresented graduate students overrepresented in teaching and outreach? *Journal of Women and Minorities in Science and Engineering, 13*(4), 391–419.

Thomas, N. R., Poole, D. J., & Herbers, J. M. (2015). Gender in science and engineering faculties: Demographic inertia revisited. *PLOS One, 10*(10), e0139767.

Tower, L. E., & Dilks, L. M. (2015). Work/life satisfaction policy in ADVANCE universities: Assessing levels of flexibility. *Journal of Diversity in Higher Education, 8*(3), 157–174.

Trix, F., & Psenka, C. (2003). Exploring the color of glass: Letters of recommendation for female and male medical faculty. *Discourse & Society, 14*(2), 191–220.

Tuitt, F. A., Sagaria, M. A. D., & Turner, C. S. V. (2007). Signals and strategies in hiring faculty of color. In J. C. Smart (Ed.), *Higher education: Handbook of theory and research* (vol. 22, pp. 497–535). Dordrecht, Netherlands: Springer.

Turner, C. (2002). Women of color in academe. *Journal of Higher Education, 73*(1), 74–93.

Turner, L. (2009). Gender diversity and innovative performance. *International Journal of Innovation & Sustainable Development, 4*(2–3), 123–134.

UM ADVANCE. (2013). *Assessing the academic work environment for science and engineering tenured/tenure track faculty at the University of Michigan, 2001, 2006, and 2012: Gen-*

der and race in department- and university-related climate factors: Executive summary. Ann Arbor: University of Michigan ADVANCE. Retrieved from https://advance.umich.edu /wp-content/uploads/2018/09/ADVANCE-2012-R1-ES.pdf.

Umbach, P. D. (2007). Gender equity in the academic labor market: An analysis of academic disciplines. *Research in Higher Education, 48*(2), 169–192.

US Census Bureau. (2016). *2016 American Community Survey: 1-year estimates*. Retrieved from https://factfinder.census.gov/faces/tableservices/jsf/pages/productview.xhtml?pid =ACS_16_1YR_CP05&prodType=table.

Valian, V. (1999). *Why so slow? The advancement of women*. Cambridge, MA: MIT Press.

Van Rijnsoever, F. J., & Hessels, L. K. (2011). Factors associated with disciplinary and interdisciplinary research collaboration. *Research Policy, 40*(3), 463–472.

Ward, K., & Wolf-Wendel, L. (2004). Academic motherhood: Managing complex roles in research universities. *Review of Higher Education, 27*(2), 233–257.

Ward, K., & Wolf-Wendel, L. (2012). *Academic motherhood: How faculty manage work and family*. New Brunswick, NJ: Rutgers University Press.

Wennerås, C., & Wold, A. (1997). Nepotism and sexism in peer-review. *Nature, 387*(6631), 341–343.

West, J. D., et al. (2013). The role of gender in scholarly authorship. *PLOS One, 8*(7), e66212.

Williams, J. C. (2000). *Unbending gender: Why family and work conflict and what to do about it*. New York: Oxford University Press.

Williams, J. C., & Dempsey, R. (2014). *What works for women at work: Four patterns working women need to know*. New York: New York University Press.

Witteman, H. O., et al. (2019). Are gender gaps due to evaluations of the applicant or the science? A natural experiment at a national funding agency. *Lancet, 393*(10171), 531–540.

Woolstenhulme, J. L., et al. (2011). Solving the two-body problem: An evaluation of university partner accommodation policies. Unpublished paper. Retrieved from http:// citeseerx.ist.psu.edu/viewdoc/download?doi=10.1.1.231.7040&rep=rep1&type=pdf.

Woolstenhulme, J. L., et al. (2015). Evaluating the two-body problem: Joint-hire productivity within the university. Unpublished paper. Retrieved from http://faculty.ses.wsu .edu/cowan/research/twobody.pdf.

Wylie, A., Jakobsen, J. R., & Fosado, G. (2007). *Women, work, and the academy: Strategies for responding to "post–civil rights era" gender discrimination*. New York: Barnard Center for Research on Women.

Xie, Y., & Shauman, K. A. (1998). Sex differences in research productivity: New evidence about an old puzzle. *American Sociological Review, 63*, 847–870.

Yoshino, K. (2007). *Covering: The hidden assault on our civil rights*. New York: Random House.

Index

accountability: hiring and, 43, 46–47, 51, 55–56, 68, 70, 72, 74, 189; lack of, 68; program evaluation and, 73; promotion and tenure and, 60, 66; strengthening structures of, 68–74

administration: accountability and, 69, 70, 73; communication and, 100, 211; dual-career couples and, 114, 118, 120; enhancing visibility of women and, 100, 102, 191–92; faculty development and, 102, 147, 151; flexible work arrangements and, 127, 135, 136; hiring/recruitment and, 23, 42–43, 55; mentoring/networking and, 162–63, 166, 169; representation of women in, 77, 79–80, 83, 85–86, 151, 212. *See also* deans; department chairs and heads; leaders; presidents; provosts

ADVANCE: community and, 4, 148; funding, 50, 91; major contributions of, 1, 40; proposals, 25; recognition, 101–2, 104–5, 154, 155, 156, 166, 183. *See also* Institutional Transformation awards; National Science Foundation

—project leaders: accountability and, 69; additional roles of, 48, 109, 115; autonomy and, 192, 195; collaboration and, 97, 104, 117, 134, 214; communication and, 103, 134, 189, 214; data collection and, 26–27, 179, 225–26; educational efforts and, 43–44; emphasis on mentoring/networking of, 52, 97, 146, 162, 164

affordances, 37, 54, 66–67, 73–74, 87, 96–97, 108, 120–21, 128–29, 137–38, 147, 156, 167, 168–69, 181, 217

allies/advocates: men as, 80, 83, 85, 86, 166, 186; mobilization of, 47, 51, 69, 97, 99, 104, 135, 213–14, 216, 218

anchoring strategies, 209–11

assessment, institutional, 64, 66, 71, 91–93, 97, 119, 142, 172. *See also* Collaborative on Academic Careers in Higher Education

awards/honors: gender inequity and, 11–12, 16–17, 99, 101–2, 157, 172, 206; improving gender equity and, 54, 59–60, 66, 92, 151–56, 183, 198, 210. *See also* grants, departmental; grants, individual faculty; Institutional Transformation awards; visibility of women and gender issues

belonging, 17, 31, 85, 95–96, 164

career planning: faculty development and, 59, 143, 151, 187, 189; inflexibility and, 14–15; leadership development and, 87; mentoring and, 64–65, 161; parenting and, 112. *See also* affordances; productivity

caregiving: accommodations and, 113, 124–27, 129, 132, 142, 150, 152, 153. *See also* childcare; parenting

Case Western Reserve University: Academic Careers in Engineering and Sciences (ACES), 44, 47, 50, 53, 65, 71–72, 84, 87, 97, 104, 105–7, 119, 126, 133, 161, 162, 180–86

change, theory of, 26, 181, 207–8, 226

change portfolios: accountability and, 74; dual careers and, 122; enhanced visibility for women and gender issues and, 109; faculty development and, 149; family-friendly accommodations and, 139; flexible work arrangements and, 129; hiring and, 55–56; identifying and framing the problem and, 24, 31, 202–4; implementation of, 212–17; improving departmental climate and, 98; individual grants and, 157; institutional context and, 26, 179, 182, 201–2, 204–6, 207–9, 220; leaders and, 88; mentoring/networking and, 162–63, 170; supporting individual women and, 141; tenure and promotion and, 67. *See also* anchoring strategies; Case Western

institutional culture: approaches to improving, 23, 27, 55, 77–78, 101, 126, 159, 167, 172, 195, 203; context and, 204–6, 220; gender inequity and, 23, 28, 76, 85, 174, 209; outcomes of interventions and, 99, 119–20, 128–29, 138, 169, 170, 190, 192, 196, 198–99, 208, 210
institutional transformation, 33, 69, 95, 99, 140–41, 201–2, 204, 213
Institutional Transformation awards: awardees, 223–24; early history of, 1, 24–25, 49–50; more recent, 29, 32, 171–76; name recognition and, 103; project evaluation and, 215; research methods and, 3, 26–27, 29, 33, 37–38, 171, 179, 225; sustainability and, 47, 52, 73, 118, 121, 146, 149, 179, 186, 190, 195, 198, 211, 213, 216–17, 220. *See also individual colleges and universities*
internalized racism, 39
intersectionality, 17–19, 32, 165–66, 174–75, 199–200

Jackson State University, 146–47, 175, 200, 203–4
job satisfaction: departmental climate and, 13, 76, 78, 89–90, 95–96, 98; dual-career initiatives and, 114, 119; evaluation and, 66, 71, 84, 95, 186, 190; work-life balance and, 15–16; workshops and, 194. *See also* retention

Kansas State University: departmental climate and, 92; flexible work arrangements and, 126, 134; grants and, 154, 155, 209; hiring/recruitment and, 44, 45, 48; promotion and tenure and, 62; research methods and, 226

laboratories: funding and, 133, 151; government, 2; harassment and, 174; lab work, 14; management of, 124, 144; underrepresentation of women and, 11, 20. *See also* sciences
Latinx: discrimination and, 18; hiring and, 8, 18, 182–83, 190, 197. *See also* ethnicity; men faculty of color; University of Texas at El Paso; women faculty of color
leaders: accountability and, 68, 70, 185; change leaders, 1–3, 13–14, 30–31, 98, 202, 205–7, 211, 213–14, 216, 217, 219; collaborative leadership, 94, 187, 189–91, 197; interviews of, 26–27, 225–27; program evaluation and, 86; senior faculty as, 23, 45, 48, 50, 53, 64, 65, 83, 100, 109, 122, 154, 161,

197, 213; underrepresentation of women, 6–7, 10–12, 77; women as, 19–20, 23, 25, 76, 98–99, 101, 150, 154, 159–60, 175, 181, 183, 188, 197, 208–9
leadership development: approaches to improving, 48, 78, 51, 63–64, 77–78, 78–86, 92, 94, 117, 141, 146, 164–65, 170, 210; outcomes of interventions and, 77, 86–88, 183, 198, 208. *See also* department chairs and heads; faculty development
Lehigh University, 46, 86, 87–88, 165, 203–4, 213
lesbian, gay, bisexual, transgender, and queer (LGBTQ) faculty, 2, 12, 13, 18, 32, 40, 174, 183, 199. *See also* gender-nonconforming faculty; nonbinary faculty; same-sex couples
life sciences, 7, 18, 192–94

marginalization: ableism, 6, 39, 172; ageism, 172; heterosexism and homophobia, 6, 17, 18, 33, 39, 172, 199; intersectionality and, 17–19, 32, 165–66, 174–75, 199–200; racism and, 3, 6, 8, 17, 33, 172, 218; sexism, 1, 6, 12, 13–14, 17, 32–33, 42, 78, 141, 172, 178, 200, 218; social class and, 6, 17
mathematics: gender inequity and, 11, 12–13, 16, 16; support for girls and women in, 22, 36, 153, 175; underrepresentation of women in, 1, 6–7, 12
men faculty: beneficiaries of gender inequity, 8–12, 12–15, 18, 21, 39, 40, 57, 58, 69, 79, 99, 111–12, 113, 123, 124, 130, 132, 150, 158, 172, 173, 194, 203; international, 199–200; mid-career, 15, 48, 59, 63, 65, 114, 132, 143–44, 145, 146, 151, 154, 155, 157, 159, 160, 161, 163, 164, 167–69, 197, 203–4; new and early-career, 41, 46, 48, 64, 123, 131, 142–43, 145, 146, 160, 161, 167, 203–4; roles as allies, 80, 83, 85–86, 166, 186, 214; senior, 23, 45, 50, 53, 59, 64, 65, 83, 85, 109, 143–44, 146, 161–62, 163, 164, 166, 168, 172, 197, 213. *See also* men faculty of color
men faculty of color: departmental climate and, 51; hiring and, 119; marginalization of, 17, 18, 44, 58, 90, 173, 194; mentoring and, 162, 166; underrepresentation of, 8, 20, 22, 45, 166; unequal workloads and, 173. *See also* Latinx; men faculty; Native Americans/ Alaska Natives; women faculty of color
men graduate students and postdocs, 15, 45, 49–50, 106, 133, 160, 163, 184

134; faculty advancement and, 65; faculty development and, 48; Leadership Education for Advancement and Promotion (LEAP), 145, 164; program evaluation and, 107, 137, 147, 167; research methods and, 225
University of Maryland, Baltimore County (UMBC), 46, 49, 64, 72, 85, 86, 152, 155
University of Michigan, 45, 50, 53, 63, 92, 102, 112, 133, 140, 153, 198 99
University of Montana, 45, 47, 48, 50, 64, 118, 127, 135, 150, 153
University of Nebraska–Lincoln, 44, 119, 214, 215
University of Rhode Island, 44, 45, 72, 92, 93, 104, 135, 146, 164–65
University of Texas at El Paso (UTEP): departmental climate and, 94; dual-career couples and, 119; faculty advancement and, 61, 126; faculty development and, 145; hiring and, 45; mentoring and, 161, 163; racial equality and, 175; UTEP ADVANCE, 187–91
University of Washington, 83, 85, 94, 117, 146, 164, 183
University of Wisconsin–Madison: hiring and, 53; informational tools and, 104; Vilas Life Cycle Professorship Program, 132, 133–34, 153, 155; Women in Science and Engineering Leadership Institute (WISELI), 51, 105, 191–96
Utah State University: data collection and, 93–94, 95–96; dual-career couples and, 117; faculty advancement and, 61, 136; family-friendly accommodations and, 134–35, 136, 211; grants and, 154; hiring and, 47; ombudsperson and, 61, 67, 72; outreach and, 105, 214

Virginia Tech, 50, 63–64, 104, 119, 136, 213
visibility of women and gender issues: approaches to improving, 99–104; barriers to, 6, 98–99, 203; educational efforts and, 106; faculty as role models, 18, 20, 31, 41, 42, 76, 105, 175; grants and, 194; mentoring/networking and, 163, 166; outcomes of interventions and, 104–7; program evaluation and, 105–6, 107–9; scholarship and, 159; significance of, 76; visiting scholars and, 50, 100, 101, 105, 107, 108, 109. *See also* awards/honors; recognition/rewards

visiting scholars: evaluation of, 107, 154, 155; funding and, 108; limitations of, 169; mentoring, 150, 153, 158, 159; networking and, 166; trainings and, 44, 102; visibility of women and, 50, 100, 101, 105, 107, 209

white women faculty, 11, 18–19, 41. *See also* men faculty; women faculty; women faculty of color
women faculty: administrators, 8, 77, 79–80, 83, 85–86, 151, 212; climate and, 12–14, 55, 89–90, 182, 194; department chairs, 101, 160, 162–63, 164, 165, 194; laboratories and, 11, 20; leaders, 19–20, 23, 25, 76, 98–99, 101, 150, 154, 159–60, 175, 181, 183, 188, 197, 208–9; mid-career, 15, 48, 57, 59, 63, 86, 114, 132, 135, 143–44, 145, 146, 151, 154, 155, 157, 159, 160–62, 164, 165, 167–69, 172, 197, 200, 203–4, 209; new and early-career, 41, 46, 48, 49, 64, 123, 131, 142–43, 145, 146, 160, 161, 167; senior, 23, 45, 48, 50, 53, 59, 64, 65, 82, 100, 101, 109, 114, 143–44, 154, 159, 160, 161–62, 163, 164, 166, 168, 197, 212. *See also* engineering; mathematics; men faculty; sciences; visiting scholars; white women faculty; women faculty of color
women faculty of color: double bind and, 17–19; hiring and, 41; intersectionality and, 17–19, 32, 165–66, 174–75, 199–200; mentoring and, 162, 165; networking and, 147; stereotypes and, 44–45; underrepresentation and, 8, 20, 202–3; unequal workloads and, 58, 173. *See also* Latinx; marginalization; men faculty of color; Native Americans/Alaska Natives; women faculty
women graduate students/postdocs, 13, 15, 20, 22, 45, 49, 50, 52, 92–93, 160, 163, 184, 194
work environments: gender inequity and, 1, 6, 13; importance to women of, 15; inclusive, 4, 19, 33, 64, 77, 135, 201–2, 208–9, 221
work/life balance: career planning and, 143; challenges to, 14–16, 58, 111, 139; data and, 104, 112, 113; grants and, 149–50; workshops and, 163. *See also* departmental climate; family-friendly accommodations; flexible work arrangements
workplace climate, 12–14, 74, 76, 140, 142
workplace culture, 12–14, 17, 174

workshops: career planning and, 48, 49, 59, 63, 64, 65, 146, 163; data collection and, 27, 33, 225, 227; departmental climate and, 92, 93, 94, 104, 193, 195; dual-career couples and, 116, 117–18; evaluation of, 66, 86, 147, 195, 215; faculty development and, 142, 143–45, 164, 192; grants and, 151, 154; hiring/recruitment and, 44, 45, 46, 51, 54, 186, 193, 194, 196; leadership development and, 82–83, 85, 87, 88, 183, 210; leading of, 214; mentoring and, 163, 165, 166; networking and, 164; support for pregnant or nursing people and, 135; sustainability of, 55, 144, 146, 148